Our Senses

TOUCH

Kay Woodward

GARETHSTEVENS
PUBLISHING
A World Almanac Education Group Company

Please visit our web site at: www.garethstevens.com
For a free color catalog describing Gareth Stevens Publishing's
list of high-quality books and multimedia programs, call
1-800-542-2595 (USA) or 1-800-387-3178 (Canada).
Gareth Stevens Publishing's fax: (414) 332-3567.

Library of Congress Cataloging-in-Publication Data

Woodward, Kay.
    Touch / Kay Woodward.
      p. cm — (Our senses)
    Includes index.
    ISBN 0-8368-4410-6 (lib. bdg.)
    1. Touch—Juvenile literature.   I. Title.
  QP451.W667   2005
  612.8'8—dc22   2004052572

This North American edition first published in 2005 by
Gareth Stevens Publishing
A World Almanac Education Group Company
330 West Olive Street, Suite 100
Milwaukee, Wisconsin 53212 USA

This U.S. edition copyright © 2005 by Gareth Stevens, Inc.
Original edition copyright © 2005 by Hodder Wayland.
First published in 2005 by Hodder Wayland, an imprint of
Hodder Children's Books, a division of Hodder Headline
Limited, 338 Euston Road, London NW1 3BH, U.K.

Commissioning Editor: Victoria Brooker
Book Editor: Katie Sergeant
Consultant: Carol Ballard
Picture Research: Katie Sergeant
Book Designer: Jane Hawkins
Cover: Hodder Children's Books

Gareth Stevens Editor: Barbara Kiely Miller
Gareth Stevens Designer: Kami Koenig

Picture Credits
Corbis: imprint page, 10 (Royalty-Free), 7 (Tom and Dee Ann
McCarthy), 12 (Ariel Skelley), 13 (Jutta Klee), 14 (Michal Heron),
15 (Joe Bator), 20 (Charles Krebs), 21 (Peter Johnson); FLPA:
19 (Hugh Clark); Getty Images: cover (Stone/Garry Wade),
title page, 8 (Thinkstock/Royalty-Free), 4 (Stone/Clarissa Leahy),
5 (The Image Bank/Don Klumpp), 11 (The Image Bank/White
Packert), 18 (Photodisc Green/Santokh Kochar/Royalty-Free);
Wayland Picture Library: 9, 16, 17, 22, 23 (all). Artwork on
page 6 is by Peter Bull.

About the Author

Kay Woodward is an experienced children's author who
has written over twenty nonfiction and fiction titles.

About the Consultant

Carol Ballard is an elementary school science
coordinator. She is the author of many books for
children and is a consultant for several publishers.

CONTENTS

Words in **bold** type can be found in the glossary.

TOUCHING EVERYTHING!

The world is filled with interesting things to **touch**. There are smooth stones and rough rocks. There are sticky sweets and springy sofas.

4

A kitten's coat feels soft, smooth, and furry.

Our **sense** of touch allows us to **feel** the many amazing objects around us. By touching objects, we find out more about them. We touch with our skin.

5

HOW YOUR SKIN WORKS

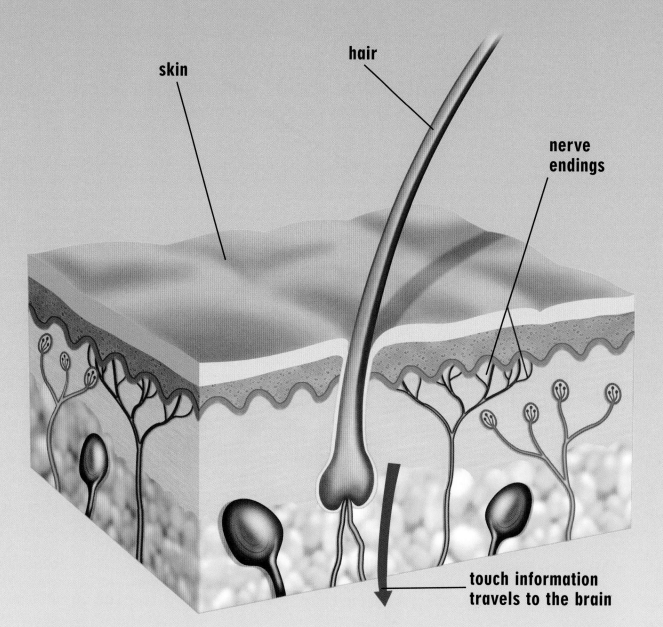

skin

hair

nerve endings

touch information travels to the brain

This is what a section of skin looks like from the inside. There are thousands of nerve endings under your skin.

When you touch something, **nerve endings** under your skin send information to your brain, which helps you learn about what you are touching. The largest number of nerve endings are in your hands, lips, face, neck, tongue, and feet. These parts of the body have a strong sense of touch. You can feel things best of all with your fingertips.

Each fingertip contains lots of nerve endings.

ROUGH AND SMOOTH

Touching tells us what something feels like. Different objects have different **textures**. The bark of a tree is rough. This page is smooth.

8

Concrete is hard. Cotton puffs are soft and fluffy. If you hold clay in your hand, it feels squishy and wet.

HOT AND COLD

When you touch something, you can tell if it is hot or cold. A mug of cocoa warms your fingertips. When you hold someone's hand, it usually feels warm, too!

A hot drink makes a mug feel warm.

10

Some things will feel cold when you touch them. Frozen treats, **icicles**, snowballs, and snowmen feel very cold. A glass filled with a cold drink also feels cold.

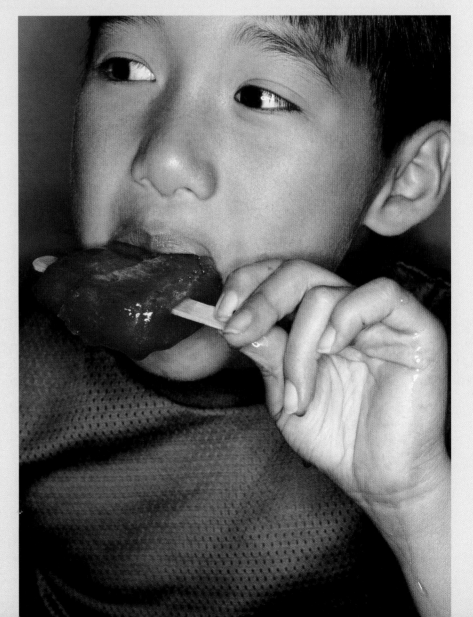

A frozen juice bar feels icy cold on your tongue.

11

OUCH!

Some things are dangerous to touch. Very hot things, such as boiling water or fire, can **hurt** you.

Stay a safe distance away from a fire.

12

Very sharp objects, such as knives, broken glass, or needles can give you a painful cut. If you ever have to touch anything sharp, be extra careful and have an adult help you.

An adult should always help you with sharp objects.

USING TOUCH TO SEE

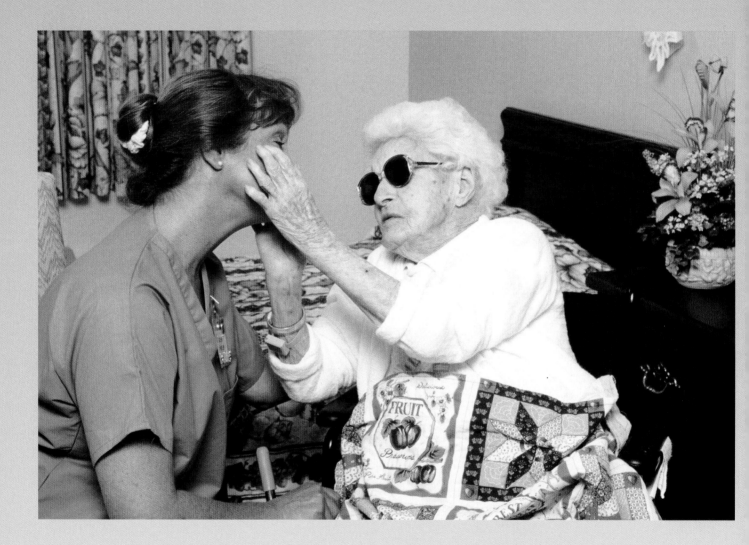

People who are blind cannot see, but their sense of touch helps them learn about the world around them. People who are blind use their hands to feel what people and objects look like.

Blind people use their sense of touch to read.

Braille is a special type of writing that can be read with the fingertips. Instead of printed words, braille uses raised dots that are arranged in different patterns. The patterns stand for letters and other characters. People who are blind read by touching the dots with their fingers.

TOUCHING

You use your sense of touch all day, every day. You touch the buttons on a telephone to make a call. You might touch your hair to push it out of your eyes. You are touching this book right now.

Your sense of touch
tells you when you are
touching something.
Without your sense of
touch, you would not feel
the chairs you sit on. You
would not be able to feel
the difference between a
sponge and a stone.

ANIMALS AND TOUCH

Animals use their sense of touch when they are in dark places. A cat's whiskers brush against the objects around them and send messages to the cat's brain. This is how a cat can find its way in the dark.

Its long whiskers help a cat feel
its way around in the dark.

Moles dig and live in dark tunnels underground. They are almost blind, so they use their strong sense of touch to find food and water. Moles use their whiskers and sensitive hairs on their noses, feet, and tails to feel movements in the dirt around them.

INSECTS AND TOUCH

Insects have tiny hairs on their bodies. The smallest breath of air will move the hairs. This movement sends information to the insect's brain.

Caterpillars have very poor sight. Instead of using their eyes to see the world around them, the small hairs all over their bodies tell these creatures about it.

WHAT DO YOU FEEL?

1. Gather a collection of different objects — some soft and squishy, some hard, some rough, and some smooth. One at a time, put each object in a box. Ask some of your friends to touch each object without looking in the box, then try to guess what each object is. How many objects did they guess correctly?

2. Touch different objects, such as wet clay, wobbly gelatin, the bark of a tree, a pillow, an ice cube, a piece of velvet, or a knitted sweater. Can you describe what each object feels like?

3. Ask a friend to shut his or her eyes. Take two pencils and lightly touch both of them to your friend's fingertips. How many pencils does your friend feel? Now do the same thing on your friend's legs. Does your friend feel two things now?

Your fingertips have many more nerve endings than do most parts of your body. This is why you find it much easier to feel things with your fingers than with your legs or other parts of your body.

GLOSSARY

feel: to become aware of an object or surroundings by using the sense of touch; to handle or touch something in order to learn about it

hurt: to cause injury or pain

icicles: thin, pointed pieces of hanging ice, formed by water that freezes as it drips

nerve endings: the tips of threadlike cells that carry messages between parts of your body and your brain

sense: a natural ability to receive and process information using one or more of the body's sense organs, such as the ears, eyes, nose, tongue, or skin. The five senses are hearing, sight, smell, taste, and touch.

textures: the look or feel of surfaces; for example, smooth and soft

touch: (n) the sense used to learn about something through contact with nerve endings in the skin; (v) to come in contact with something; to feel with a part of the body

INDEX

The Family Dinner

DINNERTIME

David asks for his dessert
Peggy wants to press her skirt
She has dance class and she's late
David says he cannot wait
Mike is giving him a ride
He'll just go and wait outside
Father tells him he will not
David mutters thanks a lot
Ann says she expects a call
Benjamin won't eat at all
Mother starts to serve the pie
Benjamin begins to cry
Mother asks him what is wrong
Father says the tea's too strong
Ann gets up to get the phone
Benjamin begins to moan
Peggy says her tights are torn
David says he hears a horn
Father says to finish first
David says that he will burst
Peggy says it isn't fair
Ann has on her other pair
Now she will be late for class
Benjamin upsets his glass
David's taking tiny bites
Ann is taking off the tights
David says the crust is tough
Mother says she's had enough
Father says it's not too bad
Mother says she's going mad
David wiggles like a mouse
That is dinner at our house.

—Mary Ann Hoberman

INTRODUCTION

WHY I STARTED HAVING FAMILY DINNER

One uneventful Wednesday night, I was sitting at the kitchen table with my family. Dessert had long since been consumed, but my two girls still lingered at the table an hour after we'd first sat down for supper. There we were, two bright, happy teenagers and I, engrossed in conversation that ranged from national politics, to binge drinking on college campuses, to who was doing what to whom at school. You know—all the stuff we crave to know but never get real answers to: what's really happening in their lives; who's mean and who's nice; who's misunderstood and why.

Wow, I thought to myself, *I have actually done something right as a parent.* This was a new feeling! Usually I'm beating myself up over all the mistakes I make on any given day. But wait, I had succeeded in luring and keeping my family at the dinner table—and talking about real issues they might have otherwise kept silent about!

What was my secret? I had insisted on the ritual of family dinner and made it a non-negotiable routine since my oldest was first secured in her high chair. Now I could see the results of that commitment on either side of me: two young people who not only enjoy eating healthy foods—an accomplishment in itself—but also listen, respond thoughtfully, and feel connected to me (and me to them!).

That night, I had to literally kick them out of the kitchen, because it was getting so late and homework still needed to be done. I, however, stayed behind at the table and soaked up a rare feeling of satisfaction along with my side order of surprise.

A decade before this savored moment, my kids were still in diapers, and as a newly minted stay-at-home mom I was frustrated that family life wasn't all I thought it would be. My husband worked seven days a week, and I had gone from having a very active career to full-time motherhood.

I was extremely lucky to be able to make the choice to stop working, but as every woman who has voluntarily left the workforce knows, the transition from career to home is bittersweet.

"I don't think there is **ONE THING MORE IMPORTANT** *you can do* **FOR YOUR KIDS THAN HAVE FAMILY DINNER."** —RUTH REICHL, former editor-in-chief of *Gourmet* magazine

"MY IDEA OF PERFECT HAPPINESS *is sitting at the kitchen table laughing with my daughters."*

—KATIE COURIC, broadcast journalist

Everyone I knew was still working. I had no mommy friends. This new isolation was just one problem. To be perfectly frank, I was completely unprepared for how challenging life can be as a new mom. I spent a lot of time pushing the stroller through neighborhood parks trying to soothe my colicky baby and searching for advice and comfort from strangers, mostly other moms who looked as bewildered to me as I must have looked to them.

When our family of three became a family of four, I started to crave the sort of meaningful family moments I had spent much of my adult life fantasizing about. Where was that charmingly chaotic and loving domestic bliss I thought automatically came with the diapers and the play-pen? I wanted that enchanted family feeling, too!

It became painfully obvious to me that achieving regular memorable family moments wasn't necessarily going to happen by itself. It occurred to me, as I sat in the park, my babies thankfully snoozing in their buggy, that dinnertime offered one place to start. We all had to eat, and everyone was generally home by six thirty, so fitting it into our busy schedules was doable.

Okay. Now what? Honestly, my childhood family dinner experiences didn't serve as very good role models for success. We had a five-night-a-week, home-cooked sit-down meal, but I barely remember a family dinner that didn't end with someone crying. Usually it was my older sister or my mother. Occasionally it was me.

I dreaded many of those meals. They were something to be gotten through quickly, with the least amount of emotional bruising. As an adolescent, my prevailing thought was always, *Who is going to go down tonight?* followed by, *How fast can I get excused from the table, out the door, and back on my bicycle?* That was not history worth repeating in my own home.

As an adult, other dissatisfying dinner experiences added to my anxiety over how to make dinner fun and rewarding instead of just a chore. The first that came to

mind was the Five-Minute Meal. As a working couple, my husband and I made a habit of them when we weren't eating in a restaurant: Zap something in the microwave and wolf it down leaning against the kitchen counter.

Oh, and let's not forget the Two-Point-Eight Dinner that friends often complain about: You lovingly prepare a meal for two hours (not counting shopping time), and then watch it get thoughtlessly devoured at record speed (eight minutes by one girlfriend's count!). There's also the Silent Supper. You know, the one where no one talks because everyone is in his or her own digestive fog, or watching the game or news on TV.

If I didn't think of a way around these scenarios, we'd be destined to a future of a million boring, predictable meals. After giving some thought to the problem, it occurred to me that my professional skills as a producer could come in handy: Why not treat dinnertime like an event! It would require cooperation from my spouse (at least a little), planning and perseverance, and most important, consistency. Oh, and maybe a few cooking classes, too. How tough could it be?

So I made family dinner into my project, and the process turned out to be not only fun but truly life changing. The key ingredient was the desire—of which I had plenty—to have everyone stop what he or she was doing at around the same time every night, and sit together for a satisfying amount of time to eat, talk, and connect as a family.

And so began the adventure. Taco Tuesday was my first big family dinner production. I enlisted the help of my girlfriend Heidi Haddad and her kids, and we quickly turned Taco Tuesday into a weekly fixture for both families. Rain or shine, busy or bored, we stuck to it.

All of a sudden, Tuesdays became sacred. For the kids, dinner during the week with "company" felt festive—like an impromptu party on a school night. It was easy and inexpensive. Heidi and I divided up the chopping and cooking tasks, while our kids used their creativity to set the table with paper flowers and mismatched place mats. We also decided to include a few age-appropriate questions for the table: If you were a fruit, which one would you be—and why? Or: If you could change your name, what would it be? Something to kick-start a conversation that everyone could enjoy and participate in.

Taco Tuesday was soon followed by Shabbat Friday (inspired by a class I took at a local temple). We would light

the candles, share a loaf of challah bread, and go around the table saying what we were grateful for. Some serious eye rolling was directed my way (from the husband, not the kids!), but determined, I made Shabbat Friday a weekly ritual too (see page 199).

From there, an easy Sunday ritual evolved. We called it "If It's Sunday, We Must Be Eating Chinese Takeout." The first of those dinners included an extended family of nieces, sisters, and cousins. Soon we were rotating who picked up and paid for the food each week. Family dinner doesn't always have to be home-cooked, and it doesn't have to be the last meal of the day, either (lunch or breakfast works, too!)—it just has to happen *together*!

I really liked the celebratory feeling that these themed nights provided. Ordinary weekdays developed a special-occasion feel to them. Miraculously, preparing dinner lost its drudgery. That enthusiasm was infectious. The kids would wake up all excited on a Tuesday morning and say, "Hey, it's Taco Tuesday!"

My cycle of meals worked well for quite a while, until my environmental work became all-consuming. The dinner hour was sacred, but out of nowhere the demands of my advocacy crept into my life 24/7. Without planning it, we had become a two-working-parent household, and the family dinner was the first thing to suffer. That's a not uncommon symptom for today's working parents. Women now make up a whopping 50 percent of the workforce—some by choice, some by necessity—but they're all asking the same question: Who's making dinner?

Some of my working friends have their moms living nearby to help out in the kitchen, making pasta sauce and lasagnas. That's one solution, if you are lucky. I have another friend whose two sisters live close by so they take turns making extra portions of food for one another's families, that

way minimizing the number of nights each is responsible for. Another strategy is to take the pressure off yourself in terms of what actually constitutes a meal. Dinner can be soup and a salad; brown rice with some veggies on top; takeout from a healthy restaurant or from the freezer. What it *doesn't* have to be is a roast and three sides, salad, and a homemade pie. Dinner is about intention much more than perfection. First and foremost, it's about sitting down together.

I did some of the above when time became an issue. Then my husband, Larry, suggested something that seemed crazy to me: hiring someone to help cook. I think the idea originally popped into his head because of his own guilt at being completely useless in the kitchen. Honestly, you couldn't even ask him to peel a cucumber unless you wanted it the size of a pencil. When I recently asked him about this period of time, he laughed and reminded me of his many personal kitchen challenges, including his fear of microwaves (won't stand anywhere near them), his distrust of toasters (stands next to them the entire time, popping them intermittently to check progress), and his inability to identify a "saucepan," thereby making him incapable of reheating anything.

Even with that handicap in the kitchen, I initially dismissed the idea of help because my middle-class upbringing made me feel uncomfortable about accepting it. How do you hire someone to do what moms are supposed to do? But with a determination to ease up on the self-imposed guilt and not think less of myself as a mom because I wasn't chopping the carrots, I finally accepted my husband's generous offer, with eternal gratitude.

The search began, and after a little trial and error we found Kirstin. Lucky for my family and me, Kirstin wasn't just any cook. She was a magical, whimsical Mary Poppins/Tinker Bell presence in our home and quickly became part of our family. She walked in and sprinkled fairy dust everywhere she went. Everything about her was unusual—starting with her name, which no one, even to this day, can pronounce correctly (*key-a-steen*).

Kirstin was raised on a large, beautiful fruit farm in Denmark (really, I'm not making this up!). Every day after school, she and her brothers would race out to the fields to pick apples or pears or whatever was in season. In the

"A FAMILY IS A GROUP OF PEOPLE WHO EAT THE SAME THING FOR DINNER." —NORA EPHRON, writer and director

evenings, she spent hours in the kitchen learning to cook alongside her mother and granny. Everyone in the kitchen cooking together is a common Danish ritual and perhaps could be one reason that the Danes are acknowledged as among the happiest people on earth.

Together, she and I began to expand and perfect the family dinner. We became great friends, co-conspirators, and dinner became our beloved nightly ritual. It improved my family life enormously; I would even say immeasurably.

From holiday dinners to birthdays, school nights and weekends, through a happy marriage, some tough times, and then divorce, one thing remained constant: dinner together around the table. This ritual has kept my family connected, kept all four of us talking through good times and bad.

Whatever your family makeup is, whatever the age range, whatever your income, whether you work outside the home or not, part-time or full-time, *The Family Dinner* gives you the inspiration, tips, recipes, and all I have learned to help draw your family to the table and keep them there. This isn't about adding more pressure to your schedule or guilt to your day. This isn't going to overwhelm you or add more "shoulds" to your life. A regularly scheduled meal can actually make your life easier and reduce your stress because you'll know much more about what your family is eating, thinking, and feeling.

Everyone will be happier as a result because, over time, you will probably start getting along better. I believe your family will be nourished in ways no multivitamin can come close to. And you'll be making dinner history yourself—by creating memories and rituals you and your kids will carry and savor forever.

STARTING NEW RITUALS

Here is a simple truth: *Dinner spreads love.* That is one of the great motivations for starting and maintaining this ritual, and it's one of the main reasons why, nine times out of ten, people grin ear-to-ear when recalling childhood family dinners. Food pioneer Alice Waters put it perfectly when she said, "My mom wasn't a very good cook but one of my fondest memories is of being three and watching her in the

"**AMONG THE MANY WONDERFUL THINGS ABOUT BEING PRESIDENT,** *the best is that I get to live above the office and* **SEE MY FAMILY EVERY DAY. WE HAVE DINNER EVERY NIGHT.** *It is the thing that sustains me."*
—PRESIDENT BARACK OBAMA

kitchen with a big pot of boiling apples. I couldn't wait to eat that applesauce. *It's a pure love memory."*

The Family Dinner is the book I wish I had when I first started raising my family and decided to embrace family dinner as a centerpiece of each day. Join us and have family dinner tonight, your own version. Start with whatever is on hand in the fridge and the pantry. You can do it with healthy take-out food, bowls of cereal, or peanut butter sandwiches. This book will help you get started whether you're an accomplished cook or a novice with a dented frying pan.

If you are a working family, *The Family Dinner* offers realistic ways to make sure that a sit-down dinner isn't sacrificed to your busy schedule. Inside these pages, you can learn how one afternoon in the kitchen can provide several meals for the week, how to turn leftovers into imaginative new dishes just by adding a few new ingredients, and how to get the conversation going in directions you never imagined.

The Family Dinner will show you ways to serve a dinner in which everyone participates—from the food to the conversation to the cleanup. When everyone is involved in the meal, they become invested in it in a new way, and are more excited to sit down and have fun. Everyone learns to be more appreciative, too!

Together, we will reconnect with our kids, eat delicious food, laugh, cry, and do it all again tomorrow! Together, one meal at a time, we can make family dinner the regular ritual it was always meant to be. Sacred time. Time to purposely be a family. Time that belongs to you and your family; time that is so important no one will dare mess with it.

So . . . what's for dinner?

Dinner Guest Recipe

GARY'S T-NIGHT TACOS

Here is the famous Taco Tuesday recipe that started our dinner rituals. Only it's not. We asked our friend Gary, a fabulous cook and designated chef for his family, to contribute the recipe for one of his kids' favorite dinners.

Without skipping a beat he said, "Oh, well it will have to be my Taco Tuesday recipe!" Yikes, awkward: We already had our own taco recipe and it had sentimental value.

What's this? Gary's recipe features black beans! And a secret ingredient—maple syrup! And a fresh and tangy salsa. Well, we might just have to have a family recipe cook-off!

Which we did, and the winner is . . . **GARY STUBER's** *Best Bean Tacos Ever!*

KIDS CAN

Peel the cucumbers.
Squeeze the limes.
Chop the cilantro.
Put the toppings in little bowls.

YOU NEED

For the Tacos

Canola oil

2 medium onions, coarsely grated

2 15-ounce cans of black beans, lightly drained (or 4 ½ cups home-cooked beans)

2 tablespoons chili powder

2 tablespoons cumin

1 tablespoon tamari soy sauce

2 tablespoons maple syrup

12 corn tortillas

For the Toppings

1½ cups shredded cheddar

1 cup sour cream or Greek yogurt

Chopped avocado

Chopped tomatoes

Chopped lettuce

Cucumber salsa (recipe at right)

Green Tip

If you use tinfoil, look for 100 percent recycled aluminum foil. It has no added chlorine or toxins and performs as well as traditional foil.

TO MAKE 12 TACOS

Heat a large nonstick pan over medium-high heat and drizzle the bottom with canola oil. Sauté the onions until they start to soften, then add the beans, spices, tamari, and maple syrup. Reduce the heat to medium low and let everything gently cook for 10 minutes.

Meanwhile, wrap the tortillas in foil and warm for 10 minutes in a 250-degree oven.

Serve the tortillas with bowls of beans and toppings on the side.

CUCUMBER GARLIC SALSA

YOU NEED

1 medium cucumber

3 garlic cloves

¼ cup fresh lime juice, divided

Pinch of sea salt

½ cup chopped cilantro

TO MAKE ABOUT 1 CUP

Peel the cucumber, cut it into cubes, and place the cubes in the blender.

Add the peeled garlic cloves, half the lime juice, and a pinch of salt.

Place the top on the blender and use short pulses to blend, adding only enough additional lime juice to liquefy.

Add the cilantro, stirring it in with a wooden spoon.

WHY FAMILY DINNERS MATTER

1

RAISE HEALTHIER, SMARTER, AND MORE CONFIDENT KIDS

Imagine sitting down and connecting with your children every day in a cheerful, significant, and meaningful way. Sound impossible or completely unrealistic? It's not. It's called family dinner. Maybe you're already cooking up a version of it that you're not completely satisfied with. Maybe you've thought about doing it but can't quite make it happen due to a nonstop stream of scheduling conflicts. Maybe you're suffering from "over-screenitis," the TV, computer, and BlackBerry sucking up most of your family's downtime. Whatever the reason, if you are missing out on regular family dinners, you are missing out on the best part of the day. The importance of dinnertime should not be underestimated, and when done well it *will* rock your world.

Family dinner—the beloved and respected ritual and a longstanding tool for raising children—was once a non-negotiable part of the day. But it is in danger of disappearing from modern life and is too often treated with as much respect as a parsley garnish. Today's overscheduled children (and adults) typically inhale fast food in the car, in front of the TV, in their bedroom, beside a computer, or standing alone at a kitchen counter.

If this sounds like your life, how many other opportunities during the day do you really have to connect as a family in a meaningful way, before your kids go to sleep, or before they shut the door to chat with friends on the Internet? Dinnertime is too important to let it slip through our fingers that easily. Everything we worry about as our kids transform from sweet, dependent, moldable toddlers to detached, hormone-raging, experimental teenagers can be improved by gathering together and sharing a nutritious, delicious, rollicking meal with them on a regular basis.

MIRACULOUS MEALS

Test after test, survey after survey, study after study have all reached the same exact conclusion: Children who have regular dinners together with their parents do better in almost all areas of life, from higher grades in school, to maintaining loving relationships, to staying healthy, safe, and out of trouble. Family meals have more to do with adolescents' self-esteem, confidence, and other positive outcomes than do income levels, after-school activities, family structure (one parent or two), or regular attendance at church. That's right, from drugs to alcohol to smoking to promiscuity, studies show that the simple habit of family dinner helps lower the odds of your kids diving off perilous behavioral cliffs.

The National Center on Addiction and Substance Abuse at Columbia University has studied the impact of

"PEOPLE SAY THEY DON'T HAVE TIME TO COOK, *yet in the last few years we have found an* **EXTRA TWO HOURS A DAY FOR THE INTERNET."** —MICHAEL POLLAN, author of *The Omnivore's Dilemma*

"If we want our kids to lead healthier lives, **WE SHOULD EAT WITH THEM MORE OFTEN."** —MIRIAM WEINSTEIN, author of *The Surprising Power of Family Meals*

A FEAST OF FACTS

As I read more on the subject of family dinner, I was completely amazed by what I learned. The positive impact a simple daily ritual can have on a whole host of family issues is revelatory. Here's just a sample of what experts say family dinners several nights a week can do for kids at every age:

- Compared with teens who rarely have family dinners, those who have them five or more times a week are 42 percent less likely to drink alcohol, 59 percent less likely to smoke cigarettes, and 66 percent less likely to try marijuana.

- Compared with teens who rarely have family dinners, those who frequently have them are three and a half times less likely to have abused prescription drugs or an illegal drug other than marijuana.

- Compared with teens who rarely have family dinners, adolescent girls who frequently eat meals with their families appear less likely to use diet pills, laxatives, or other extreme measures to control their weight, even five years later.

- One in three American children are overweight or obese. Regular family dinner can reduce the incidence of childhood obesity.

- Compared with teens who rarely have family dinners, teens who have frequent family meals are 40 percent more likely to get A's and B's. Children ages seven to eleven who did well on school achievement tests were the ones who ate meals and snacks with their families more frequently.

- Family dinners are a key ingredient in helping children develop language skills, expand vocabulary, learn how to tell stories, and articulate feelings and thoughts.

- Teens who have regular family dinners are more likely to be well adjusted. They're less likely to be depressed, are more motivated at school, and have better peer relationships.

family dinner for years. Its president, Joseph Califano, believes, "Our nation's drug problem is not going to be solved by legislation; it's going to be solved across the kitchen table." Years of research have led Califano to the conclusion that parents still have the strongest influence on kids. "I call the ages ten to twenty the killer decade," he says. "That's when drugs and alcohol rear their ugly heads, and family dinner falls apart, just when it's most important."

The family dinner begins to work its magic as soon as our children are old enough to sit at the table. According to child development specialist Dr. Harvey Karp, meals are important even to the youngest children. "Having predictable routines for toddlers lowers stress, increases their confidence, and makes them feel smarter because they love knowing what to expect. Routines like dinner are an island of calm in a world of change. They are predictable and anchoring," he says. In short, dinner makes a difference, and the sooner you start the more rewards you will reap. Establishing a dinner routine with your young children will serve you well when your kids are older and the issues with them more complex. But the good news is that it is never too late to start—whatever the age of your children, everyone will gain by sharing family meals.

SCREENING FOOD

There is so much tearing at the family fabric these days; anything we can do to make the cloth stronger is surely something we should embrace—and how lucky for us this effort includes food! Heaven knows, we can use all the help we can get, because our challenges as parents today are much more difficult than even a decade ago. Sure, our parents had to worry about us in terms of sex and drugs, but they didn't have to deal with the complete inundation of the COMPUTER and CELL PHONE (all-caps because I am yelling them!), including but not limited to IMing, texting, Twitter, Facebook, and

"One of the most powerful **MEDICINES AGAINST BREAST CANCER IS FAMILY DINNERS.** *It's the single most potent way to improve your nutrition, manage your weight, feel support, find love, have fun, and create a family legacy of healthy eating."* —MARISA WEISS, MD, president and founder of Breastcancer.org

"ADOLESCENTS ENJOY EATING MEALS WITH THEIR FAMILIES *and feel they eat healthier when they eat more often with them."* —DIANNE NEUMARK-SZTAINER, PhD, Division of Epidemiology and Community Health, School of Public Health, University of Minnesota

video games. **On average, kids today spend almost seven and a half hours a day using some form of electronic media!** (This stunning statistic shocked even the people who were doing the research.) We really need to take a moment to consider the implications of that. More technology time means less family time (online spikes start as early as 7 AM). School is also contributing to the problem by sending kids home every day right back on to their laptops for homework, providing the perfect cover for playing computer games and social networking, eating into what little time is left in the day. I can't count the times I have asked my kids to get off the computer only to hear, "I'm doing homework, Mom." Yeah, right. Let's face it: The computer is keeping our kids inside and in their own isolated world, making it more difficult for us to stay engaged in their lives and for them to stay engaged with us.

Throw into that stew overscheduling, after-school practices played right through the dinner hour, and peer pressure. Mix in a big cultural shift of two working parents, longer work hours, economic challenges, exhaustion, guilt (there

---

The recent study "Household Routines and Obesity in U.S. Preschool-Aged Children" by Sarah E. Anderson, PhD, and Robert C. Whitaker, MD, found that kids as young as four already have a lower risk for obesity if they had three basic routines in their life:

- FAMILY DINNER
- ADEQUATE SLEEP
- LIMITED WEEKDAY TV VIEWING

---

1 OF 5 MEALS ARE EATEN IN THE CAR.

is always plenty of that) . . . well, you start to get the picture about why such an important ritual is losing ground.

And let's not forget the biggest screen of all, the television. This screen is flipped on like a light switch in multiple rooms in the house. No more group votes on what to watch and everyone snuggling together on the couch. These days, there can be more TVs in the average U.S. home than people, making it easy for everyone to watch their favorite shows *by themselves.* This is another big cultural shift affecting family life. If you're not watching together, there is zero chance of any conversation and discussion.

A 2006 Kaiser study concluded that TV helps parents cope with the everyday tensions we all face. "In many homes, parents have created an environment where the TV is a nearly constant presence, from the living room, kitchen, dining room to the bedroom." As one mom puts it, "If he's watching TV, I can get things done. I don't have to constantly watch him."

I know I overused the TV when my kids were little to calm them down from tantrums and to give myself some breathing room, but overuse often comes with a hefty price tag. Using TV to accompany meals cuts off communication and puts an end to any meaningful social interaction. Here is a sobering stat for you: For every hour spent online or watching a screen at home, forty-one minutes less is spent with family.

Moreover, screens aren't just antisocial—they can be fattening, too. We overeat when we aren't paying attention. Research shows that kids who are overweight eat 50 percent of their meals in front of a television.

While we are on the topic, we should also factor in the enormous amount of advertising for unhealthy food and drink products kids are bombarded with during

"MY CAR HAS REPLACED THE HEARTH *as the center of my family life."* —Overheard comment by mom in carpool line

their favorite shows. Depending on how much TV a child watches, they could see more than seventy-six hundred food ads a year. Of those, 70 percent are for foods in the lowest category of nutritional quality. Brilliant, sparkly ads glamorizing fast food, candy, sugary cereals—making our job teaching good nutrition even tougher.

STARVED FOR TIME

Most of us would agree that today's families face a "time famine." Ellen Galinsky, president of the Families and Work Institute and author of *Mind in the Making*, studies this problem and says many parents feel that they have too much to do and not enough time to do it. "A majority of employed parents—75 percent—feel that they don't have enough time with their kids; they are distracted and find it hard to come up for air," she says. Not surprisingly, when Galinsky asked a nationally representative sample of kids what their concerns are, the largest proportion responded that they wished Mom and Dad would be less stressed and less tired. "Kids feel that their time with their parents is rushed, and parents feel that, too." Among Galinsky's conclusions: Families need to find ways to slow down and zero

"A MEAL *is about* **CIVILIZING** *children. It's about* **TEACHING THEM TO BECOME A MEMBER OF THEIR CULTURE."** —ROBIN FOX, PhD, professor of social theory at Rutgers University

in on one another. "Focus is one of the essential skills we need to practice and teach our children," she says.

Rituals to the rescue! As a family, you don't need dozens of them to help you stay connected, but you do need a few. There is something so powerful about the accountability of committing to come to the table most nights that works. My family members know that every day, they are going to have to reconnect with me. **Family dinner acts as a motivator, a deterrent, and a safety net.** Because we interact with one another every night, no one can get too upset, depressed, or confused without someone in the family noticing. And that gives us all a chance to help and be helped when we need it.

Family therapist and nutrition expert Ellyn Satter puts it perfectly when she says, "Meals are as essential for

67% OF TEENS IN AMERICA WANT TO HAVE MORE TIME WITH THEIR PARENTS.

"CHILDREN WHO FEEL LISTENED TO, *become better able to listen to others."* —ELLEN GALINSKY, president of the Families and Work Institute and author of *Mind in the Making*

nurturing as they are for nutrition. Meals provide us all with reliable access to food and they provide children with dependable access to their parents. Without meals, a home is just a place to stay."

Because family dinner provides consistent parental access, it adds glue to a family. It builds relationships, encourages open communication, and provides security for all family members.

So many healthy lessons are learned at the family table, including portion control, how to make healthful choices, how to experiment with new foods, and how to develop your palate.

Regular family dinner—one meal for everyone (no separate orders; allergies and diet concerns excepted of course)—pays other huge dividends as well, including getting picky eaters to open their minds (and mouths). Experts say it can take trying a food up to a dozen times, sometimes taking just one bite, before you acquire a taste for something. That's why it is so important to never give up exposing kids to new foods.

Hey, we haven't even mentioned the all-important, could-take-years task of teaching good table manners. Honestly, there was a year when I didn't think one of my daughters would ever improve her manners (she knows who I am talking about!). It was really starting to get embarrassing. Then one night, I realized that phase had finally ended. She was actually using her fork instead of her fingers to eat! It wasn't my nagging that did it; in fact, the more nagging I did, the worse it got. Instead, all the modeling done by

"THE DINNER TABLE *is the* **CENTER FOR THE TEACHING AND PRACTICING** *not just of table manners but of conversation, consideration, tolerance, family feeling, and just about all the other accomplishments of polite society except the minuet."*

—JUDITH MARTIN (Miss Manners), writer and etiquette authority

...⌘...

DINNER
And That's an Order

"Be home for dinner by six" is a command that comes not from home but from the top brass of the U.S. Army. In this case, Fort Hood, America's largest military base. The policy, initially issued by Lieutenant General Rick Lynch to all soldiers stationed there, acknowledges the importance of family dinner. "It does more than make everyone happy," Lynch says. "It creates a more resilient soldier, one less likely to abuse drugs or alcohol, injure himself in a traffic accident, or fall to suicide." Since the policy was instituted in February 2009, Fort Hood has seen a noticeable reduction in traffic accidents and suicides. And it's an order service members and their families really look forward to following.

everyone, every night, including the many guests at our table, made her finally notice that there is a socially acceptable way to eat. Today, she's the manners police at our table . . . go figure!

Family dinner is an opportunity to carve out the time to influence, engage, and entertain one another. It's a time to learn how to listen, communicate, and socialize with adults and peers, and to learn how to sit and share. Family dinner teaches your small community the proper skills to become healthy, contributing members of the larger community. It's the perfect opportunity to teach your kids how to be good citizens. And every time you sit down together, you are building that foundation for their future. It doesn't happen overnight, but it does happen over time, meal after meal after meal.

Your table is also the perfect training ground for building confidence and self-esteem, respect for others, debating skills, and all-around good composure. This point was made beautifully in a *New York Times* interview with Carol Smith, a respected businesswoman and VP and publishing director for *Bon Appétit* and *Gourmet*. Smith says that when she is serious about hiring someone, she always takes that person out for a meal. "You learn so much in a meal. It's like a microcosm of life. How they order, what they order, how they give instructions to a waiter, can they keep a conversation going ... these are all the things I look at."

Wow. Who'da thunk it? Family dinner might help your kids get a job!

Regular family dinner will give everyone, including you, a chance to look one another in the eye, relate, connect, eat, talk, and laugh, enjoying the great pleasures of a shared expe-

rience. If dinner isn't an option don't give up; make breakfast your family time ritual, or lunch, or before-bed teatime.

Meals are an opportunity to take a break from our worries and feel, at least once a day, that we are all in this life together. Taking time to share dinner lets every family member know, "You are important to me—so important that this time is sacred for all of us." And of course, it's a chance to make and eat some really yummy food.

Like everything worthwhile in life, dinner gets better the more you do it. Every day we get a new chance to practice and experiment. So let's get started—I'm starving!

It Starts in

PRESCHOOL

MARY HARTZELL *is a child development specialist, author, and director of*
First Presbyterian Nursery School in Santa Monica, California.

LAURIE: I had the good fortune to send both my children to your preschool, where you have been guiding new and returning parents through the early years for a long time now. What do you see as the big challenges facing parents today?

MARY: Both parents and children are overscheduled. As a result, family time isn't given the value it deserves. Family dinner isn't considered important. Too often it's just squeezed in and rushed through. There isn't much joy, conversation, or bonding in rushing through meals.

LAURIE: Why is dinner so important, in your view?

MARY: Dinnertime is an opportunity to build and deepen relationships. The foundation of our family is loving, respectful relationships. All of us, adults and children, learn through our relationships, not only about others but about ourselves, too. At dinner, when parents sit down at the table, they are generally focusing on the wrong things. They focus on how much food the child is putting into their mouth. They miss the opportunity to have a connecting,

joyful experience, to listen to their children and engage in a shared dialogue. For the most part, we don't know how to listen well. The ways our culture is eating today—fast food, solitary eating, eating on the run—don't support relationships. Parents aren't slowing down, and this can mean a missed opportunity every day to build our sense of belonging through shared mealtimes.

LAURIE: I remember when my kids were little, I was constantly watching what they were eating. How many bites of broccoli she took, whether she touched the chicken or not.

MARY: Toddlers are really working on their autonomy. When a parent gets overly involved with how much food their child is eating, children usually eat less. They don't want to eat because the parent is trying to *make* them eat. It's a classic power struggle between the parent and the child, and guess who usually wins? Eating is your child's job. Your job is to provide healthy, tasty food. What and how much they are eating is not a worthy topic of your dinner conversation.

"OBESITY IS GROWING *faster than ... any other public health condition in the country's history."* —KENNETH THORPE, PhD, professor and chair, Rollins School of Public Health, Emory University

TEN

SIMPLE STEPS

to Successful Family Dinners

2

These ten steps—or rules—have been the key to success for my family dinners. They are not arbitrary or voluntary. They level the playing field by giving everyone the same chance to have a positive experience. Pay no attention to the inevitable complaining. It is human nature to resist, and your job to insist! Enforcement must be the same for everyone, no exceptions for Dad or excuses for Mom. Consistency is crucial.

If you are starting family dinner from scratch, follow two or three steps to get you started and add more as you go along. They will save you time, energy, and aggravation. Your big reward for this effort will come the day *you* try to skip one and your children bust you! They will loudly and firmly insist you adhere to the rules. You will at first be shocked, and then pleased. I speak from personal experience, naturally.

RECITE TONIGHT

A child should always say what's true
And speak when he is spoken to,
And behave mannerly at the table,
At least as far as he is able.

—*Robert Louis Stevenson*

STEP ONE: *It's a Date!*

Set a regular time for the family dinner. This rule will save you the monotony of having to repeatedly answer the question "When's dinner?" When my kids were little, we had a five thirty start . . . a few years later we adjusted the time to fit our changing schedules to six o'clock . . . today it's six thirty sharp. By the time this book comes out, we should be at a very civilized 7 PM.

STEP TWO: *Everyone Comes to the Table at the Same Time*

No late stragglers, no showing up when you feel like it. "I'm not hungry" is not an acceptable excuse for skipping dinner. Even if you don't eat, you still have to participate (in my experience, the non-hungry participants usually forget they weren't hungry and end up eating the whole meal).

STEP THREE: *No Phones*

Do not answer the phone at dinner. Do not bring a phone or BlackBerry to the table. No ringing, vibrating, answering, or texting allowed. If someone mistakenly brings their phone to the table and has the misfortune to accidentally glance at it, it's yours, for as long as you decide to keep it. Try that policy out and see how quickly the violators learn to leave their phones elsewhere. Trust me, it works!

If you have to dry the dishes
(Such an awful boring chore)
If you have to dry the dishes
('Stead of going to the store)
If you have to dry the dishes
And you drop one on the floor
Maybe they won't let you
Dry the dishes anymore.

—*Shel Silverstein,* A Light in the Attic

"In my house growing up, you basically had to **HAVE A NOTE FROM YOUR DOCTOR NOT TO SHOW UP FOR DINNER!"**
—ELLEN WEISS, senior vice president for news, NPR

STEP FOUR: *One Meal, No Substitutions*

This rule was very important when my kids were young, and it still is. I served meals that I thought everyone would like, but they weren't "kid meals." They were adult meals with kid-friendly ingredients (roast chicken, crunchy potatoes, green beans with teriyaki sauce). This really helped them learn to eat—and like—what they were served. You're not really doing your kids a favor by making it okay not to eat what's served. Be prepared for initial stubbornness and a few uneaten meals, but that phase won't last long. Tough it out or you'll end up as a short-order cook and never actually get to sit down yourself.

STEP FIVE: *Everyone Tries Everything*

This is very different from the old adage "Eat everything on your plate." The rigid insistence in the old days on eating all of your vegetables only accomplished one thing—it turned kids into stealth veggie Houdinis. I became an expert at the veggie disappearing act; my sister Lisa was my mentor, the dog, my accomplice. When Farfel the pooch refused

an item, I would resort to the "hide the peas in the napkin" trick. Cloth, paper, it didn't matter. Just hide those darn peas. Once, a few rolled out of my sister's napkin and blew our cover sky-high. To this day, Lisa cannot tolerate even a single pea on her plate, and she is fifty-five years old!

Tasting everything is an important rule. It shows respect to whomever prepared the food and respect for yourself. Why not give your taste buds an opportunity to be pleasantly surprised? Recently we had a six-year-old guest at the table whose first reaction to the homemade tomato soup was "yuck." Her father nicely but firmly told her she had to try it, which she did. Two bowls later she declared tomato soup her new favorite food!

STEP SIX: *No Television*

Of course, that also includes *any* electronic device. Maybe we should just call this rule "No screens." Your kids will argue with you that they can do three things at the same time (watch TV, eat, *and* listen closely to your every word, maybe even IM, too!), but it doesn't matter. Here's the good news: On special occasions the television is invited to dinner and as a result of the novelty, it is a really fun treat. In my house those times include presidential debates, election returns, Olympics, award shows, and a final of a big game.

STEP SEVEN: *Tap Water Only, Filtered if Needed*

No individual plastic bottles allowed in the kitchen, period. Serve it cold and preferably from a filtered tap in a clear glass pitcher. Garnish with slices of lemon, lime, cucumber, oranges, apples, or sprigs of mint. Adding whole fresh or frozen strawberries, raspberries, or blueberries to their glasses makes kids want to drink even more water in their attempts to reach the berry treasure at the bottom!

This was one of the early rules I insisted on, and I am so grateful now that I followed my instincts. First, it's a serious nutritional issue. Water is essential for good health, and most people don't drink enough of it. Juice is loaded with sugar. Soda is loaded with sugar and chemicals. Milk was never an option for me because my kids were lactose-intolerant. Don't forget, in your kitchen you are establishing patterns that will last your children a lifetime and hopefully

SIX SMART STRATEGIES
for Ensuring Mealtime Success

On the subject of healthy family eating, dietitian and family therapist **ELLYN SATTER** *is wise, wise, wise. Her book* Secrets of Feeding a Healthy Family *is a commonsense guide to making mealtimes simple and nutritious.*

1. MAKE THE TIME. In terms of supporting your child's overall social and emotional welfare, family meals are more important than organized activities.
2. FEED YOURSELF, FEED YOUR CHILDREN. Parents often are not very competent eaters themselves. They have a tendency to feed the children rather than feed themselves. The family meal works best if parents put on a meal for themselves and "invite" the children to join in.
3. PLAN SNACKS. The key word being *planned* in place of grazing—snacks are mini meals that help sustain children between meals, and guarantee that they will be hungry when they sit down for dinner.
4. SET THE STANDARD. Feeding children appropriately requires a division of responsibility. Parents are responsible for the what, when, and where of feeding. Children are responsible for tasting, trying, and determining how much they will eat of what's served.
5. SERVE IT UP ALL TOGETHER! Put everything on the table at the same time (including something to mop up spills), sit down, and don't get up till you're finished. Children behave exactly as their adults teach them to behave. If you hover and jump up and chase after and respond to every little demand for attention, your child will ask for it all and more. If, however, you help your child get served, serve yourself, and refuse to be distracted from your own meal, your child will attend to his or her own meal rather than try to get you to perform.
6. COOK IN A HURRY IF YOU MUST, BUT DON'T EAT IN A HURRY.

"FAMILY DINNER IS A WAY TO DE-STRESS *and—if managed correctly—***A TIME TO HAVE FUN.*** *By that I mean don't use it as a period of inquisition or a recounting of shortcomings. Keep it light, keep it fun, make it a highlight of the day."* —PEGGY DREXLER, PhD, assistant professor of psychology, Weill Cornell Medical College

Guess Who's

COMING TO DINNER?

To American television audiences, she is known as the not-to-be-messed-with **JUDGE JUDY SHEINDLIN,** *but to her eleven grandchildren, ranging in age from five to twenty-one, she is just Nanna. One night she planned a formal family dinner, invited her children, their spouses, and their offspring. Oh, and one more special guest: a manners expert hired from the Internet!*

LAURIE: Is it true you hired an etiquette expert to have dinner with your family?

JUDGE JUDY: Yes, but let's start with why. My father was a fastidious manners person. He had a thing for good table manners, and I grew up hearing the words, "Close your mouth when you chew," "Bring the food to you," "Don't talk with your mouth full." If dinner was twenty minutes, it was twenty minutes of "Sit up straight" and all the rest. I believe I taught my children reasonable table manners, but not all of their mates had the same upbringing. I also think people today are so busy with just trying to maintain order at home with two parents working and shuffling back and forth between tennis lessons and bongo lessons and soccer that somehow the importance of good manners has gotten lost.

LAURIE: So one motive was perhaps to refresh the adults as well as the kids?

JUDGE JUDY: Sometimes a little bit of a brush-up is a good thing. Doctors, lawyers, CPAs go for continuing education. Why not do the same when you parent children? Not to mention the grandkids, who are wonderful and well schooled, but not all of them know how to hold a fork!

LAURIE: How was this idea received?

JUDGE JUDY: The children were very excited about coming to a fancy dinner party at Nanna and Poppy's where they were going to learn etiquette and manners. They got all dressed up. There was really no fooling around. We started right away with how to sit down at the table the appropriate way, and for the young men to stand until the women were seated. They learned that when a bread basket is passed, you politely take a roll, you put a little pat of butter on your bread plate, and then you butter your roll.

LAURIE: Did you learn any new manners that evening?

JUDGE JUDY: I did. I learned that when you eat in a restaurant and you get up to go to the restroom, if you're not finished with your meal, you are supposed to leave your napkin on the chair. But if you are finished with your food, your napkin goes on the table.

LAURIE: Your dad would be very pleased with your experiment!

JUDGE JUDY: He would have loved it. I remember, after I became a judge, going out to dinner with my father and ordering soup. He gave me a gentle reminder, "Darling, the whole spoon does not go in your mouth, sip it from the side." He wasn't afraid to say this to his daughter who now had a prestigious position. You're never too old to be reminded!

"We have done research showing that even kids as young as two are more willing **TO TRY SOMETHING NEW IF THEY OBSERVE AN ADULT TRYING IT.** *Dinner provides all sorts of modeling opportunities, like portion size, food sampling, etc."* —LEANN BIRCH, PhD, distinguished professor of human development, Penn State University

the lifetimes of your grandchildren. My kids learned at an early age to expect water at meals, and they got used to it pretty quickly. A decade later, they now associate meals with water—crave it really, even when they are in restaurants.

It's also a financial issue. Check your grocery bills and add up what you spend on needless, unhealthy sugary drinks over the course of a month. You might be shocked. Not to mention the energy you spend lugging all those cans, bottles, and jugs into the house and then out to the curb for recycling.

This rule doesn't mean you can never serve other drinks, but they should be considered special-occasion choices. For instance, when oranges are in season, squeeze them and make spritzers. Mulled cider with a cinnamon stick is fun when winter winds blow. And of course, wine with dinner is a grown-up's choice—in addition to a glass of water.

STEP EIGHT: *Friends and Family Welcome*

I always encourage my kids to invite their friends and even their friends' parents to dinner. "The more the merrier" really puts everyone in a happy mood at the table, and everyone is on their best behavior, too. Dinner is always fun when there are guests; it becomes an event, the evening's activity! Manners improve, conversation ramps up, everyone lingers.

STEP NINE: *You're Excused*

No one leaves the table until after dessert. Okay, I know that insisting everyone stay for dessert doesn't seem like a tough one, but having this rule keeps everyone focused on the meal and not what they want to do next. It also provides an opportunity for parents. If, say, Act One doesn't work out so well (maybe you all get into a squabble, someone's feelings get hurt, or it's a night where everyone has an attitude and the compliments on the food are scarce), at least you know there is going to be a second act to resuscitate the family spirit. No one can leave at intermission.

By the way, when I say dessert, I don't mean chocolate mousse or cheesecake every night. Dessert can just as easily be orange slices, or a few fresh strawberries, or just a cup of warm tea.

STEP TEN: *Everyone Helps Clean Up*

No exceptions. It's more fun and cleanup is faster when everyone chips in. "Many hands make light work," as they say. Rotate the duties so nobody gets stuck always taking out the trash or washing pots and pans.

Feel free to add more guidelines to this list to make it your own and to suit your family's needs. I do promise you that eventually the rules become second nature to everyone, and will rarely be broken.

"Wally, there is nothing **OLD-FASHIONED ABOUT POLITENESS."**
—WARD CLEAVER to his son at dinner, *Leave It to Beaver*

SETTING
THE SCENE
3

"Do ordinary things with extraordinary love."
—MOTHER TERESA

Kirstin says: It all starts with a fork, and a plate, a white cloth napkin, or maybe just a big green leaf beneath a sandwich. It does not take much to set the scene so that it is a little different, a bit exciting, and very memorable. And that is what matters, isn't it?

Put a little effort into making the ordinary count. Throw takeout dinner on a plate, plop it in front of kids, and pay them no mind, and they will not be impressed. But change the setting once in a while, add some whimsy, a bit of ethnic flair, a dash of the unexpected, and you'll have their attention. Have an Italian spaghetti dinner on Sunday with a red-checkered tablecloth, candles, and Sinatra playing in the background. Set the table with your fancy china one night, get dressed up, wear hats, and serve sandwiches and tea. One of the quickest ways to set a new scene is to pack up your food and go . . . even if it's just to the rug in the next room!

They will be pleased with the new adventure (even if they are too cool to tell you so), and dinner will be fun, funny, and memorable. All you need is a little thoughtfulness, some love, and a few minutes spent focusing on what might make someone smile today.

SETTING THE TABLE

Setting the table is one of the first chores a child can learn how to do. I have asked quite a few teenagers to set the table, with cataclysmic results. So unless you want your child embarrassed by some future in-law, let's teach them how to set the table.

Once they know how to set the table correctly, it's time to have some fun and bend the rules. For example, on those days when you have invited people for dinner, but you are not sure exactly how many are going to show up, put the food on a buffet with plenty of plates on the side. And down the center of your table line up glasses, each with a napkin, fork, and knife inside. That way you won't have to reset the table each time someone walks in the door, and you also don't have to remove any sad empty place settings. Another day find some pretty vessels, like silver vases, small ice buckets, or flowerpots, arrange your silverware, napkins, and flowers in each, and put them in the center of the table.

Other ideas: Put your utensils in the center of the plate; to one side; fan them; balance them on the glass; just have fun with it. Simple changes make setting the table a creative project as opposed to a chore.

Paint Your Dinner Fancy

For nights the kids have friends over . . . Cover your dining table with a big piece of craft paper. Put out crayons, water paints, and pens. Have them draw the fanciest, fun, or craziest table settings, flower arrangements, and name cards right on the paper.

THE LAZY SUSAN

The lazy Susan is anything but! Named for hardworking servants whose names, oddly, were frequently Susan, the spinning platter was first advertised in *Vanity Fair* magazine in 1917. Usually circular, these rotating trays are placed on top of a table to help pass food with a gentle glide of the wrist. They are wonderful additions to any table and have the added bonus of making any meal more fun. But beware, most families have at least one lazy Susan abuser in their midst. For that I have the golden rule: "Overspinning will lead to a temporary loss of your lazy Susan privileges!"

Setting a Picnic Scene Inside or Out

Pack up a tablecloth, real silverware, and candlesticks. None of these things break, but they all make a picnic pretty and memorable. Also, any day is a good picnic day. So surprise your family with a picnic dinner on a Wednesday, inside or out.

Setting the Table for Take-Out Chinese

Get the kids to help you while you wait for the food to come. Hide the forks, put out your reusable chopsticks and little bowls for condiments, set the table with your blue-and-white china, or get out your lucky red linens. Float a few flowers in shallow bowls; brew a pot of jasmine tea.

"I'm a **WORKING MOM** *so I often get* **TAKEOUT, BUT I PUT IT INTO NICE BOWLS.** *It takes that moment, you pause and you're* **NOT JUST EATING OUT OF THE PLASTIC, YOU'RE GIVING GRACE TO THE FOOD.** *Not letting it be rushed shows you care."*

—JILL, mom of three

Green Tip

Our favorite picnic item is a tiffin tin—that wonderful Indian stackable lunchbox, usually three-tiered, stainless steel, and reusable forever. Fill these with your salad and snacks and marvel at how easy they are to serve, clean up, and store leftovers in. Find inexpensive ones in Indian or Asian markets and online. (See Resources on page 231.)

The Special Bowl of Treasures: Show-and-Tell at the Table

Try this for a week or a year, especially if your kids are the kind whose pockets are always spilling with found objects. Place a bowl in the center of your table. As the week progresses and objects are found, either by chance or on special treasure-seeking expeditions, the empty nests, the magical marbles, the rock that looks like Uncle Bob's nose, acorns, perfect pebbles, and strange seeds are all placed in the bowl. At the end of the week, let each person explain what he or she has found, and why it is so special.

This not only gives you something to talk about, and perhaps a new appreciation of someone else's finds, but also makes you look at your world in a different manner as you search for objects that are beautiful, odd, or surprisingly meaningful.

Flowers

Flowers do not have to cost much, if anything. (They *grow* right outside in sidewalk cracks!) They bring beauty, color, and nature to your table. In the spring, go for a walk with your kids and find three budding branches, put them in a vase in the center of your table, and over the next few days watch the blossoms slowly unfurl.

Go to your local grocery store and buy some daisies (the cheapest flowers in the land, but is there anything sweeter than a bunch of happy daisies smiling on your dinner table?).

Float one rose in each of three of your grandmother's teacups. You get to enjoy flowers and the fancy china that has spent too much time locked up in a dark cabinet.

If you are having a dinner where herbs are added at the last minute, put them instead in a vase and place them in the center of the table so your family can add the herbs themselves.

At some point, your long-stemmed flowers will start to droop and look sad. Worry not! There is a second chance. Cut the stems very short and stuff the flowers into a low container: a bowl, a cup, or an old toy truck that deserves its chance to be admired.

"IN MY HOUSE *the living room, children's playroom, and kitchen are basically one large room. Traditionally kitchens were considered an embarrassment and therefore conveniently tucked away from the more important rooms of the house. Nothing could be more ridiculous.* **THE KITCHEN SHOULD BE THE CENTER OF THE HOUSE** *and everyone should eat in them. Dining rooms should be abolished. Cooking and eating should be* **INSEPARABLE.** *Especially in the minds of children."* —KEITH MCNALLY, owner of eight wildly popular New York City restaurants

Napkins

Having fun with folding napkins is one of the easiest and most charming ways to enhance the look of your table. One of my first jobs was working on a cargo ship that traveled between Denmark and Greenland. (If that job is ever offered to you, say no thank you.) Hundreds of miles out to sea, I was desperate for any kind of creative outlet, so I started folding the napkins in fanciful ways for the sailors. Get this: They noticed and appreciated it! Napkin folding could become something fun for your kids to do—teach them a few simple tricks, or let them have at it and see what they come up with. Teach them to fold a napkin like an envelope, and slip in an encouraging note or a funny poem.

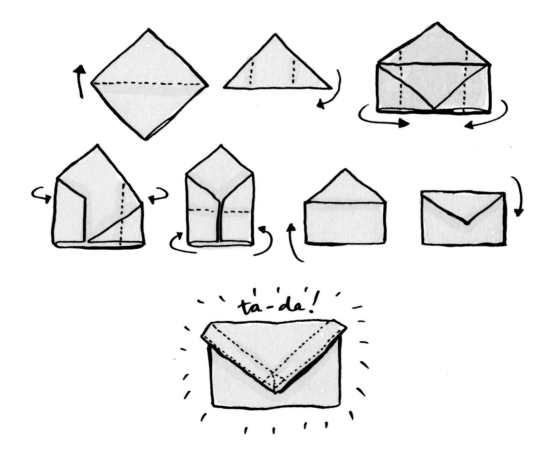

Flowers and Food

One of the sweetest ways to decorate food is with edible flowers. Throw nasturtiums, pansies, or blue borage into a salad and suddenly it is a beautiful edible garden on your plate. Just a few rose petals on a platter make a dessert extra-special, even if it is just a store-bought cookie you dust with powdered sugar. Gently tear or cut flower petals into strips, throw them on top of a dish, and no one will even know they are flowers; they'll just see sparkling bits of color scattered about. Flowers are the easiest way to make a store-bought cake beautiful. Snap off the stems, arrange the flowers on the cake top, and stick them to the sides. A frosting flower may be sweet, but it will never be as beautiful as the real thing.

EDIBLE FLOWERS
You Can Grow

Nasturtiums
grow like weeds;
plant them anywhere

Roses

Snapdragons

Chrysanthemums

Pansies

Sweet Alyssum

Borage

Geraniums

Blossoms of herbs

One note of caution: Always be sure the flowers you use are edible, and have not been sprayed with pesticides.

"ENJOY THE LITTLE THINGS, *for one day you may look back and* **REALIZE THEY WERE THE BIG THINGS."**

—ROBERT BRAULT, writer

The Wreath Around the Plate

Birthdays at my house meant flowers! Not in a bouquet, but in a beautiful wreath around the breakfast plate. It's a great way to make anyone feel special, anytime. How about a wreath for a grandparent who has traveled from afar, or "Hurray, Pete got an A today," or "Thanks, Dad, for all you do" night. It does not have to be flowers; it can be leaves, pinecones, a wooden train, alphabet magnets or Scrabble letters spelling out a surprise, anything that makes the person seated there know, "Today you are very special indeed."

Use Your Heirlooms

Really! Take them out of the cupboards, dust them off, and appreciate them. Let your kids hear about why the special dishes are special, who owned them, and where they came from. If you don't tell them, how will the next generation know?

When we used my mother's family silverware, I always thought of the seven years during World War II that those forks and spoons spent deep in a hole in the backyard, hidden from harm. And I imagined the first dinner after the war, when it was dug up, polished, and set at a peaceful table. Take a walk through your home, collect the knickknacks that hold stories about your travels or celebrations, and gather them on your table for an evening of storytelling.

Bring your old photo album to the table and find family traits in the faces of ancestors. Best of all . . . tell about that most embarrassing time when Auntie Augusta . . .

"THERE IS SOMETHING MYSTICAL *and* SACRED *about the preparation of the meal. The meal itself becomes a* CELEBRATION *of working together."* —THE REVEREND ED BACON, rector of All Saints Episcopal Church in Pasadena, California

MEET THE NEELYS
Pat and Gina

Maybe you've already seen this dynamic husband-and-wife duo on their hit Food Network show
Down Home with the Neelys, *bought their cookbook of the same name, or soaked up BBQ sauce at one*
of their restaurants in Tennessee. If so, you know the **NEELYS** *have it going on! Their secret?*
Let me give you a hint: It's got something to do with food, family, and fun!

PAT: One of the reasons we are so connected as a family is our long tradition of cooking and eating together. Both Gina and I grew up with that, and it's important to us to continue that tradition with our two girls. It's a fantastic way of bonding with your children and staying connected with them.

We both came from large families and were pretty much forced to have dinner together at home because we couldn't afford to eat out. My mother always prepared these big meals, and having five boys and one girl, we couldn't wait to start in on it. As soon as the food was ready, we would be at the table eating and laughing.

GINA: When our kids were younger, I still had a corporate job and Pat did all the cooking. I'd come home from the bank and jump right in to help. On Fridays, we had a ritual called "Friday Free for All." That's when the kids could have pizza or whatever they wanted.

PAT: Getting dinner ready was a time for Gina and I to connect in the kitchen and talk about our day. And our kids would be sitting nearby doing their homework so socializing in the kitchen started even before the meal was ready.

Then we all would sit down to eat and, according to our kids, that was considered strange. Our kids would tell us, "Mary doesn't have dinner with her family," but because of this ritual, we have the most open relationship with our children. They talk to us about anything.

GINA: Maybe a little too much! But really, we can see the difference in our girls. We can see the impact that it's had on their upbringing and even compared to their friends how different they are from those who didn't have family dinner.

PAT: We try as hard as we can to keep our family grounded and stick to those values we were raised with. We say grace before our meals, we hold hands. We go to church together as a family on Sunday. We watch movies together. I even sit through all those girlie movies they watch just to be with them. It's very important because no matter how successful you become, if you lose connection to your family, nothing else matters.

GINA: You got that right!

PAT: My advice, don't wait till Sunday to have a family meal! We have family meals all week long. Do you know how easy it is to prepare baked chicken, green beans, some potatoes, and some bread on a Wednesday? It's so simple! You season some thick chicken thighs in the morning, you get home from work, you turn the oven on 350, and you throw them in. Take some green beans or some broccoli, blanch them quickly in a pot of water. Put some potatoes on, bring them to a boil, take some heavy cream out, and after they become soft, mash them and put garlic in it or bacon if you like.

While your chicken is baking, if you need to go take a shower or do other things go ahead, it's going to cook itself. When you're ready, throw your sides together, and by six thirty on a Wednesday evening you have a meal most people would eat on a Sunday. It's not that difficult. It's just about putting the emphasis on it and making it important.

I came home a week ago and I walked into the house and Gina had some cabbage and vegetables on and there was music playing. It was the middle of the week, both my girls were there, they were deep in conversation with Gina, the dog was running around and having a good time, and I paused for a moment and I said, *Wow, what a lucky man I am. What a peaceful home I have, what a dynamic experience this is, and I hope this stays with me for the rest of my life because truly it's what a home is really all about.*

"Our kids call us **OLD-FASHIONED** *—we take that as a compliment."*—PAT NEELY

Candles

Every dinner table should have a lit unscented candle (to avoid the perfume interfering with your delicious home-cooked aromas). Lighting a candle slows time down; it says, "Now it is time to focus on those who are lit by its light and put aside everything that is not."

Do the same at after-school snack and teatime, the little flickering light saying, "Hey, welcome home."

Find a bunch of mismatched candlesticks, at least five or six, some tall, some short. Gather them in the center of your table like a candelabra. Your table will *glow*!

Water

Fancify your water! All it takes is a cinnamon stick, a few mint leaves, cucumber slices, or wedges of citrus, and suddenly tap water becomes thirst-quenching spa water.

Serving Platters and Bowls

Look at the dishes you have and use them in new ways. Pour soup into teacups with saucers. Serve pudding from a big soup terrine, or a little egg cup. Present your sandwiches or pizza on a big wooden cutting board. Instead of putting your dinner in lots of bowls, how about arranging it all on one big platter? Secure a plate firmly on top of a mug with Play-Doh and *ta-da*—you have a temporary cake platter for a tea party. Put desserts in wineglasses, wine in short juice glasses, and hot chocolate in small bowls (so French).

"I have given and received some of my **LIFE'S MOST IMPORTANT HUGS** *with those big oven-mitt* **POTHOLDERS** *on both hands."*

—BARBARA KINGSOLVER, author of *Animal, Vegetable, Miracle*

HEART OF THE HOUSE

NANCY WILSON *grew up close to her sisters. In fact, work is a family affair. Nancy and her sister Ann are the central duo of the enormously successful rock band Heart. And offstage, sister Lynn handles wardrobe. Family dinner played a key role in all of their lives. Here is what Nancy remembers:*

"We had family dinner almost every single night. My sisters and I always helped cook and clean. My mom always had candles lit and music on. Weekends we would all get a break from kitchen chores. We liked to call it 'Pig Night.' Out came the TV trays and our mom would make burger patties with lettuce wedges on the side, and just throw some mayo with salt and pepper on it. Or we would just heat up TV dinners and watch our favorite shows with our trays lined up much like a dinner train. It was so deliciously informal!

"At dinner we talked a lot, about our day, about politics, history, philosophy, spirituality, and people we knew. We often had a lot of our extended family and friends over for dinner. Our mom was an avid family historian and she liked to tell long tales about the history of our relatives, stories that dated back to covered wagons and even earlier. Some of our relatives were the first settlers that came over in the 1600s! It gave us kids a deep sense of connectedness to history.

"On Sunday mornings, our mom and dad started another great food ritual. It was amazing. Opera and pancakes! My parents would put on *The Mikado* or *Madame Butterfly* and we would have eggs, fruit, pancakes, sausage, and syrup, and make a big occasion out of it. Singing at the table was obviously *allowed*. After breakfast, my sisters and I would end up 'air-conducting' the orchestra with our dad in the living room, or doing interpretive dancing around the house, play-acting to the themes of the opera.

"It's a great gift to my twin boys to make sure we have some of that ritual still in place around our dinner table. We take time for talking by candlelight and music. We share stories about our day and our lives, tell jokes. At the family table, they come to know they can share anything that's in their hearts. It's a safety zone.

"I want to give them what I was so lucky to have and I cherish the solid family I came from."

"IF I SING *when I cook, the food is going to be happy."* —PASQUALE CARPINO, chef

Music

A big part of setting the scene is setting the mood for *yourself*. To aid in that effort, we have asked some of our favorite rock-and-roll girlfriends to give us their list of top five CDs they play in the kitchen when making dinner. Listen to any of these and sing your way through chopping and prepping!

BETTE MIDLER I have to say that for cooking and cleaning up after, anything goes, but we never play music during dinner; it's practically grounds for divorce. We talk and catch up with everything that's going on in our lives . . .

- *The No. 1's* by Diana Ross and the Supremes
- *Jump, Jive an' Wail: The Essential Louis Prima*
- *The Wild Tchoupitoulas*
- Anything by Gilbert and Sullivan
- *The Very Best of Sheryl Crow*

CARLY SIMON My dinners growing up were very formal. Everyone had to be dressed up, every night! My dinners today are more casual and relaxed.

- *Tea for the Tillerman* by Cat Stevens
- "Sexual Healing" by Marvin Gaye
- *Stylefree* or *I, John* by John Forté
- *The Best of Caetano Velosa*
- "The Pearl Fishers" *Duet* by Jussi Björling

CAROLE KING It wasn't easy to settle on a "top five," but the CDs below are definitely among my favorites, and you might enjoy them while rolling out a piecrust.

- *That's the Way of the World* by Earth, Wind & Fire
- *Continuum* by John Mayer
- *The E.N.D.* by the Black Eyed Peas
- *The Best of James Taylor*
- *Speak for Yourself* by Imogen Heap

NANCY WILSON Growing up, music and dinner went hand in hand at my house. It still does.

- *Ronroco* by Gustavo Santaolalla
- *Blue Incantation* by Sanjay Mishra
- *Ingénue* by k. d. lang
- *Together Through Life* by Bob Dylan
- *Harvest Moon* by Neil Young
- *Baby Guitars* by Nancy Wilson (*I'm throwing this one in. I made it to help babies fall asleep to, but it's also a really nice dinner thing.*)

SHERYL CROW I'm always listening to music. When I cook, I might put on any one of these.

- *Greatest Hits* by Al Green
- *Back to Black* by Amy Winehouse
- *Madame Butterfly* by Giacomo Puccini
- *Tea for the Tillerman* by Cat Stevens
- *Tumbleweed Connection* by Elton John

FAST RECIPES

That Can Save Weekday Dinners

4

STAGING QUICK DINNERS from a Well-Stocked Kitchen

A well-stocked kitchen will save you money in the long run, especially if you buy in bulk, but more important it will save you time. So take a look in your pantry and throw out the old, the dusty, and the unknown. Take your list of must-have pantry items (and a canvas bag) to your grocery store. If you can buy in bulk, great. If you can buy from bulk bins, even better! You get to go home and put everything in your own containers. We prefer the big glass canning jars, mostly because they are inexpensive, but also because they are so cool looking and practical. They keep your food safe from invaders (bugs, not kids), and you can see exactly what it is and how much you have.

If it's 5:49 PM and you have not a clue what your family is going to have for dinner, never fear, your well-stocked pantry is near! Here is a list of helpful items to keep in your kitchen and a few quick things you can cook from it.

IN YOUR PANTRY
- Olive oil, vegetable oil
- VINEGARS: balsamic, apple cider, red wine, seasoned rice wine
- Salt and pepper
- SPICES: cumin, chili, cinnamon, allspice, cardamom, cayenne, vanilla extract
- CANNED BEANS: white and black, refried beans, dried beans, dried peas and lentils
- Quinoa, rice, and your favorite grains
- Canned (or in a carton) vegetable and chicken stock
- Canned (or in a carton) good-quality tomatoes, jarred tomato sauce
- Canned tuna
- Pasta, couscous
- All-purpose flour, oatmeal, cornstarch, baking powder, baking soda, chocolate chips
- Quick-cooking grits or polenta
- Sugar, honey, maple syrup
- Soy sauce, fish sauce
- Salsa
- Whole wheat crackers
- Panko bread crumbs
- All-natural peanut butter, jam, tahini
- Potatoes, sweet potatoes
- Garlic and onions
- DRIED FRUIT: raisins, apricots, apples

IN YOUR FRIDGE
- Butter
- Milk
- Eggs
- Greek yogurt
- Dijon mustard, mayo
- Yeast
- CHEESE: Parmesan, a good melting cheese (mozzarella cheddar, provolone), and a tasty snacking cheese
- Carrots, celery, broccoli
- GREENS: salad greens, kale, cabbage
- Apples, oranges, lemons, lime

IN YOUR FREEZER
- Peas
- Corn
- Bread (the "par-baked" loaves are great—you just take them out of the freezer and pop them in your oven)
- Tortillas
- Shrimp
- Nuts
- Italian sausage
- Chicken breasts
- Homemade cookie dough
- Homemade tomato sauce
- Leftovers (don't forget to label them)

IN YOUR GARDEN, or on your stoop or window sill
- Rosemary, basil, thyme, oregano, parsley, mint, cilantro
- …And if you have room for salad greens and tomatoes, that would be fantastic!

What do we mean by greens? Any sturdy leafy green like…

Cook's Tip

kale, spinach, turnip tops, escarole, chard, and collards.

The purple tops of beets aren't green, but that doesn't mean we don't love them.

QUICK DINNERS MADE FROM YOUR PANTRY

EGGS IN PURGATORY

Warm 2 cups salsa in a small skillet. Crack 4 eggs into your skillet, cover, and cook until the eggs set. Slide onto a bed of warm tortillas, topping with hot sauce and grated cheese.

PIZZA POTATO

Make a deep slit in prebaked potatoes, then stuff with some pasta sauce, shredded mozzarella, and steamed broccoli. Bake at 400 degrees until the cheese melts.

QUICK SOUP with Greens

In your soup pot, sauté some onions and plenty of garlic, add a small handful of white rice or quinoa, simmer in 5 to 6 cups of stock for 15 minutes, add chopped greens, and simmer for an additional 5 minutes or until the grains are very tender. Serve with grated Parmesan and a squeeze of lemon.

A Bowl of POLENTA HAPPINESS

Spoon tomato sauce over soft-cooked grits or polenta, then top with leftover vegetables and some cheese. Put under the broiler until bubbling.

ANGELHAIR with Broccoli and Cheese

Chop a head of broccoli into little bits, boil in the same pot as a pound of angelhair pasta, then toss with butter or olive oil, red pepper flakes, and Parmesan cheese. (If you use pasta of another shape, throw the broccoli in the pasta water just in the last minute or two before you drain the pasta or the broccoli will overcook.)

WHITE BEANS with Shrimp

Drain a can or two of white beans and sauté with a drizzle of olive oil, garlic, some shrimp, and a sprig of rosemary. Cook, stirring, until the shrimp are pink and done, about 4 to 5 minutes. Top with chopped tomatoes, spritz with some lemon juice, and serve on slices of toasted bread. (Of course, you can leave out the shrimp.)

COUSCOUS with Mediterranean Greens

Mix 1 part couscous with 2 parts boiling water, cover, and let it rest until tender (10 minutes). Top with tomato sauce, sautéed greens, and feta cheese slices that you've stuck under the broiler and broiled until soft and golden.

VEGETABLE AND BEAN Wrap

Make wraps of leftover roasted vegetables, warm white beans, lettuce, tomato, and a drizzle of tahini rolled up in a big flour tortilla.

"TUNA CEVICHE"

Drain canned tuna (packed in water), toss with lots of lime juice, diced red onions, tomatoes, and cilantro, and serve on lettuce, tostada shells, or tortilla chips.

QUESADILLA

Put your favorite melting cheeses on half of a large flour tortilla, then top with minced onion, refried beans, or chopped tomatoes. Fold the tortilla over and brown on both sides in butter or oil on a medium-hot skillet, until the cheese is melted. Serve with salsa and guacamole.

PASTA CARBONARA

In a large bowl, whisk 4 egg yolks. Add 1 cup Parmesan. Cook 1 pound pasta. Working quickly, add the drained pasta to the yolk mixture and toss to combine. Add 4 strips of cooked crumbled bacon (or a handful of chopped smoked almonds), ½ cup chopped parsley, and salt and pepper to taste.

ALMOST-AS-QUICK
Dinners from the Pantry and the Store

If you have time to run to the store, here is also a list of recipes from the book that only need one or two extra ingredients:

SAVORY SAUSAGE AND WHITE BEAN STEW, page 51. You just need to buy the fresh herbs.

BANG, BANG CHICKEN PARMESAN, page 55. You just need the frozen breaded chicken breasts (which are good to keep in the freezer as well).

CHICKEN PICCATA, page 59. From the store, you need capers and herbs.

ESCAROLE AND QUINOA SOUP, page 79. From the grocery store, you need escarole.

CABBAGE AND NOODLES, page 51. Shop for the cabbage and optional caraway seeds.

DEEP DARK BLACK BEAN SOUP, page 82. You would need a can of chipotles in adobo, and various optional toppings.

CARAMELIZED SWEET POTATOES WITH QUINOA AND GREENS, page 116. Go get fresh ginger and leafy greens.

EASY CHEESY DINNER FRITTATA, page 127. All you need is asparagus and fresh herbs.

DANISH MEATBALLS, page 185. You need . . . ground chicken and fresh parsley.

CRUNCHY CHICKEN SCHNITZEL, page 45. Fetch some buttermilk for the mashed potatoes, along with sugar snap peas.

PASTA ALLA CHECCA, page 54. Find some fresh sweet tomatoes and basil.

IN THE KITCHEN
with Alice

ALICE WATERS *is a beloved American restaurateur, author, and advocate who has long been a champion of locally grown and organic ingredients. Forty years ago when Alice decided to open Chez Panisse, her groundbreaking Berkeley eatery, she knew it should feel like home.*

"When I first started the restaurant I wanted it to smell right . . . garlic and rosemary, the smell of the bread baking. Good aromas bring people to the table and open their senses and then their minds." In 1995, Alice founded the Edible Schoolyard program, which works to integrate growing organic food into school curriculums, and now reaches almost a thousand students in California and across America.

Alice knows what she is talking about and can easily explain it to us in simple principles. Here are four out of her famous nine:

See Alice's recipe on page 42.

1. **COOK SIMPLY.** Plan uncomplicated meals; let things taste of what they are; and enjoy cooking as a sensory pleasure: touch, listen, watch, smell, and, above all, taste.
2. **COOK TOGETHER.** Include your family and friends and especially children. When children grow, cook, and serve food, they want to eat it.
3. **EAT TOGETHER.** No matter how modest the meal, create a special place to sit down together, and set the table with care and respect.
4. **FOOD IS PRECIOUS.** Never take it for granted. Good food can only come from good ingredients. Its proper price includes the cost of preserving the environment and paying fairly for the labor of the people who produce it.

DINNER GUEST RECIPE

ORGANIC CHICKEN LEGS

Braised with Tomatoes, Onions, and Garlic

BY ALICE WATERS

Here is a simple, delicious dinner for family and friends. Leftovers can be chopped and made into a tasty chicken salad sandwich (very good for a bag lunch).

Season, the day before if possible:

4 chicken legs

with:

Salt and fresh-ground black pepper

Heat a heavy-bottomed pan over medium heat. Add:

2 tablespoons olive oil

Place the chicken legs into a pan skin-side down and cook until crisp and brown, about 12 minutes. Turn and cook for another 4 minutes.

Remove the chicken and add:

2 onions, sliced thick (or diced large)

Cook until translucent, about 5 minutes. Add and cook for 2 minutes:

4 cloves garlic, sliced thin

1 bay leaf

1 small rosemary sprig

Add and cook for 5 minutes, scraping up any brown bits from the bottom of the pan:

4 tomatoes, diced coarse, or 1 small (12-ounce) can organic whole tomatoes, diced (including juice)

Arrange the chicken in the pan, skin-side up, and pour in any juices that have collected. Pour in:

1 cup chicken broth

The liquid should reach halfway up the chicken; add more if needed. Bring to a boil and then turn down to a simmer. Cover and cook at a bare simmer or in a 325-degree oven for 45 minutes. When done, pour the braising liquid into a small bowl and skim the fat. Discard the bay leaf and rosemary. Taste for salt and adjust as needed. Return to the pan and serve.

VARIATIONS: Before adding the tomatoes to the onions, add ⅓ cup dry white wine and reduce by half.

Garnish with 1 tablespoon chopped parsley mixed with 1 garlic clove, chopped fine.

Substitute 2 breasts for 2 of the legs. Brown them but do not add them to the braise until the legs have been cooking for 30 minutes.

Use basil, oregano, or marjoram instead of the rosemary.

—From *The Art of Simple Food*

CHIPOTLE ORANGE SHRIMP

with Caramelized Bananas and Black Beans

Fancy food fast! Nestle smoky, tangy shrimp on a bed of sweet bananas and savory black beans, drizzle a bit of sauce onto the plate, and you'll be so happy you stayed home for dinner tonight.

YOU NEED

For the Marinade

½ cup frozen condensed orange juice, defrosted

Grated zest and juice of 1 orange

2 tablespoons soy sauce

¼ cup vegetable oil

2 medium cloves garlic

½ cup chopped fresh cilantro

½ chipotle chile in adobo sauce from a can*

Salt and pepper to taste

For the Shrimp

1½ pounds large shrimp, peeled and deveined

Squeeze of lime

Cilantro or scallions, for garnish

You can use more or less depending on how spicy you like it; if you want it much less spicy, just use a tablespoon of the sauce from the can, not the chile itself.

TO MAKE 4–6 SERVINGS

Combine the marinade ingredients in a blender and blend until smooth. Taste for seasonings. Is it tangy, sweet, and salty with a little heat?

In a nonreactive bowl (the acid in citrus revolts in aluminum or iron bowls), mix the shrimp and marinade. Let this sit in your fridge for 15 to 30 minutes.

With tongs, fish out the shrimp. Pour the remaining marinade into a small pot and bring to a gentle simmer over medium heat.

Meanwhile, put the shrimp on an oiled baking sheet. Place the baking sheet under the broiler and cook the shrimp until sizzling and starting to brown, about 4 minutes. Using tongs, flip and broil until the second side is pink, 1 to 2 minutes longer. Alternatively, you can use the same method to grill the shrimp.

Squeeze the juice of 1 lime into the sauce and taste for seasonings. Garnish with sauce and herbs.

CARAMELIZED BANANAS

YOU NEED

3 bananas, peeled and sliced into inch-long diagonal slices

3 tablespoons honey or maple syrup

1 tablespoon olive oil

Pinch of cayenne pepper

Pinch of salt

TO MAKE 4–6 SERVINGS

Gently toss the bananas with the remaining ingredients. Put them on an oiled baking sheet and place them under the broiler until golden and soft, about 6 minutes.

QUICK BLACK BEANS

YOU NEED

1 tablespoon olive oil

1 medium onion, chopped

2 cloves garlic, chopped

2 teaspoons chili powder

1 tablespoon cumin

2 15-ounce cans black beans, drained

1½ cups low-sodium chicken or vegetable stock

Salt and pepper

Squeeze of lime

2 tablespoons chopped fresh cilantro leaves

LET'S PLAY!

DO YOU KNOW...
What your parents' first three jobs were?

TO MAKE 4–6 SERVINGS

Heat a drizzle of the oil in a heavy-bottomed pot over medium heat. Add the onion and cook until golden. Stir in the garlic, chili powder, and cumin and cook until fragrant, about 1 more minute.

Stir in the beans and chicken stock and gently simmer for about 15 minutes, adding more stock to moisten, if needed.

Season with salt, pepper, and lime, to taste. Stir in the cilantro.

SPEEDY PASTA IN A PAN

Although this isn't really lasagna, the concept is the same: layers of noodles, with cheese and sauce in between. But instead of spending four hours making sauces, boiling pasta, and layering this and that—not to mention washing all those dishes—this will only take you about thirty minutes to make, and your kids won't have to wash the pan after they have licked it clean.

YOU NEED

2 tablespoons olive oil

1 medium onion, chopped

3 cloves garlic, chopped

1 14-ounce can organic, diced tomatoes, undrained

1 tablespoon each chopped fresh basil and oregano

1 pound fresh or defrosted frozen cheese ravioli

½ cup freshly grated Parmesan cheese

3 cups tomato sauce, homemade or store-bought

8 slices fresh mozzarella, or 3 cups shredded mozzarella

Heat a large nonstick pan and drizzle in the olive oil. Over medium heat, sauté the onion and garlic until golden.

Add the diced tomatoes, basil, and oregano. Stir and simmer for 5 minutes.

Remove half the tomato mixture. Top the tomatoes in the pan with a layer of uncooked ravioli, then a sprinkling of Parmesan cheese, a cup of the tomato sauce, and the remaining tomato mixture. Nestle the last raviolis into the pan, topping with the tomato sauce and the mozzarella. Cover the pan with a lid or a layer of foil and simmer over low heat for 15 minutes.

Let the dish relax off the heat for a few minutes, just so all the excited juices can calm down. Serve with pride straight out of the pan.

Cook's Tips

Sauté a pound of Italian sausage with the onions. • If you have some leftover pesto, you can add a few dollops before serving. • Add cooked vegetables, like broccoli, asparagus, spinach, or squash, and layer in between the pasta. • Double the recipe by making two pans and slip half into an oven dish to freeze for a rainy night.

CRUNCHY CHICKEN SCHNITZEL (or You May Call It a Large Chicken Nugget) with Tangy Buttermilk Mashed Potatoes and Big Peas and Little Peas

When I was a kid and it was my turn to pick what we were going to have for dinner, it was often Wienerschnitzel. The name is pretty fancy, but the dish is not, and to a kid it's really just a big, flat chicken nugget.

In this recipe I use chicken cutlets, but if you want to use pork or turkey cutlets instead, go ahead. I have also modernized it using the fantastically crispy Japanese panko bread crumbs.

KIDS CAN

Remove the tails and tips of the sugar snap peas.

YOU NEED

3 cups panko crumbs (or unseasoned bread crumbs)

1 cup finely shredded Parmesan cheese

1 cup flour seasoned with salt and pepper, for dredging

4 large eggs, beaten

1½ pounds thin-cut boneless, skinless chicken breasts, trimmed, preferably kosher and/or organic

Vegetable oil, for sautéing

2 lemons, sliced

TO MAKE 6 SERVINGS

Mix the panko crumbs and Parmesan in a wide, shallow container. Fill another wide, shallow container with flour and a third container with the beaten eggs.

Dredge the chicken breasts in flour, pat or shake off the excess, and then dip them in egg, letting any excess drip off. Coat the cutlets in the panko mixture by pressing them hard down into the crumbs, then flipping them and pressing the other side into the crumbs.

Heat a large nonstick skillet over a medium flame and drizzle in enough oil to cover the bottom. Gently sauté the cutlets for 3 to 4 minutes on each side, or until golden and just cooked through. You might have to do this in a few batches; just keep the finished ones warm in the oven.

Serve the cutlets garnished with a lemon slice. And Honey Mustard Sauce (page 134) on the side if you like.

Leftover Tip

Make a few extra breaded chicken breasts, wrap them well, and freeze them to make Bang, Bang Chicken Parmesan (page 55) another night.

*"The love of **RITUALS** and repetition led me to the kitchen."*

—THOMAS KELLER, chef and author of *Ad Hoc at Home*

TANGY BUTTERMILK MASHED POTATOES

YOU NEED

2 pounds potatoes, peeled and cut into 1-inch chunks

¼ cup (½ stick) room-temperature butter, cut into small pieces

1¼ cups buttermilk, at room temperature (buttermilk has less fat than low-fat milk but all the tangy goodness of sour cream)

Salt and pepper to taste

Perhaps some chopped chives or parsley, for garnish

TO MAKE 6 SERVINGS

Place the potatoes and 1 tablespoon salt in large saucepan. Add cold water to cover by 1 inch. Bring to a boil over high heat, then reduce the heat to medium and simmer until the potatoes are soft when poked with a knife, about 15 minutes.

Drain potatoes and return them to the saucepan set on the still-hot burner. Add the butter to the pot and mash the potatoes with a masher or a fork (never, never use a food processor, unless you need some glue).

Add the buttermilk to the potatoes, stirring gently until just incorporated. Now please taste your potatoes and add salt and pepper until they are really good, then garnish.

Big PEAS and Little PEAS

YOU NEED

½ pound sugar snap peas

⅓ cup water

Pat of butter

1 pound frozen peas, defrosted

Salt and pepper and a grating of nutmeg

Fresh mint, parsley, or chives (optional)

LET'S PLAY!

ROSES AND THORNS

Just like they do at family dinner in the Obamas' White House, tell everyone about the best thing that happened to you today—the Rose. Then talk about the worst—the Thorn.

RECITE TONIGHT

I eat my peas with honey;
I've done it all my life.
It makes the peas taste funny,
But it keeps them on the knife.
—*Anonymous*

TO MAKE 6 SERVINGS

Remove the tips and tails from the sugar snaps, and if they have a string, pull that off as well.

In a medium pot, bring the water to a boil, adding the pat of butter. Throw in both kinds of peas, cover with a lid, and boil for 3 to 4 minutes.

Drain the peas and season with salt and pepper. Toss with the herbs and nutmeg. Serve right away.

SOY GOOD MAPLE-GLAZED SALMON with Edamame Succotash

Savory soy sauce, sweet maple syrup, and luscious salmon . . . all come together in a perfectly quick and delicious dinner.

So good your kids will love it! So easy you will, too.

YOU NEED

For the Marinade

1 cup maple syrup

½ cup low-sodium soy sauce

3 cloves garlic, finely chopped

2 tablespoons peeled and grated fresh ginger

2 tablespoons Asian fish sauce* (optional)

¼ teaspoon chili flakes (more or less depending on how spicy you like it)

For the Salmon

6 salmon fillets, 4–6 ounces each

Salt and pepper to taste

Found in the Asian section of your supermarket.

RECIPES

Combine the first six ingredients in a medium-sized pot and bring to a simmer for about 15 minutes, or until the sauce has thickened and has the same consistency the maple syrup had.

Cool the marinade to room temperature (you can make this in advance). Put the salmon in a small container and pour half the marinade over it, making sure the salmon is submerged. Save the rest of the marinade for a glaze.

Marinate the salmon in the fridge for at least 20 minutes, preferably 1 to 2 hours.

Preheat your broiler.

Take the salmon out of the marinade and blot it dry with paper towels. Discard the marinade. Put the salmon on an oiled broiler pan if you have one; an oiled baking sheet will also work just fine.

Put the salmon under the broiler 5 to 6 inches from the heat source. Broil for about 4 minutes on each side, until the salmon is just cooked through and golden brown on top. Be careful—it does like to burn.

In the meantime, gently heat up the remaining glaze.

To check if the salmon is done, stick a pointy knife into the center of the thickest fillet, then touch the tip of the knife. If it's warm, the salmon is ready.

Scatter some herbs on a platter, put the salmon on top, and drizzle with the warm maple soy glaze.

Serve with the succotash (recipe at right) and perhaps a little wild rice on the side.

Leftover Tip

The next day, make a green salad, top with the leftover succotash and salmon, serve with an Asian vinaigrette, and call it Asian Salmon Salad Delight.

Health Tip

The omega-3s in salmon act as "health heroes" against hypertension, breast cancer, and depression.

SUCCOTASH WITH SOYBEANS (EDAMAME)

YOU NEED

1 small red onion, chopped

Pat of butter and some olive oil

1 clove garlic, minced

2 cups freshly shucked or defrosted frozen corn kernels

2 cups defrosted and shelled soybeans

1 red pepper, chopped

1 teaspoon grated fresh ginger

Handful of chopped mint, basil, or cilantro

Salt and pepper to taste

TO MAKE 6 SERVINGS

Sauté the onion in a little olive oil with a pat of butter. When it's soft, throw in the next five ingredients. Sauté for about 8 minutes, or until the vegetables are done to your liking (I like them still a little crunchy). Season with fresh herbs, salt, and pepper.

ASIAN BEEF STIR-FRY

Tonight let's eat the Asian way, where meat is an accent in a dish and the main focus is on bright flavors and crisp vegetables. In this stir-fry, a little beef is marinated until it packs a lot of flavor, then is quickly stir-fried with a tangy sauce and plenty of green vegetables. Spoon with pleasure onto fragrant jasmine rice or a tangle of rice noodles.

YOU NEED

For the Beef and Marinade

¾-pound skirt or flank steak cut in half lengthwise, and into thin strips against the grain

1 tablespoon brown sugar

2 tablespoons soy sauce

1 tablespoon Asian fish sauce*

1 tablespoon vegetable oil

For the Stir-Fry Sauce

¼ cup seasoned rice vinegar

¼ cup white wine

¼ cup soy sauce

2 tablespoons Asian fish sauce*

For the Vegetables

Vegetable oil, for the stir-fry

4 scallions, cut into 1-inch pieces

1½ pounds asparagus, cut into 1-inch pieces, woody ends snapped off

2 cups sugar snap peas, tips and strings tossed

1 tablespoon peeled and chopped fresh ginger

4 cloves garlic, chopped

1 lime

Found in the Asian section of your supermarket.

TO MAKE 6 SERVINGS

Combine the beef with the marinade ingredients in a small bowl, cover, and refrigerate for at least 30 minutes. An hour would be even better.

Meanwhile, whisk all the ingredients for the stir-fry sauce in a small bowl. Set aside.

Drain the beef and discard the liquid. Pat the beef dry.

Heat a large skillet or wok over high heat and drizzle in enough vegetable oil to cover the bottom. Add half of the beef to the skillet, let it sizzle without stirring for 1 minute, then flip the pieces and leave them until they are brown, about 30 seconds more. Transfer the beef to a medium bowl. Heat another drizzle of oil in the skillet, and repeat with the remaining beef. When the second batch of beef is done, add it to the first.

Wipe out the skillet, drizzle a bit more oil into it, and, when it's hot, toss in the vegetables and stir-fry them for 3 minutes. Add the ginger and garlic; stir for a minute. Now add the beef and the stir-fry sauce.

As soon as it is hot and sizzling, serve with white or brown rice and a tangy squeeze of lime.

"I always add **EXTRA ONION** *... we are onion people."* —ROMY, age thirteen

...ℰ✺ℰ...
THE IRON MAGNOLIA

Raised in Jackson, Mississippi, by a family of Greek restaurateurs, **CAT CORA** *has cooking in her blood. She pioneered Greek fusion foods and in 2005 became the first female Iron Chef. She's also authored several cookbooks, including* Cat Cora's Kitchen: Favorite Meals for Family and Friends.

"I have really strong family memories growing up around food. Being from a boisterous Greek American (and Southern) family, everything we did revolved around being together and food. My parents believed that every supper, the TV went off and we sat at the table together and talked about our day. And even as we became teenagers on the move, Sunday supper was a must in our house.

"I grew up in a family of great cooks who had their own specialties that I learned from. My mom made sure she taught all the kids to cook, and my dad made sure everyone could make a good marinade and knew how to grill something. I have memories of great parties at our house that always started with happy hour, which was cheese and crackers with olives, peperoncini, and other trimmings, juice for the kids and wine for the adults.

"We sit down for dinner today as often as possible. Having twin babies as well as a six-year-old and a two-and-a-half-year-old definitely makes it more difficult to have every meal together. But we sit and have cheese and crackers or a salad with our older boys while they eat their dinner or while we feed our six-month-olds.

"For people in similar situations, I suggest planning ahead. Use a slow cooker or prep some things the night before or that morning for dinner. A slow cooker is great to put a roast in and leave on low to cook all day while you are at work. (Chili and meat sauces work well also.)

"The most important thing is connecting and having that one-on-one quality time. It is not as important *what* you are eating, but that you are gathering around something comforting together—and that can be whatever you create."

RECIPES

CABBAGE AND NOODLES

Soft, silky cabbage and savory browned onions tangle with egg noodles. My dear friend Marti introduced me to this recipe that her grandmother had brought from Hungary. You would think this dish would make everybody happy. And it usually does, except for once. I made it for a gaggle of Kennedy children, who all happily finished their dinners and ran off to cause mischief somewhere else. Except for the smallest child. He was left alone with his father at the darkened table, his hands in his lap, stubbornly refusing to try the cabbage. Then, finally, his small voice wailed, "But it's poison!" and after some thought his father let him go. You win some, you lose some.

This one is usually a winner.

YOU NEED

2 tablespoons olive oil plus 1 teaspoon for tossing

2 large onions, sliced

2 teaspoons brown sugar

1 teaspoon salt

1 12-ounce package wide egg noodles

1½-pound white cabbage, thinly sliced

1 tablespoon apple cider vinegar

2 tablespoons butter

1 teaspoon caraway seeds (optional)

Salt and pepper to taste

TO MAKE 6 SERVINGS

In a large nonstick pan, drizzle 2 tablespoons of olive oil. Keep the oil bottle handy, as you might need to add more now and then if the pan gets "dry." Add the onions; sprinkle with the brown sugar and 1 teaspoon salt. Slowly sauté over medium-low heat, stirring occasionally, for about 15 minutes, until the onions are softened and golden with a few dark crunchy bits.

Meanwhile, start cooking the noodles by bringing a big pot of water to a boil. Salt it so it tastes like the sea, add the pasta, stir well, and cook the pasta according to the package directions. Drain, toss with a teaspoon of olive oil, and put aside.

When the onions are done, add the cabbage to the pan and sauté for about 10 minutes or so, stirring occasionally. When the cabbage and onions are soft and happily married, add the apple cider vinegar just to keep life from getting boring.

Turn the heat back up to medium high, add the cooked noodles, and stir until hot. I like to let the noodles get a little crispy as well, but that is up to you. Toss with the butter and caraway seeds. Taste for seasonings.

Green Tip

It takes about seven gallons of water to grow a single serving of lettuce. Roughly twenty-six hundred gallons are required to produce one portion of steak.

SAVORY SAUSAGE AND WHITE BEAN STEW
with Crispy Sage Topping

Cassoulet is one of the wonderful iconic French dishes. To make it takes lots of peering into cookbooks and hours spent poking in the kitchen.

Here is a quick and lighter weeknight version of it.

No, we cannot call it cassoulet—the French would be unhappy if we did—but we can call it delicious.

We highly recommend doubling this recipe. It freezes beautifully, and you will be very happy to defrost it on a night you are too busy with life to cook.

YOU NEED

¼ cup olive oil, divided

4 medium-size organic Italian-style sausages, turkey, chicken, or pork

1 cup bread crumbs (I prefer panko bread crumbs because they are crunchier; or if you make your own bread crumbs out of day-old bread, that would be great, too)

3 fresh sage leaves, chopped

5 cloves garlic, finely chopped, divided

½ cup Parmesan cheese

1 medium onion, sliced

1 bay leaf

1 sprig rosemary, chopped

1 cup white wine

1½ cups canned diced tomatoes, drained

3 15-ounce cans white beans, rinsed and drained (cannellini or great northern), or 5 cups home-cooked beans

2 cups chicken stock

Salt and pepper to taste

Juice of 1 lemon

Handful of chopped parsley

TO MAKE 6 SERVINGS

Drizzle a large skillet with 2 tablespoons of olive oil and over medium heat, sauté the sausages so they are golden brown and crisp on each side, about 10 minutes. Then slice them thickly on the bias, or into small bite-size pieces . . . you can even leave them whole. Whatever makes you happy. Put them aside.

In the same pan, sauté the bread crumbs, sage, 1 clove chopped garlic, and Parmesan until they are crunchy and golden brown. You might need to add a little olive oil. Put the bread crumbs aside as well.

Wipe out the pan, add 2 more tablespoons olive oil, and sauté the onion until it is caramel-colored and has little crispy edges. Add the remaining garlic, bay leaf, and rosemary, stir for a moment, then add the wine and tomatoes, letting it all simmer for 2 or 3 minutes.

Add the beans and chicken stock, then nestle the sausage into the pan among the beans. Let it all gently simmer until the sauce has evaporated a bit and the beans are lovely and creamy. Season with salt and pepper.

Top with the bread crumbs, lemon juice, and a shower of parsley.

Serve with a simple mixed green salad and whole-grain mustard.

Leftover Tip

Cut a baguette into slices on the bias. Grill or toast the bread. Place the toast in the middle of a plate, top with arugula and a heaping spoon of the warm beans, scatter a few halved baby tomatoes about, and add a drizzle of balsamic vinegar and olive oil. Finally, strew on a few shards of Parmesan cheese and your "leftovers" won't be left over anymore.

...⌘:⌘...

For the

LOVE OF BEANS

LYNNE ROSSETTO KASPER *has a gift. She can rattle off how to make anything, right off the top of her head. When she explains how to cook, it's always as simple as 1, 2, 3. No wonder the food show she hosts on NPR, The Splendid Table, is an enormous hit. As one of America's leading food authorities, Lynne lets us in on her must-have for any family dinner!*

"Make friends with the bean world. No two taste alike—and there are dozens to try. For instance, dried chickpeas cook up to be amazingly sweet and meaty. Mix beans with any kind of whole grain, or serve with a piece of whole wheat bread or corn bread and you've got a complete protein! For a buck fifty, you can buy a pound of organic beans. And that pound of beans is going to turn into six or eight cups of cooked beans. They are good on their own, but you can also turn them into all kinds of things, from bean burgers to stews to soups to salads. My Tuscan grandmother's method for cooking dried beans was simple—she'd cook them with garlic and sage. But the best part was the bean water. It was called 'crazy water' and was a fabulous broth. I've blindfolded people and served them bean broth, and they thought they were eating chicken soup, that's how good it tastes."

1. Cover the beans with boiling water; soak for 1 to 2 hours. Drain them.
2. Take a little olive oil, a little celery, a carrot, and an onion. Sauté until it's all soft.
3. Add the beans, cover with 2 inches of water, and cook at a low, slow bubble until they're tender—about 45 minutes to an hour.

Veggie Tip

Leave out the sausage; instead, with the beans, stir in a big handful or two of greens—like escarole, chard, or chopped kale—to make a beautiful rustic stew. Top with the bread crumbs and Parmesan cheese.

...༄໐༄...
LET'S PLAY!

Everyone name three things you
can't live without and why.

RISOTTO

A Chef's Secret: It's Not Fancy, It's Fast

People will tell you there is a "right" way to make risotto, and I promise you it will be different from someone else's "right" way. The only right way to cook anything is the way you think it tastes best. So here is a way to cook risotto. It's easy, quick, and perfect for a weeknight dinner.

KIDS CAN

Stir and stir and stir the pot.

YOU NEED

6–7 cups low-sodium chicken or vegetable broth

3 tablespoons olive oil

¼ cup very finely chopped shallots or onion

2 cups Arborio rice (short-grained risotto rice)

2 cloves garlic, finely chopped

½ cup white wine

½ cup freshly grated Parmesan cheese

1–2 tablespoons butter

Salt and pepper to taste

TO MAKE 4 SERVINGS

In a large pot, bring the broth to a simmer over medium heat.

In a medium-size heavy-bottomed pot (heavy so the rice doesn't burn), heat the olive oil until it shimmers. Add the onion and sauté for about 3 minutes, until soft and translucent. Now pour in the rice and add the garlic as well, stirring until the grains are translucent around the edges, about 3 or 4 minutes. Stir in the wine and cook until absorbed.

Begin adding the hot broth 1 cup at a time, stirring with a wooden spoon until it is absorbed, before adding the next cup. This is one of those times you need to stand at the pot and pay attention most of the time, but it will only take about 20 minutes—enough time to whistle three good songs or call your mother on the wireless and brag about cooking risotto on a weeknight.

The risotto will be ready when it is tender but not mushy, with a little bit of firmness in the center. Gently fold in the Parmesan cheese and butter—this will also add silkiness and shine. Season to taste. I prefer risotto when it is thick enough to barely hold its shape when you spoon it into a bowl, but loose enough to spread out when you slap the table and shout, "This is so good!"

TASTY ADDITIONS TO THE RISOTTO

Summer in a Bowl

After you add the wine, add 1 cup fresh corn kernels and 1 cup chopped ripe tomatoes. Just before serving, stir in ½ cup chopped fresh mozzarella and some fresh basil. Garnish with chopped baby tomatoes tossed with salt, balsamic vinegar, and basil.

A Fall Favorite

Halfway through cooking the risotto, add 1 cup cubed roasted butternut squash, 1 cup diced cooked turkey sausage, ½ cup chopped apple, and 3 leaves of fresh sage. Just before serving, fold in a bit of cubed smoked Gouda or some Parmesan cheese.

More Peas Please

Puree 1 cup of defrosted frozen peas. Just before serving the risotto, throw in this puree along with 1 cup whole defrosted peas with a dollop of pesto (page 115). Heat and eat. Fancy and pretty, too.

Leftover Delight

Open your fridge. What do you see? Some leftover vegetables/chicken/shrimp? Great! Chop them up and throw them in at the end.

ANGELHAIR PASTA Alla Checca

"Alla checca" is the simplest, most beautiful tomato sauce there is. Its few ingredients are just thrown together raw and left to taste how nature intended them to taste. So the secret is to get the very tastiest ingredients you can. Summer-ripe sweet tomatoes are best—and if you can get the colorful heirloom ones, even better.

YOU NEED

3 cups chopped ripe tomatoes, the tastiest you can find

2 cloves garlic, sliced

¼ cup or so fresh basil, torn into small pieces, a few whole leaves saved for garnish

½ cup good-quality extra-virgin olive oil

1–2 balls of fresh mozzarella, cut into cubes, or 8 ounces of the tiny bocconcini mozzarella balls

2 tablespoons balsamic vinegar

Salt and pepper to taste

1 pound angelhair pasta

TO MAKE 4–6 SERVINGS

Combine all the ingredients (except the pasta) in a bowl to make the checca sauce. Cover and let stand at room temperature for half an hour.

Boil the pasta according to the manufacturer's instructions, in water that tastes like the sea.

Toss with the checca sauce and garnish.

Cook's Tips

If your tomatoes are a little lackluster, you can cheat a bit by adding ½ teaspoon of sugar or honey, and a bit more vinegar. ※ This is a bruschetta sauce as well. Put a spoonful onto slices of toasted baguette, then top with a leaf of basil and a drizzle of balsamic vinegar.

Leftover Tip

Serve the pasta as a cold salad the next day, with a little more balsamic vinegar plus some arugula, pine nuts, black olives, and capers.

BANG, BANG CHICKEN PARMESAN
(Please Don't Tell Anyone How Easy This Is)

My mom calls this "bang, bang" food. You open a jar, "bang"! You toss it all together, "bang"! You slam the oven shut, "bang," you are done!

Then you throw down a red-and-white-checkered tablecloth, light some candles, and hum "Amore" while you toss a salad. When everyone finishes their plate, smile sweetly. Just don't give out the recipe, please.

YOU NEED

8 breaded frozen, not defrosted, chicken breasts (Trader Joe's or Bell & Evans are great)

1 pound penne

6 cups of your favorite tomato sauce, divided

½ cup grated Parmesan cheese

12 ounces fresh mozzarella, sliced (or the shredded mozzarella from a bag)

Handful of fresh parsley or basil, chopped

TO MAKE 6 SERVINGS

Preheat your oven to 425 degrees.

Place the chicken breasts in a large oiled baking dish. Bake in the oven for 15 minutes, flipping them halfway through.

Meanwhile, boil the pasta in salted water until al dente. Drain and toss the pasta with 4 cups of the tomato sauce.

Remove the chicken from the oven and take it out of the baking dish. Pour the pasta into the baking dish and top with the chicken breasts. Sprinkle the Parmesan cheese over the chicken. Bake for 15 minutes.

Take out the baking dish, dollop the remaining tomato sauce over the chicken, and arrange the mozzarella on top. Bake for 10 minutes or until bubbly. Top with the fresh herbs and serve with a green salad.

Veggie Tip

For the chicken, substitute vegetarian meatballs or breaded eggplant, both found in the freezer aisle.

Cook's Tips

Since this is such a quick dish to make, why not buy double the ingredients, make two, and freeze one for a busy day? • Feel free to add chopped vegetables to the pasta, like broccoli, grated carrots, or frozen peas. • Instead of chicken, use 1 pound sliced, cooked Italian sausage or meatballs.

Leftover Tip

If you have chicken breasts left over, make sandwiches. Put them in rolls with lettuce and tomatoes, and serve the pasta as a side dish.

RED THAI CURRY WITH SHRIMP

This is one of the fastest recipes in the book. Spend a few minutes chopping and assembling the ingredients, and once that is done it all cooks in 10 minutes. You will be rewarded with a Thai curry that you won't believe you made yourself!

The secret is the Thai curry paste. Let it do all the work for you. Thai curry paste usually comes in a small can or jar. The next time you see it at an Asian market or a well-stocked supermarket, make sure you pick up a few jars along with some cans of coconut milk and a bottle of fish sauce.

The vegetables are just suggestions; use what you have and what is in season.

YOU NEED

Vegetable oil

1 large red onion, sliced into wedges

3 large cloves garlic, sliced

1 tablespoon grated fresh ginger

2 tablespoons Thai red curry paste* (more or less depending on how spicy you like it)

1 14-ounce can unsweetened coconut milk*

1 cup low-sodium chicken broth

2 tablespoons Asian fish sauce*

1½ tablespoons brown sugar

1 cup diced tomatoes

1 cup snow peas, tips and tails removed

1 cup chopped asparagus, woody ends snapped off

1 pound uncooked large shrimp, peeled and deveined

Salt and pepper to taste

Chopped fresh cilantro

Lime wedges

Found in the Asian section of many supermarkets.

TO MAKE 6 SERVINGS

Heat a large nonstick skillet over medium heat and drizzle in enough oil to film the bottom. Add the onion and sauté until soft and beginning to brown, about 4 minutes. Add the garlic and ginger and sauté until the garlic is golden.

Reduce the heat to medium. Add the curry paste; stir until fragrant, about 1 minute.

Add the coconut milk, chicken broth, fish sauce, and sugar; bring to a low simmer.

Add the remaining vegetables and simmer for 2 minutes.

Add the shrimp and cook, stirring often, for about 3 minutes, or until the shrimp are pink and curled. Taste for seasonings.

Transfer the curry to a large, shallow bowl. Garnish with cilantro and lime wedges. Serve with rice.

RECITE TONIGHT

It's such a shock, I almost screech,
When I find a worm inside my peach!
But then, what really makes me blue,
Is to find a worm who's bit in two!

—*William Cole*

LET'S PLAY!

WHO ARE YOU?
Describe yourself in three adjectives (a word used to describe a noun). Personal favorites include *juicy*, *crunchy*, and *luscious*. Round two: Assign three adjectives to everyone else at the table.

MAC 'N' CHEESE PLEASE

Sometimes the day calls for plain ol' comforting stovetop mac 'n' cheese, and when it does, here is the recipe.

YOU NEED

For the Crunchy Topping

1 cup panko bread crumbs or crushed saltines

1 tablespoon butter, melted

½ cup Parmesan cheese

For the Noodles

3 eggs

2 12-ounce cans evaporated milk

4 cups of any good melting cheese, like cheddar, Monterey Jack, mozzarella, or Gruyère (the sharper your cheese, the cheesier your mac will be)

2 teaspoons dry mustard

Salt and pepper to taste

1 pound elbow macaroni, shells, or other small pasta shape

2 tablespoons olive oil or butter

½ cup grated onions

TO MAKE 8 SERVINGS

Preheat your oven to 350 degrees.

Mix the topping ingredients together. Put them on a baking sheet and bake, giving them a stir once or twice, until golden and crisp, 10 to 15 minutes.

Meanwhile, mix the eggs, evaporated milk, cheese, and mustard in a small bowl. Season with salt and pepper and set aside.

In a big pot of salted water, cook the macaroni until tender, then drain (check the package for cooking times).

While the noodles are cooking, heat a heavy-bottomed pot over medium heat. Add the olive oil or butter and onions. Sauté the onions until soft and translucent.

Add the drained noodles to the onions, stir, then pour the egg mixture into the pot, reduce the heat to medium low, and keep stirring until thoroughly combined and cheese has melted, about 3 minutes. You do not want the mixture to boil, as the eggs will set too stiffly—just heat it up nice and slow. Top with the toasted bread crumbs and call the kids in for dinner.

Cook's Tip

Pack leftover mac 'n' cheese into a square baking dish. When it's cold, cut into individual serving-size squares, wrap each one tightly with foil, label what it is and when it was made, and drop it into your freezer. Next time you need one serving, remove the foil and pop a frozen serving into the microwave or oven. Heat until warm.

...⟨⟩...

LET'S PLAY!

NAME YOUR SUPERPOWER

Name a superpower you would like to have and why.

Assign a superpower to everyone at the table.

Five Questions for Chef
MARIO BATALI

CHEF BATALI *owns fifteen restaurants, has written eight cookbooks, has starred in a host of TV shows, owns a vineyard in Italy, and is the father of two boys. He is home most nights for family dinner between six and seven o'clock. Thursday is always fish taco night. He does not answer the phone during that time, so don't try calling.*

1. What were family dinners like when you were growing up?

We had dinner together most every night. Sometimes it would be as simple as pasta and salad or roasted chicken with lemon and olives. More serious dinners were on Sundays with extended family at Grandma's house.

2. Do you have any advice for people who say "I can't cook" or for people who say "I don't have time to cook"?

Make or find time to cook something. It can take as little as twenty minutes to make a great salad and delicious pasta or a simple sauté, broiled fish, or a chicken dish. Everyone in the family is happier and calmer when dinner is homemade.

3. What are a few of the "must-haves" in your refrigerator and in your pantry?

Great olive oil, anchovies, Parmigiano Reggiano, salami, pasta, real balsamic vinegar, olives, good pickles from the Greenmarket on Union Square, white wine, champagne.

4. There is a trend in America for people to eat on the run or in front of the television. What do you think they are missing by eating that way?

People who cannot find a way to turn off their cell phones and e-mails are truly selling their families short. A completely unplugged and interruption-free family dinner should happen at least a couple times a week, if not every night. People who cannot make that work do not develop the connections in their lives with their family members, and family structure diminishes as the family members drift apart and lose attachment. The obvious implications are loss of meaningful communication and the comfort and reassurance it provides, especially for children as they face the challenges and fears of increased expectations in school and social strata.

5. You have had family dinners all over the world. What are the ingredients you've observed that unite them all?

In our foodie family, I find that the presence of good ingredients that speak of the specific location in the world create and provoke passionate and interesting conversation all by themselves, whether it be salmon and oysters in Seattle, or whitefish and cherry pie in Michigan, or linguine with tiny briny clams from the lagoon in Venice. Taking the time to enjoy the meal, and lingering an extra half hour over the last bites—as opposed to quickly moving on to the next event—is one of my favorite times.

"IF YOU'RE COOKING . . . YOU'RE ULTIMATELY MAKING THE BIGGEST STATEMENT *because you're cutting down on how much is being processed and manipulated before it gets to your kitchen."*

—DAN BARBER, executive chef and co-owner, Blue Hill, Blue Hill at Stone Barns, and Blue Hill Farm

CHICKEN PICCATA
with Crispy Smashed Potatoes

Chicken Piccata is a tangy, tasty dish that is made in one skillet. As for the potatoes . . . somehow I always lose some between the kitchen and the table. It might have something to do with the kids wanting to make sure the potatoes are "okay." So this recipe gives you a few more than you need . . . just in case.

KIDS CAN

Smash the potatoes. But it's one of the best jobs around, so make sure they let you do a few!

YOU NEED

1½ pounds thin-cut boneless, skinless chicken breasts, preferably kosher and organic

1 cup flour

2 tablespoons grated Parmesan cheese

1 teaspoon salt

2 tablespoons olive oil

3 shallots, finely chopped

½ cup white wine

2 cups canned low-sodium chicken stock

3 medium-size lemons

1 teaspoon honey

Salt and pepper to taste

A couple of tablespoons capers (if they are the kind stored in salt, wash the salt off)

2 tablespoons chopped parsley

TO MAKE 6 SERVINGS WITH LEFTOVERS

Cut each piece of chicken in half crosswise. Mix the flour, Parmesan, and salt, and dredge the chicken in it. Gently shake off any excess flour.

Heat a large nonstick skillet over medium heat and drizzle in enough oil to cover the bottom. Put the chicken into the pan and sauté it for 3 minutes on each side. You will probably have to do this in two batches.

Put the chicken aside, wipe out the skillet, and add another drizzle of olive oil. Sauté the shallots until soft and translucent, then add the wine and stock and simmer until reduced by half, about 8 minutes.

Meanwhile, remove the lemon zest (the fragrant yellow part of the lemon rind) from 2 of the lemons with a

grater. (Be careful not to zest any of the white pith under the yellow skin or your sauce will be bitter!)

Squeeze the juice of the 2 lemons into the pan, add the honey and lemon zest, and whisk to combine. Taste the sauce—is it too tart for you? Add a little more honey. Need a little more zing? Add more lemon. It will need salt and pepper as well.

Nestle the chicken breasts into the sauce. Thinly slice the last lemon, arrange the slices among the chicken pieces, and top with the capers and parsley.

Bring back to a simmer, serve out of the pan.

Cook's Tip

Capers are actually tiny flower buds. If you dry them well and fry them in hot oil, they will pop open into the lovely little flowers they are.

Leftover Tip

Put slices of chicken on a bed of greens (arugula would be lovely) and serve with "Ranch" Dressing (page 70) on the side.

CRISPY SMASHED POTATOES

YOU NEED

About 20 walnut-sized small potatoes

½ cup extra-virgin olive oil

1 clove garlic, grated

Salt and pepper

TO MAKE 6 SERVINGS

Preheat the oven to 450 degrees.

In a large pot of salted water, boil the potatoes until they can easily be pierced with the tip of a knife, 15 to 20 minutes.

Drain the potatoes well. Toss them with olive oil and garlic. Put them on an oiled baking sheet.

With a rimless pot lid, or with the heel of your hand (be careful if they are still hot), press down on the potatoes so they flatten.

Roast in the oven for 30 minutes or until they are golden and crispy. Season with salt and pepper.

Monina's WHEAT BERRY SALAD

Our neighbor Monina is a great and generous cook. She has taught us how to make beach plum jam, crunchy green tahini salad, and this delicious wheat berry salad that is so good you could eat it as a meal several days in a row without getting tired of it.

Your kids will love the chewy goodness and the combination of a little tart, a bit sweet, and a handful of crunchy.

YOU NEED

2 cups wheat berries (wild rice or farro also are good)

1 cup dried cranberries or cherries

⅓ cup canola or toasted walnut oil

Zest and juice of 2 oranges

Zest and juice of 1 lemon

Salt and pepper to taste

1 cup frozen edamame beans, defrosted (no need to cook)

1 cup toasted pecans or walnuts

Optional additions: feta, chopped dried apricots, chopped scallions, parsley, dill, arugula, spinach, pine nuts, or whatever else your heart desires

TO MAKE 6 SERVINGS

In a large pot, combine the wheat berries with 6 cups of water. Bring to a boil and cook, uncovered, for about 60 to 80 minutes, bearing in mind that they are quite unpredictable, so start tasting them after 45 minutes. When they are tender but still chewy, drain and let cool.

Toss the wheat berries with the cranberries, oil, and zest and juice of the oranges and lemon. Season generously with salt and pepper.

Let the salad hang out for at least 2 hours so the ingredients get to know each other. Just before serving, toss with the edamame and nuts.

Leftover Tip

If you (intentionally) cook too many grains, serve them warm for breakfast with milk, honey, and a splash of vanilla.

Crunchy GREEN TAHINI SALAD

A crunchy green surprise salad. Surprising because your kids are really going to love it.

YOU NEED

For the Salad

2 bunches kale leaves, stems and tough ribs removed, leaves cut into fine strips

Tahini Dressing to taste (recipe below)

Optional Additions

½ head raw cauliflower, finely chopped

1 cup chopped parsley leaves

½ cup chopped fresh mint

1 pound warm roasted potatoes

Dried cranberries

Toasted pine nuts or almonds

Orange segments

TO MAKE 4–6 SERVINGS

Put the kale and any optional additions into a salad bowl. Toss with enough dressing to make you happy.

TAHINI DRESSING

YOU NEED

2 tablespoons well-stirred tahini (Middle Eastern sesame paste—yummy on toast, too)

⅓ cup water

½–⅔ cups fresh lemon juice (depending on how tart you like your dressing)

⅓ cup olive oil

3 cloves garlic, chopped

2 tablespoons Bragg Liquid Aminos* (optional)

¼ teaspoon sugar (optional)

Salt and pepper to taste

* Available in most supermarkets. Also great sprayed on popcorn!

TO MAKE 1 CUP

Place all the dressing ingredients in a blender or food processor and blend thoroughly.

Your QUICK-FIX DINNER IDEAS

Anything served on a stick or a spear almost always goes over extremely well. This can get very sophisticated. It can include folds of sliced lunch meats, such as smoked salmon, ham, or turkey (even veggie dogs), steamed veggies, cheese cubes, or bread cubes, served with fun dipping sauces.

TOM, father of Luke, Milo, and Charley

If I have leftover rice (usually from the Chinese take-out box), I will sauté it in a big pan with some thinly sliced garlic and cabbage (cooked broccoli and peas are good, too). When the rice is good and hot, I throw in a few eggs beaten with soy sauce and sesame oil. Sauté for a few more minutes until the eggs are cooked.

KIKI, aunt of Elias, Noah, Felicia, and Victoria

Here's what I do in a pinch, and I always keep these ingredients in the fridge and freezer; taco salad night is always a hit at our house! We sauté ground turkey and onions, and add a packet of taco seasoning. Then we chop up lettuce and tomatoes. Throw everything in a big bowl, add some shredded cheese, crunch up a handful of tortilla chips, add sauce and some dressing. Toss all of it together, and you have dinner in one bowl! The whole family loves it—kids included!

DEANNE, mother of Jaclyn and Jeramy

A kielbasa sausage is always in our fridge. I slice it into coins and sauté them. I'll roast some broccoli in the oven with olive oil, salt, and pepper. The kids call it "crispy broccoli and sausage night"! Add half an avocado that they can scoop out with a spoon and you have a pretty great meal.

KAISA, mother of Alex and Elsa

We do "breakfast for dinner" nights and we get into our pajamas and make pancakes or French toast and turkey bacon. I thought I was fooling my children but they call my pancakes and French toast "science experiments" because I make the batter with pumpkin and agave and protein powder . . . depends what I have on hand. It tastes great and is much healthier . . . but they think it's hysterical to call me a "mad scientist" behind my back.

JAMIE, mother of Jordan and Gray

Our last name is Henry and we make "Henry Salad." Everyone gets to pick out something to put in the salad, and everyone has a job. My husband and son wash and cut veggies; I deal with cutting the meat, eggs, bacon, or whatever; and my daughter with special needs likes to put the dishes, salad dressing, and napkins on the table. That keeps her busy, and she gets to help, too!

DEBBIE, mother of Gracie and Caleb

KALE IS A SUPER-FOOD.
GREAT RAW OR COOKED, IT BOASTS VITAMINS C, A, AND K, AS WELL AS OMEGA-3S.

We take steamed broccoli and chop it really, really fine. Throw it in a pan with some olive oil and a little butter. Keep stirring until browned. Season with salt and pepper. Cheese is good to add, too. Mmm, yum. Hot or cold, kids beg to take leftovers to school.
LIBBY, mother of Ella and Alec

I use a wide frying pan to fry up some diced onions and chopped cooked potatoes until they are nice and brown, then add whatever other leftovers we have in the fridge (cooked vegetables, turkey, diced ham). It becomes a big tasty mish-mosh that we top with fried eggs.
RENATE, mother of Torsten, Henrik, Benjamin, and Kirstin

I keep frozen pizza dough from the local Italian bakery in my freezer. I let it thaw during the day, and when we get home, the kids play baker and roll it out to pizza size. We spoon on some sauce and add whatever cheese and veggies I have in the fridge. Bake it in the oven (according to the dough directions), make a salad, and by the time the homework is done, pizza dinner is ready!
JENNIFER, mother of Alex, Ben, and Rebecca

It's hard for us to do family dinner, so we have breakfast together instead. Seven AM, everyone shows up, I make a full breakfast: granola, corn bread, muffins and pancakes, smoothies or juice. I like the kids to go out feeling full. I have very fond memories of my mom being up just a little before us; it was very comforting.
VERONICA, mother of Molly, Leo, Maggie, and Seamos

I sauté onion, carrots, celery, and thyme in a saucepan with olive oil. Then I add chicken stock, some shredded rotisserie chicken from the grocery store, and finally throw in some cooked pasta and peas.
We call it . . . *Soup.*
ROSITA, mother of Sasha, Shaya, and Joshua

For more quick-fix recipes and to share your own, go to **THEFAMILYDINNERBOOK.COM.**

How the Microwave
ZAPPED FAMILY DINNER

Buyer beware! Although it sits quietly in the corner of your kitchen, do not underestimate the power of the microwave to be a menacing influence on your family's togetherness! Sure, it revolutionized the task of preparing food . . . but was it for the better?

Initially intended to reheat food when it first hit stores in 1947 (and cost $5,000 and weighed 750 pounds!), the microwave went on to spawn a multibillion-dollar industry of processed, prepackaged, high-fat, salty, and preservative-laced foods for you to buy and "conveniently" microwave. No need for a home-cooked meal with fresh ingredients! Now everyone can grab his or her own individual meal choice and zap away (in just the past three years, microwave use has gone up 20 percent). We don't even have to sit together—in fact, we can't. Since the microwave is cooking for us, everyone's meal is ready at different times.

Will the homes of tomorrow feature a microwave in every room? (Hey, don't scoff. It happened with televisions!) Will the day come when we won't even have to bump into one another heading for the cupboard for things to nuke? Food historian Felipe Fernandez-Armesto sums it up in his book *Near a Thousand Tables*: "In the microwave household, home cooking looks doomed. Family life must fragment if people stop having shared meals. Instead of a bond, meals are becoming a barrier. The microwave makes possible the end of cooking and eating as social acts."

Wow. Okay, he's a little down on microwaves. To be fair, they do make life easier when time is of the essence (and they're great for cooking yams!). But it is also true that the microwave encourages people to eat less nutritious foods, faster, and alone. Make sure you're the boss of it, not it the boss of you or your family!

"COOK" TOGETHER AT THE TABLE

5

So here is our trick: Leave the final touches of dinner for your family to finish at the table. By involving them this way, they will feel . . . well, involved! Now everyone takes pride in the final result, eats better, and has more fun!

Here are some great recipes designed to foster a little ownership in the meal. If you cook it, they will come . . . and help finish it themselves!

PASTA AS YOU LIKE IT
(And How Your Kids Like It, and Their Friends Like It . . .)

L o n g noodles, short noodles, dried noodles, fresh noodles, tiny pastina, huge rigatone—whatever noodles you use, they will make your kids happy because they get to create their own pasta plate.

Boil two or three types of noodles, some of them short some of them long, put them out on a platter side by side or in different serving dishes, if you like, along with a few sauces in separate bowls and the toppings on the side.

Let everyone pick and mix pasta, sauces, and toppings.

KIDS CAN

Be in charge of the toppings.
Arrange them in bowls.
Pick out the bowls for the sauces and pastas.
Pick the pasta shapes.

TOPPINGS: Choose Some or All
In little bowls, arrange . . .

Steamed broccoli

Fresh tomatoes, chopped

Mozzarella sliced or diced

Sliced grilled chicken

Parmesan cheese and a grater

Chopped sun-dried tomatoes

Pesto (page 115)

Olives

Fresh or defrosted frozen corn or peas

Chopped grilled vegetables

"Life is a combination of **MAGIC** *and* **PASTA."** —FEDERICO FELLINI, **film director**

Here is the recipe for a basic tomato sauce, with three variations. Make one, or all three (to make enough sauce for all three, double the recipe).

TOMATO SAUCE

YOU NEED

¼ cup extra-virgin olive oil

1 medium onion, finely chopped

4 cloves garlic, finely chopped

2 28-ounce cans crushed tomatoes (Muir Glen or San Marzanos are good)

A few fresh basil leaves

1 teaspoon chopped fresh or dried oregano

1 teaspoon salt or to taste

TO MAKE 8 CUPS

Combine the olive oil, onion, and garlic in a medium pot. Heat up gently and stir until the onion is translucent and the garlic is fragrant.

Stir in the remaining ingredients and heat to a gentle simmer. Simmer for about 30 minutes and taste for seasonings.

LET'S PLAY!

A TRUTH AND A LIE
Each person tells two stories that happened to them that day, one that is true and one that is made up. Everyone guesses which story was true, and which was not.

PINK SAUCE

Just before serving, take out 4 cups of the tomato sauce, put it into a different pot, add ½ cup cream and ½ cup Parmesan, and gently reheat the sauce.

Health Tip

For low-fat pink sauce, replace the cream with 1 cup nonfat dried milk dissolved in ¼ cup hot water, stirred well.

PUTTANESCA SAUCE

YOU NEED

2 anchovies, chopped (optional)

10 black pitted kalamata olives

2 tablespoons capers

¼ teaspoon red pepper flakes

2 tablespoons chopped fresh parsley

Take out 4 cups of the tomato sauce, put it into a different pot, and add all the ingredients.

Simmer for a few minutes and taste for seasonings.

ALL'ARRABBIATA (SPICY TOMATO SAUCE)

Take out 4 cups of the tomato sauce, put it into a different pot, and add ½ teaspoon red pepper flakes (or to taste) and 2 tablespoons chopped fresh parsley.

Green Tip

Boil two types of pasta in one pot of water. First, bring a big pot of salted water to a boil. Boil the pasta that takes the longest time. When the pasta is done, remove it with a big slotted spoon and put it in a colander to drain; cover it to keep it warm. Bring the water back to a boil and add a quick-cooking pasta like angelhair, or a fresh pasta that only takes a few minutes. Ta-da.

"Cooking is at once **CHILD'S PLAY AND ADULT JOY.** *And cooking done with* **CARE IS AN ACT OF LOVE."** —CRAIG CLAIBORNE, author of *The New York Times Cookbook*

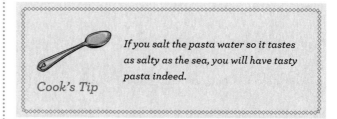

Cook's Tip

If you salt the pasta water so it tastes as salty as the sea, you will have tasty pasta indeed.

THAI CHICKEN WRAPS

At the table, fill lettuce leaves with flavorful minced chicken, vegetables, and pieces of torn herbs. Add a squeeze of lime or some peanut crunch, and roll it up.

Serve with some steamed brown rice on the side, and you have a perfect summer dinner.

KIDS CAN

Help tear the mint into little pieces.

Pinch the tips and tails off the green beans.

Wash the vegetables.

Taste to make sure the chicken is perfect.

YOU NEED

For the Chicken Filling

1 tablespoon vegetable oil

2 cloves garlic, finely chopped

2 tablespoons grated fresh ginger or ½ teaspoon ground ginger

¼ cup water or stock

1 pound ground chicken

¼ cup chopped fresh mint leaves

2 tablespoons sliced shallots

1 teaspoon Asian chili sauce or to taste

1 sliced Thai chile pepper (very spicy, so optional)

¼ cup lime juice

2 teaspoons brown sugar

2–3 tablespoons Asian fish sauce

YOU NEED

For the Wrappings and Toppings

18 whole large lettuce leaves (about 3 lettuce heads)

½ pound young raw green beans, thinly sliced on the diagonal

2 cups bean sprouts

1 cucumber, cut into strips with your peeler or mandoline

1 large carrot, shredded

Some fresh mint, cilantro, and basil

Cut limes

Asian chili sauce

½ cup chopped peanuts

For the Dipping Sauce

¼ cup lime juice

¼ cup sugar

½ cup water

¼ cup Asian fish sauce

1 clove garlic, minced

TO MAKE 4–6 SERVINGS

Mix all the ingredients for the dipping sauce in a little bowl. Set aside.

In a medium nonstick pan, heat the vegetable oil and sauté the garlic and ginger over medium heat until light brown. Add ¼ cup water or stock, then add the chicken and stir well, separating the chicken into small bits. This should take you about 4 to 5 minutes. Drain out the water.

Transfer the cooked chicken into a mixing bowl. Add the remaining ingredients for the filling and mix well. Taste and season until there is a good balance among the sweet, tart, and savory flavors. You might need a bit more fish sauce, another squeeze of lemon, a little more hot sauce . . .

On a large platter, mound the vegetables, herbs, and chicken. Serve with little bowls of the dipping sauce, cut limes, fish sauce, chili sauce, and chopped peanuts.

THE **MINT FAMILY** CONTAINS ABOUT 3,200 SPECIES, AND FROM IT WE GET MINT, BASIL, AND OREGANO.

RECIPES

YOUR FAVORITE GRILLED CHEESE for Dinner!

There is no reason why you shouldn't have lunch for dinner (or breakfast, for that matter). You probably even have the ingredients for this in your fridge right now.

The fun part of this dinner is that everyone gets to create their own sandwich.

You simply assemble the ingredients, lay them out in an attractive manner, and let your family pile all their favorite cheeses and toppings on the bread. Then you grill them either on a pan, in the oven, or on the grill ... just make sure not to confuse whose is whose, as people get very attached to their own masterpiece (I write the names on little heart-shaped pieces of parchment paper, and stick them on the sandwiches). Here is a list of suggestions, but the ingredients happily depend only on what your favorite combinations are ... and what you happen to have in the fridge.

BREADS: Any Kind You Like, Perhaps . . .

Some baguettes

Fruity, nutty dark bread

Soft, squishy and white loaf

Hard, crunchy and small rolls

CHEESES: Any Cheese You Love, Sharp or Mild

Mozzarella

Smoked Gouda

Brie

Swiss

Feta

Goat cheese

Cheddar

LET'S PLAY!

NAME YOUR SANDWICH

If it was featured in a deli, what would it be called?
The Serendipity, the Heartthrob . . .

TOPPINGS: Perhaps . . .

Caramelized onions (slice onions, season with salt and a pinch of sugar, and sauté in olive oil over medium-low heat, stirring often, 20–30 minutes)

Sliced apples or pears

Sliced tomatoes

Sun-dried tomatoes

Sliced avocado

Fresh basil

Prosciutto, salami, ham, sautéed bacon

CONDIMENTS: Why Not . . .

Olive tapenade

Pesto (page 115)

Aioli (page 134)

Honey

Mustard

Fig jam

Apple butter

TO MAKE ANY NUMBER OF SERVINGS

As each sandwich is put together, brush each side with either olive oil or garlic butter, then grill, broil, or sauté the sandwiches over medium heat until they are golden brown and the cheese is melted. You can also make these in a panini pan, if you have one.

Serve with pickles, a simple green salad . . . and perhaps, on a rainy day, with tomato soup (page 81) and a lit fire.

RECITE TONIGHT

I wonder if the cabbage knows
He is less lovely than the Rose;
Or does he squat in smug content,
A source of noble nourishment . . .

—*Anonymous*

A Crunchy, Tasty, Fresh MAKE-YOUR-OWN-SALAD BAR

On a hot or busy night when you don't want to turn on the stove, why not set up a salad bar in your kitchen? The sky and your taste buds are the limit to ingredients on this one. Before you go shopping, take a peek in your fridge: Is there some leftover chicken that can be diced? Some pizza that can be cut into little squares and served on the side? Are there some slices of bread that can be cubed, tossed with a little olive oil, and toasted as croutons? Even better, is there a vegetable growing on your sill or in your garden that can be the guest of honor tonight?

Here is a list of ingredient suggestions. Pick five or fifteen—just remember to add plenty of things that crunch, and include your family's favorite vegetables. Then get the kids involved setting up the "salad bar." Have fun arranging everything in pretty bowls and platters. An old restaurant trick is to mound your ingredients TALL instead of spreading them FLaaaaaaaT.

YOU NEED A FEW OF THESE FAVORITES

Vegetables

Any kind of pea: sugar snaps, snow peas, green peas (defrosted frozen or freshly shucked)

Carrots, cubed or shredded

Cucumbers, cubed or sliced

Baby tomatoes, or big sliced tomatoes

Mushrooms, sliced

Corn, raw and cut off the cob, canned, or defrosted frozen

Celery, sliced

Sprouts

Avocado slices

Salad Greens

Romaine, sliced

Mixed baby greens

Spinach

Kale

Watercress

Arugula

Bibb lettuce, torn into pieces

Iceberg, in crunchy chunks

Toppings

Crumbled tortilla chips

Croutons

Sesame seeds

Sunflower seeds

Almonds

Pecans

Walnuts

Raisins

Protein

Chickpeas

Cooked lentils

White beans

Kidney beans

Shredded roast chicken

Cubed or sliced turkey

Canned tuna

Cheese

Feta, cubed

Blue cheese, crumbled

Cheddar, shredded

Goat cheese, in chunks

"RANCH" DRESSING

YOU NEED

¾ cup buttermilk

2 tablespoons low-fat mayonnaise

2 tablespoons plain yogurt

1 tablespoon chopped fresh basil

Quick Tip

On days when you're in a rush, you can really cheat on this one. If a grocery store or health food market nearby has a salad bar, you can go there and get all the items already precut and prepared. Keep all the items separate so you can put them in bowls when you get home. Try to stick with the leafy greens and the raw vegetables, and please stay away from the mayonnaisey-potato-pasta-egg "salads." (Salads? Really?) Not only are they bad for you, but they are unusually heavy, making it an expensive salad if you pay by weight. All you have to do now is go home and arrange the "salad bar" on your counter or lazy Susan.

1 tablespoon chopped fresh chives

2 tablespoons chopped parsley

2 teaspoons vinegar

1 small shallot, minced

½ teaspoon sugar

Salt and pepper to taste

TO MAKE 1¼ CUPS

Put all the ingredients in a blender and blend until smooth. Taste and adjust the seasonings.

ASIAN APPLE VINAIGRETTE

YOU NEED

½ unpeeled red apple, cored and chopped

¼ small red onion

⅓ cup seasoned rice wine vinegar

⅓ cup canola oil

2 tablespoons toasted Asian sesame oil

1 tablespoon soy sauce

½ tablespoon minced fresh ginger

Salt and pepper to taste

TO MAKE 1¼ CUPS

Put all the ingredients in a blender and blend until smooth. Taste and adjust the seasonings.

SIMPLE VINAIGRETTE

YOU NEED

1 small shallot or garlic clove, minced

¼ cup red, white, or balsamic vinegar

2 teaspoons Dijon mustard

¾ cup olive oil

1–2 teaspoons chopped fresh herbs if you have them

Salt (about 1 teaspoon) and pepper to taste

TO MAKE 1¼ CUPS

The easy way: Put all the ingredients into a jelly jar and shake, shake, shake. Or you can put everything in a blender and blend. Taste and adjust seasonings.

·❦· A WELL-SPICED LIFE

MARICEL PRESILLA *is a Latin American cooking expert, popular Hoboken, New Jersey, restaurateur, and author of* The New Taste of Chocolate: A Cultural and Natural History of Cacao. *Cucharamama offers artisanal South American cuisine and some of the best mojitos on the East Coast; right down the block, Maricel's Zafra serves authentic Cuban fare. Presilla's amazing Latin cuisine has also been served at the White House.*

"In my culture we eat a big lunch—lunch is dinner. The whole family sits together. That is a given. Dinner should be a habit. I don't have kids but I do it with my husband and with my employees; they are family to me. Sitting down to a meal is a joyful occasion. It brings everyone closer together. Once you share a meal something changes. It brings a level of wonderful intimacy and it relaxes everyone.

"I had four aunts who were fantastic cooks. We would always eat at my maternal grandfather's house on Sundays. The preparation of that lunch was a ritual. I saw so many wonderful traditional foods prepared in my grandfather's kitchen, seasonal foods like tamales. I come from eastern Cuba, and corn season coincided with carnival time. The making of the tamales was a big family affair. You need a lot of people to help, and I remember my aunts each doing a chore and then the kids husking the corn or helping to grate it. The smell of damp earth that corn has when you're boiling the tamales is something that I will never forget.

"I can tell you that growing up, the act of cooking as a group is one of my best memories. I think that's why I am a cook today. My relationship with food was always about being gregarious and sharing. It's about being able to sit down and enjoy a meal with others."

RECIPES

VIETNAMESE SOUP in a Teapot

Sweet and tart, crunchy and soft, hot and cool... In Vietnam, pho soup is traditionally served for breakfast, but it is so beautiful and delicious that it can be eaten any time of day.

At the table, each person adds his or her favorite garnishes to their bowl. Perhaps some slippery rice noodles, a bit of bright mint and other herbs torn from the centerpiece, fiery chile peppers, some chicken, and crunchy peanuts can top it off. Then a teapot filled with the pho broth is passed to pour over the garnishes. Enjoy your very own bowl of happiness.

YOU NEED

For the Pho Broth

8 cups low-sodium chicken broth

1 whole onion, peeled and cut in half

4 cloves garlic, smashed

2-inch chunk ginger, peeled

2 whole star anise

1 cinnamon stick

2 tablespoons brown sugar

1 pound boneless, skinless chicken breasts, trimmed

2 tablespoons Asian fish sauce, or to taste

Juice of ½ lime

Salt and pepper to taste

For the Garnishes

1 package flat rice noodles soaked in hot water for 15 minutes and drained (or angelhair pasta cooked according to the package)

1 tablespoon vegetable oil

A bunch of fresh leafy herbs, washed (for example: mint, basil, Thai basil, and cilantro)

1 cup fresh bean sprouts, rinsed and drained

2 tablespoons sliced scallions

2 medium carrots, peeled and grated

1 fresh red or green chile, sliced very thin

Lime wedges

2 thinly sliced shallots or 1 small red onion, sliced (optional)

Asian chili sauce, more fish sauce, hoisin sauce

TO MAKE 6 SERVINGS

In a large pot, bring the chicken broth, onion, garlic, ginger, star anise, cinnamon stick, and brown sugar to a boil. Turn down the heat and simmer for 15 minutes. Add the chicken and simmer for 10 to 15 minutes or until it is done. Skim the scum off of the surface of the soup. Take out the chicken and shred or cut it into bite-size pieces.

Bring a pot of salted water to a boil for the rice noodles. Cook them in the boiling water, stirring, for 45 seconds. Drain the noodles in a colander, and rinse under cold water. Toss with the vegetable oil and put in a serving bowl.

Arrange the herbs in a glass of water as if they were a flower arrangement, and put them on the dinner table.

Put the chicken and remaining garnishes into individual serving bowls.

Bring the broth back to a simmer. Stir in the fish sauce and lime juice; add salt and pepper if needed. Strain the broth into a teapot. Keep the remaining broth hot on the stove.

To serve, give each person a bowl, a spoon, and chopsticks. Let everyone fill their bowl with the noodles, adding chicken, squeezing lime, tearing off bits of herbs, then passing the teapot to pour the hot broth over.

Finally, adjust the flavors of your own soup to taste with the sauces and fresh chiles.

IN CHINA
IF YOU FIND AN UNEVEN PAIR OF CHOPSTICKS AT YOUR TABLE SETTING, IT MEANS YOU ARE GOING TO MISS A BOAT, PLANE, OR TRAIN.

LET'S PLAY!

WHERE WILL YOU GO?
Where would you like to travel with your family?
Where would you like to travel with a friend?
Where would you like to travel all alone?

RECIPES

Tasty, Tangy SHRIMP TOSTADAS

Here is a great, quick dinner with no "cooking" involved. Just throw all the ingredients together and put them in bowls on the table. Let your family "stack" their own tostadas.

KIDS CAN

Pick out interesting bowls for the fixings and fill them.
Squeeze the citrus juices.
Make the guacamole.

YOU NEED

For the Citrus Shrimp

1 pound cooked shrimp, peeled and deveined

½ cup fresh lime juice

½ cup fresh lemon juice

¼ cup fresh orange juice

¼ cup chopped red onion

1 teaspoon salt

1 cup chopped celery

½ cup chopped red pepper

1 tablespoon minced jalapeño, seeds and white pith removed (optional)

2 tablespoons chopped fresh mint and cilantro (optional)

For the Cabbage Salad

½ small white cabbage, finely shredded

1 small jicama or 1 medium-size seeded hothouse cucumber, peeled and cut into matchsticks

½ cup seasoned rice vinegar

Chopped fresh mint and cilantro (optional)

For the Fixings

Guacamole (store-bought or see page 134)

Salsa (store-bought or see page 133)

Tostada shells (the flat kind) or tortilla chips

Limes, cut in half

Cilantro

Hot sauce

A drizzle of Mexican crema or sour cream

TO MAKE 4 SERVINGS

Mix all the ingredients for the citrus shrimp together in a bowl and put this into the fridge for at least 10 minutes but no longer than 30 minutes. In the meantime, mix together all the ingredients for the cabbage salad, and make the guacamole.

To make your own, put the shrimp, cabbage salad, and fixings in separate bowls. Let everyone make their own tostadas.

Or, if you want to plate the tostadas, put a tostada shell or a handful of tortilla chips on a plate for each person. Top with the cabbage salad, then a layer of the shrimp, a dollop of guacamole, some tomatillo or tomato salsa, a jauntily placed sprig of cilantro, and half a lime on the side. Serve and enjoy.

Cook's Tip

Should you buy shrimp fresh or frozen? If you can get local fresh shrimp, you are very lucky. Buy them. However, most shrimp you see in the market have been frozen and defrosted. There is nothing wrong with that, but why let the fishmonger defrost them (who knows how long ago that was) when you can do it yourself? If you want to cook shrimp that is still frozen, bring a big pot of water to a boil. Salt it; you can also add a few bay leaves and some lemon slices. Throw the still-frozen shrimp into the pot. Just as soon as the water starts to boil again, take the pot off the heat, and when the shrimp are pink and curled—this should take 2 to 3 minutes more— they will be done.

Green Tip

Whatever kind of seafood you are buying, it is always a good idea to go to www .montereybayaquarium.org and check whether your seafood was sustainably caught or responsibly grown. Not only because you want to take care of the sea and its creatures, but also to educate yourself, so you choose fish that has the least amount of mercury, and to protect your family from seafood that has been fed funky food and medications.

RECIPES

TORTILLA SOUP FOR AMIGOS A Hearty Mexican Soup with Lots of Toppings to Add . . . or Not!

What is a perfect dinner on a cold October night? Tortilla soup! But it's also the perfect dinner on a hot summer night, when you don't want to spend too much time in the kitchen.

Make the soup and, while it is simmering, arrange the toppings into bowls or on a large platter. (The latter makes the cleanup quicker, but if your kids are doing the dishes, go ahead and use a lot of little bowls.)

When dinner is ready, serve the soup and let everyone heap on their own toppings. Some will be spicy, some will be cheesy, and yours will be just right.

KIDS CAN

Crumble the corn tortillas.
Chop the avocados.
Put toppings in bowls.

YOU NEED

For the Broth

2 tablespoons olive oil

1 large onion, sliced into wedges

4 cloves garlic

1 tablespoon ground cumin

2 teaspoons chopped fresh oregano or 1 teaspoon dried oregano

1½ cups of your favorite tomato salsa

8 cups chicken stock, homemade or store-bought

1 pound boneless, skinless organic chicken breasts

1 cup torn corn tortillas

For the Toppings: These Are Just Suggestions—Use Them All or Just a Few

1 cup shredded or crumbled cheese: cheddar, feta, or Cotija

1 cup crumbled tortilla chips (I like the low-fat baked kind—they are just as crunchy, and I promise you will not miss the fried part.)

Handful of chopped fresh cilantro

½ cup low-fat sour cream or Greek yogurt

1 cup shredded cabbage, white or purple

1–2 chopped avocados

Limes cut in half for squeezing

Hot sauce

TO MAKE 6 SERVINGS

In a large pot, heat the oil until shimmering. Add the onion, garlic, and cumin and sauté for 3 or 4 minutes, until fragrant. Add the oregano, salsa, stock, and chicken breasts; bring to a gentle simmer over medium heat. Simmer for 15 minutes and then remove the chicken breasts.

Add the corn tortillas and simmer until they are soft, about 5 minutes. In a blender, or with a handheld blender, blend the soup until smooth. You might have to do this in a few batches.

Shred the chicken. Put it along with all the other toppings into little bowls, or arrange them on a large platter.

Pour the soup into each bowl and let everyone add their own favorite garnishes.

To make this soup vegetarian, skip the chicken, use vegetable stock, and add tofu or cooked beans for protein.

Veggie Tip

Rinse and save your take-out containers. They are great for storing leftovers and for transporting your kids' lunches.

Green Tip

SOUPER DINNERS

Sometimes All You Need
Is a Good Bowl of Soup

6

> Beautiful soup, so rich and green,
> Waiting in a hot tureen!
> Who for such dainties would not stoop?
> Soup of the evening, beautiful soup!
> Soup of the evening, beautiful soup!
>
> —*Lewis Carroll*

ESCAROLE and QUINOA SOUP

This is a simple, comforting soup. Double the recipe and make plenty for tonight, tomorrow, and to store in the freezer, too.

If you also add a cup of cooked white beans, a cup of chopped tomatoes, and some turkey sausage meatballs, it transforms from a simple soup into a substantial supper.

YOU NEED

2 tablespoons olive oil

1 small onion, finely chopped

3–4 cloves garlic, minced

1 medium carrot, finely chopped

1 celery stalk, finely chopped

6 cups low-sodium chicken or vegetable broth

1 sprig thyme

A Parmesan cheese rind if you have one, or ¼ cup grated Parmesan, plus more for garnishing

½ teaspoon red pepper flakes

½ cup quinoa, rinsed under cold water

1 small bunch escarole, chopped or torn into 1-inch pieces—about 4 cups loosely packed

Squeeze of lemon

Salt and pepper

TO MAKE 6 SERVINGS

Heat up your soup pot and film the bottom with a drizzle of olive oil. Sauté the onion, garlic, carrot, and celery over medium heat until the veggies start to soften and get fragrant, about 5 minutes.

Add the broth, thyme, Parmesan rind or grated Parmesan, and red pepper flakes; bring to a boil. Add the quinoa and turn down the heat. Simmer, covered, for 20 minutes.

Throw in the escarole and continue to simmer gently until the escarole wilts down, just a few minutes, then remove the thyme twig and Parmesan rind.

Add lemon juice, salt, and pepper to taste. Serve with Parmesan cheese for sprinkling, and toasted slices of good bread.

SIMPLE SAUSAGE MEATBALLS

Remove ½ pound raw, organic Italian-style turkey sausage from its casings. With wet hands, roll it into walnut-size balls. Drop the meatballs into the soup at the same time as you add the quinoa.

TUBE FOOD
Frozen in Time

For some cultural historians, the ascent of the frozen TV dinner in postwar America was the first meatball thrown in the food fight pitting housewives' growing fascination with "quick and easy" against the traditional "slaving" over a hot stove. The trays of compartmentalized sliced turkey and sweet potatoes, or Salisbury steak with peas and carrots, were seductive solutions for a generation of women who were ready to loosen their apron strings.

Frozen, prepackaged meals hit their stride around 1954. The timing was perfect. The clever marketers at the Swanson Food Company sensed the growing restlessness among housewives and the growing appeal of that new glowing box—television—that had begun invading the living rooms of middle-class homes. Why not let Mom relax and warm up a few just-like-homemade meals in the oven—a different kind for each person! Originally Swanson produced just five thousand dinners, but when moms got a taste of their ease, demand skyrocketed: The company sold more than ten million its first year. Today the combination of eating processed food in front of the television no longer seems like such a good idea.

DANISH YELLOW SPLIT PEA SOUP with Crispy Brown Onions and Bits of Bacon

When I was a kid, there were a couple of years we had fields of yellow peas growing down by the woods. After the peas dried on the vine, they would be harvested and sold. But my parents would always keep a big sack for themselves in the cellar. Being as frugal as they were, they had figured out that by using our peas, bacon from Uncle Emil's farm, and some cheap onions, they were able to make a dinner for pennies, yet it was fit for a (Danish) king.

The trick is to pile the bacon and onions on top of the soup, spoon a bit of soup from the edge of your bowl, dip it into the middle and get some of that goodness on your spoon, then say, "Nej hvor ER det lœkkert" (yum, this is SO delicious).

Serve with toasted and buttered rye bread and a crock of mustard to dip your spoon into now and then.

Traditionally we have crêpes for dessert (page 214)... but that is up to you.

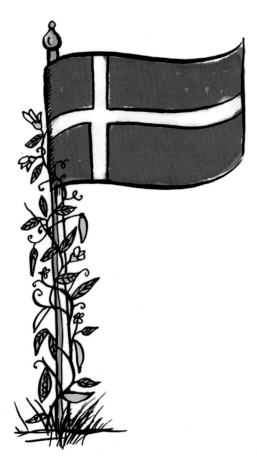

KIDS CAN

Be official taste testers.
Put the bacon and onions into the middle of each bowl.
Sprinkle on the parsley garnish.

YOU NEED

For the Soup

2 tablespoons olive oil

2 medium onions, chopped

2 stalks celery, diced

2 carrots, peeled and diced

¼ celery root, diced (optional, but very Danish)

6 cups chicken broth

2 cups dried yellow split peas, rinsed

1 smoked ham hock or smoked turkey leg (optional)

1 sprig thyme

1 bay leaf

¼ cup chopped parsley, divided

Salt and pepper to taste

For the Topping

8 pieces bacon, chopped

2 medium onions, sliced

TO MAKE 6 SERVINGS

In your soup pot, heat the olive oil and sauté the onions until golden.

Add the remaining ingredients, including half the chopped parsley. Over medium-low heat, let the soup simmer under a lid for 1 hour. The soup will be done when the peas are soft, and your house smells wonderful.

In the meantime, sauté the bacon in a medium skillet until crisp. Remove it with a slotted spoon and let it drain on some paper towels.

IT WAS THE YEAR 2000 WHEN **SALSA** REPLACED KETCHUP AS AMERICA'S **FAVORITE CONDIMENT.**

RECIPES

Pour most of the bacon drippings out of the pan, add the onion slices, and sauté until golden with crispy, dark edges. Return the bacon to the pan and keep it warm.

When the soup is ready to serve, remove the bay leaf and thyme sprig. If you're using the ham hock, take it out of the pot, and if there are any morsels of ham on the bone, cut them off and add them to the soup. Taste the soup for seasonings.

Pour the soup into wide bowls, topping each with onions, bacon, and a sprinkling of parsley.

Slow Cooker Option

Sauté the vegetables and put them, along with the remaining ingredients, into your slow cooker. Cook on low for 8 to 10 hours or high for 6 hours.

Veggie Tip

Leave out the ham and bacon, use vegetable stock, and skip the bacon garnish (or use chopped smoked almonds).

RAINY-DAY TOMATO SOUP WITH GRILLED CHEESY CROUTONS

Late in the day on a rainy fall afternoon, as it's getting dark outside and the Halloween leaves are falling from the trees, put this soup on the stove and make some grilled cheese sandwiches.

Have a cozy soup dinner together. And while you are listening to the wind and the rain, talk about all the things that make you feel lucky.

YOU NEED

2 tablespoons olive oil

1 large onion, chopped

1 small carrot, peeled and chopped

4 cloves garlic, chopped

1 sprig thyme

1 28-ounce can good-quality diced tomatoes, undrained

1 tablespoon tomato paste

1 tablespoon red wine vinegar

A Parmesan cheese rind (optional) or ¼ cup grated Parmesan cheese

3 cups vegetable or chicken broth

Salt to taste

Pepper or red pepper flakes to taste

A few leaves of basil

TO MAKE 6 SERVINGS

In your soup pot, heat the olive oil over medium heat. Sauté the onion and carrot until the onion is soft and translucent.

Add the garlic and thyme; stir for a moment. When the garlic is warm and fragrant, add all the other ingredients except for the basil. Let the soup simmer under a lid for 30 minutes.

Remove the thyme stem and the Parmesan rind if you used it. Stir in the basil and blend the soup in a blender until it is very smooth. You will have to do this in a couple of batches; only fill the blender a little less than half to avoid a soup explosion. If you want the soup even smoother, pour it back into the pot through a strainer.

Bring the soup back to a simmer and taste it. Does it need more salt? Perhaps some pepper or red pepper flakes?

Serve with a drizzle of olive oil, a basil leaf, and a Grilled Cheesy Crouton (page 82) or two.

RECIPES

GRILLED CHEESY CROUTONS

YOU NEED

8 slices of your favorite bread

Butter

2 cups shredded cheese

TO MAKE A FEW CROUTONS FOR EACH BOWL

Preheat your oven to 400 degrees.

Butter both sides of the bread and put into the oven on a baking sheet. When the toast is golden, take it out. On the lightest side of each piece, evenly sprinkle the cheese. Top 4 slices with the other 4 and bake for about 8 minutes more or until the cheese has melted.

Cut the sandwiches into long fingers, small croutons, fancy wedges, or any shape that you think looks good by your soup.

Cook's Tip — *If you have any sun-dried tomato, olive, or pesto spread, it would be very tasty if you spread it on the bread, under the cheese, before baking.*

DEEP DARK BLACK BEAN SOUP WITH FIXINS

Why do little kids like black beans? Even some of the "I only eat foods that are white" kids like black beans. This is great, because black beans are a great source of antioxidants, protein, calcium, and fiber. Since the soup is so dark and mysterious, you can also swirl in a cup or two of chopped spinach or broccoli and no one would ever know . . .

Serve it with a bunch of toppings on the side, perhaps with a scoop of brown rice as well, and enjoy a nutritious, tasty, inexpensive dinner that kids all over love.

KIDS CAN

Crumble the oregano.

Put the garnishes in bowls.

Taste to make sure the soup is perfect.

YOU NEED

2 tablespoons olive oil

2 medium onions, chopped

5 medium cloves garlic, finely chopped

1 tablespoon ground cumin

1 teaspoon dried oregano

1 15-ounce can of diced tomatoes, undrained

3 15-ounce cans of black beans, drained (or 5 cups home-cooked beans)

4 cups vegetable or chicken broth

½ chopped chipotle pepper, from a can of chipotles in adobo sauce (optional, and only if you want your soup spicy)

1 tablespoon brown sugar

Salt and pepper

Optional Toppings

½ cup sour cream, to dollop

3 limes, cut in half, for squeezing

Small handful of cilantro, to add some flair

Shredded or crumbled cheese, to make you happy

½ cup salsa, because it is America's favorite condiment

TO MAKE 6 SERVINGS

In your soup pot, heat up the olive oil, add the onions, and sauté until soft, 4 to 5 minutes. Add the garlic and cumin, and sauté for another 2 minutes.

Toss in the remaining ingredients and simmer over medium heat for at least 30 minutes.

Pour half of the soup into a blender, blend until smooth, and stir it back into the pot. (If you have a hand immersion blender, you can stick it into your pot and blend for a moment instead.) Taste for seasonings.

Serve in big bowls with the toppings on the side.

Slow Cooker Option

Sauté the vegetables and put them, along with the remaining ingredients, into your slow cooker. Cook on low for 8 to 10 hours or high for 6 hours.

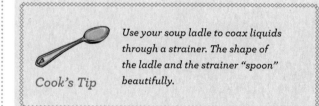

Cook's Tip — *Use your soup ladle to coax liquids through a strainer. The shape of the ladle and the strainer "spoon" beautifully.*

WHITE BEAN AND TINY PASTA SOUP with Parmesan and Pancetta

You have a choice: You can pay a lot of money for one bowl of pasta e fagioli in a fancy restaurant, or for the same amount of money you can stay at home, hang out with your kids, and make a big pot of your own fancy soup. Hey, why not double up on the recipe and give some to your neighbors? Even better, invite them and their kids over for dinner.

YOU NEED

8 ounces tiny pasta, like orzo, tiny shells, or small macaroni

2 tablespoons olive oil

4 ounces pancetta or bacon, chopped (optional)

1 medium onion, chopped

3 large cloves garlic, chopped

2 celery stalks, chopped

2 carrots, peeled and chopped

3 15-ounce cans cannellini or great northern beans, drained (or 5 cups home-cooked beans)

6 cups vegetable or chicken broth

1 cup diced tomatoes, canned or fresh

A Parmesan cheese rind (optional, but very tasty)

1 sprig fresh rosemary

Salt and pepper to taste

Optional Garnishes

1–2 tablespoons olive oil

1–2 tablespoons balsamic vinegar

¼ cup grated Parmigiano Reggiano cheese

Slices of rustic bread, brushed with olive oil and toasted

Chopped parsley

RECIPES

LET'S PLAY!

TELL US ABOUT...
Your wildest winter storm.
Your hottest summer.

TO MAKE 6–8 SERVINGS

In a large pot, cook the pasta according to the package directions. Drain and set aside.

Heat up your soup pot and drizzle in enough olive oil to cover the bottom. Sauté the pancetta with the onion until golden. Add the garlic, celery, and carrots and sauté until fragrant, about 2 minutes more.

Add the remaining ingredients and simmer under a lid for at least half an hour. (This soup is happy to sit and simmer quietly on your stove for an hour, although you might need to add a little broth.)

Remove the rosemary stem and Parmesan rind. Puree a cup or two of the soup in your blender. Even easier, stick a hand immersion blender into the soup for a quick moment, just until it thickens a bit.

Fold the cooked pasta into the soup. (If you have little kids, perhaps you should save a bit of pasta and use it as garnish, to assure them that there is something they like in the soup.)

Taste for salt and pepper.

On the rim of each soup bowl, balance a slice of toast, ladle the soup on top, garnish with a drizzle of olive oil, a few drops of balsamic vinegar, and a shower of Parmigiano Reggiano and parsley.

LENTIL STEW with Potatoes and WARM INDIAN SPICES

Here is a gentle Indian lentil stew, its flavors soft, fragrant, and comforting. But by all means, stir in some cayenne pepper if you are looking for some excitement.

YOU NEED

2 tablespoons olive oil

2 medium onions, chopped

3 cloves garlic, finely chopped

2 tablespoons grated fresh ginger

1 tablespoon good quality garam masala (see the Cook's Tip)

1 cup diced carrots

1 large potato, peeled and cut into small cubes

2 cups brown lentils, rinsed

1 14-ounce can diced tomatoes, undrained

1 cup unsweetened coconut milk (or light coconut milk)

5 cups vegetable or chicken broth

1 cup frozen peas, defrosted

Salt and pepper to taste

Yogurt, for garnish

TO MAKE 4–6 SERVINGS

In your soup pot, heat the olive oil and fry the onions until wilted and golden, then add the garlic, ginger, and spices and stir for a moment until they are fragrant. Be very careful not to burn the spices, as this will make them bitter.

Take half of this mixture and set it aside for later. Add the carrots, potato, lentils, tomatoes, coconut milk, and stock. Let the stew simmer, without a lid, for about 30 to 40 minutes until the potatoes and lentils are tender.

Fold in the remaining onion-and-spice mixture. Add the peas to the stew last to keep their brilliant color. Simmer for another few minutes until the stew is heated through. Season with salt and pepper.

Serve with a dollop of yogurt, warm naan bread or pita, and perhaps some brown rice, plain or cooked with a cardamom pod.

Cook's Tip

Garam *is the Indian word for "warm" or "hot," and the blend of dry-roasted, ground spices known as garam masala* (gah-RAHM mah-SAH-lah) *adds a sense of "warmth" to both palate and spirit. You can find a blend in the spice aisle of any well-stocked grocery store, or see Resources on page 231.*

Leftover Tip

The next day, put the stew into a blender and blend until smooth. Then thin it with a bit of milk, broth, or coconut milk so it becomes a soup and give it a fancy new name, like Princess Jahanara's Wedding Soup.

TAKE IT SLOW

Cook Today, Eat Tomorrow—
or Freeze for Another Day

~ 7 ~

MOROCCAN CHICKEN TAGINE (Fancy Word for "Stew") with Apricots, Almonds, and Olives

Take your family on a trip to faraway Africa with this dish. Imagine having dinner in a billowing Bedouin tent upon velvet pillows. Outside, the desert night sky is filled with a thousand stars.

Why don't you take the dinner plates off the table, throw down some pillows, and have your dinner Bedouin-style right on your own magic carpet?

YOU NEED

2 tablespoons olive oil

1 large onion, sliced into wedges

1½ pounds skinless, boneless organic chicken thighs, trimmed

1 tablespoon grated fresh ginger

1 cinnamon stick

½ teaspoon turmeric

½ teaspoon cumin

4 cloves garlic, finely chopped

1½ cups chicken broth

½ cup small pitted green olives, like picholines

10 dried apricots

Salt and pepper to taste

Lemon juice to taste

Handful of whole blanched almonds

Handful of chopped fragrant tender herbs, like cilantro, parsley, and basil

---

DID YOU KNOW?
COUSCOUS IS TINY PASTA.
OFTEN YOU CAN GET IT MADE WITH WHOLE WHEAT. SINCE YOU REALLY CAN'T TASTE THE DIFFERENCE, YOU MIGHT AS WELL CHOOSE THE WHOLE-GRAIN GOODNESS.

TO MAKE 6 SERVINGS

Heat up a heavy-bottomed pot and drizzle in the olive oil. Add the onion and sauté until it's soft and golden. Add the chicken and remaining ingredients, saving the almonds and herbs for later. Let the tagine gently simmer, covered, for 30 minutes.

In the meantime, toast the almonds in a dry skillet until they are golden. (Watch them carefully. Every chef I know has burned more nuts than we care to think about. Nuts are sneaky that way.)

Just before serving, taste for seasoning, remove the cinnamon stick, and sprinkle on the herbs. Top with the toasted almonds.

Serve with couscous cooked according to the package, then toss with plenty of lemon juice, and a mixed green salad with fresh sliced oranges topped with a sprinkle of cinnamon.

SUNDAY-AFTERNOON CHICKEN with Lentils and Leeks

Maybe you've had a tough week. Everyone's cranky and tired, even the dog. It might be time for some aromatherapy. How about the scent of rosemary, garlic, and thyme? Dinner slowly roasting in your oven, making your house smell like a quiet Sunday afternoon.

While the chicken is cooking, make a simple green salad, light some candles, and let your dinner table be the calming anchor of your home.

YOU NEED

For the Lentils

1½ cups lentils

2 carrots, chopped

6 sun-dried tomatoes in oil, drained and chopped

2 cups chicken broth, plus more if needed

1 cup red or white wine

2 tablespoons olive oil

6 leeks, washed very well, white and pale green parts thinly sliced

6 medium cloves garlic, left whole but smashed a bit

For the Chicken

¼ cup Dijon mustard

1 tablespoon olive oil

2 teaspoons fresh thyme leaves

2 teaspoons honey

2 cloves garlic, chopped

1 4-pound chicken cut into 8 pieces, skin removed (preferably free-range, organic, and kosher)

Salt and pepper to taste

TO MAKE 4–6 SERVINGS

Preheat your oven to 450 degrees.

Into a medium-size roasting dish, pour the lentils, carrots, tomatoes, 2 cups of broth, and the wine. Put the dish into the oven so the lentils can start to cook.

Heat a large nonstick skillet over medium heat and drizzle in 2 tablespoons olive oil, or enough to cover the bottom. Sauté the leeks and the garlic until they have softened and are turning golden.

Mix the Dijon mustard with 1 tablespoon olive oil, thyme, honey, and the chopped garlic, then spread evenly on the chicken pieces.

Take the lentils out of the oven, layer the leeks on top, and tuck the chicken into them. Scatter any leftover herbs all about. Roast uncovered for 30 minutes. Check if the lentils need a little more broth. Continue roasting for 10 to 20 minutes more or until the lentils are tender, the chicken registers 170 degrees on a thermometer, or the juices run clear, not pink, when pricked with a knife.

Slow Cooker Option

Pour the lentils, carrots, tomatoes, 2 cups of stock, and the wine into the slow cooker. Sauté the leeks and garlic; add these to the cooker. Rub the chicken with the Dijon mixture and put it on top of the lentils and leeks. Cook on low for 6 to 8 hours.

Cook's Tip

Why so picky . . . organic kosher chicken? Organic because it is healthier for you and kosher because it has been brined so it stays moist (neat trick, huh?).

ASIAN SHRIMP CAKES
with Sesame Asparagus

Golden and crunchy, these little shrimp cakes are bursting with the bright flavors of Asia. Serve them with the Sesame Asparagus, steamed rice, and Toasted Sesame Aioli (page 134).

YOU NEED

1½ pounds peeled deveined shrimp

2 tablespoons chopped fresh cilantro

1 tablespoon finely minced peeled fresh ginger

2 medium-size cloves garlic, minced

¼ cup finely minced celery

2 tablespoons finely minced red bell pepper

1 egg

¼ cup mayonnaise

1 teaspoon Asian fish sauce (optional)

1 teaspoon Asian chili sauce (optional)

1½ cups panko bread crumbs, divided

Vegetable oil

TO MAKE 4–6 SERVINGS

Either by hand or in a food processor, coarsely chop the shrimp until it holds together but still has a few pea-size pieces in it. In a food processor, this will only take a few pulses, so be careful.

Mix everything else, apart from the panko bread crumbs and oil, in a bowl. Add the shrimp and ½ cup panko crumbs. Let the mixture rest in the fridge for 15 minutes so it can firm up.

Place the remaining bread crumbs on a plate. Drop a heaping tablespoon of the shrimp mixture into the crumbs and turn to coat. In your hand, shape it into a small patty. Coat and shape the remaining shrimp mixture.

Now you can either sauté the cakes on an oiled nonstick skillet over medium heat for about 8 minutes, flipping them halfway through, or spray them with olive oil and bake them on an oiled baking sheet in a 400-degree oven for 15 minutes or so, turning them over halfway through, until they are golden and crispy.

SESAME ASPARAGUS

YOU NEED

2 tablespoons soy sauce

2 teaspoons brown sugar

1 tablespoon toasted sesame oil

2 tablespoons vegetable oil

2 large cloves garlic, chopped

1 tablespoon chopped fresh ginger

1½ pounds asparagus, ends snapped off

4 teaspoons sesame seeds

Salt and pepper to taste

TO MAKE 4–6 SERVINGS

Stir together the soy sauce, sugar, and sesame oil in a small bowl. Set aside.

Heat the vegetable oil in a large nonstick pan. Add the garlic and ginger and stir until fragrant, about 30 seconds.

Add the asparagus and stir-fry until crisp-tender, about 4 minutes.

Add the soy mixture and sesame seeds and toss until the asparagus is coated, about 1 minute longer. Season with salt and pepper to taste.

Picnic Tip — *Bring some large lettuce leaves, the shrimp cakes, some shredded cabbage, a batch of Thai dipping sauce (page 67), and some rice noodles. Everyone takes a lettuce leaf, tops it with the fillings, rolls it up, and pops it in their mouths. No plates or forks needed, just a lot of napkins!*

APPLE CIDER CHICKEN
with Caramelized Onions and Apples

Tangy apples, sweet golden onions, and cider—it's as if fall fell into your pan . . .

KIDS CAN

Pull the leaves off the rosemary twig.

Taste the apple cider and determine what vintage it is.

YOU NEED

1½ cups apple cider

½ teaspoon salt

1 teaspoon chopped fresh rosemary

1½ pounds boneless, skinless organic chicken thighs, trimmed, each piece cut into 2 pieces

1 tablespoon olive oil

...~⚬~...

Sunday Lessons of
LOVE AND LINGUINI
By Lori Mozilo

The most important things my mother taught me, I learned in her kitchen. Her food was the backdrop, the fuel, for my fondest childhood memories. When she was cooking, baking, or serving, there was no hint of what doctors diplomatically referred to as "her nerves." Once she tied on her apron, she was the Zen Buddhist of ziti, the Goddess of ganache.

My mother's food was the edible expression of her creativity and love. The kitchen provided her the freedom of invention. Seeing us enjoy her food made her almost levitate with pride.

Her tour de force was Sunday dinner. Preparations began early, and I woke up to the incongruous smell of frying meatballs and simmering tomatoes at 7 AM. She'd rush us off to church, staying behind to continue cooking. It was a mortal sin to miss Mass, but if I challenged her, my mother would say, "God understands, I have to make the braciole." We'd

get back as she was mixing dough for homemade pasta and, without prompting, my sister and I spread clean sheets on our beds, sprinkling them with flour, knowing that's where we'd lay the "macaroni" to dry.

My mother affixed the pasta machine to the edge of the kitchen counter and passed the dough through two metal cylinders by turning a crank on its side. Eight times, one of us would click the wheel and turn the handle, each pass making the dough thinner, until it came out in long, almost transparent sheets. We'd fight for control of the crank, and then argue about which kind of pasta we wanted. Then my sister and I floured our hands and held them out. My mother loaded us up with the freshly cut pasta, and we'd march our delicate cargo into the bedroom, and onto the sheets.

My mother passed away two years ago. But I stay connected to her through our shared passion for food. Like her, I put a family meal on the table every night. *Because* of her, I know how to make that meal delicious. But in my mother's kitchen and at her table, I learned some things that are even more valuable: If you don't have exactly what you need, improvise, it'll still turn out fine; and most important, everything is better when you share.

(continued from page 89)

2 onions, cut into wedges

3 slices bacon, chopped (optional; you can also use turkey bacon)

2 tart apples, peel left on, cut into wedges

1½ cups chicken broth

3 tablespoons flour

¼ cup apple cider vinegar

TO MAKE 4–6 SERVINGS

In a large bowl, combine the apple cider, salt, rosemary, and chicken. Set aside.

Preheat your oven to 350 degrees.

In a large ovenproof nonstick pan, drizzle the olive oil and heat until shimmering. Add the onion wedges and bacon. Sauté over medium heat until the onions are wilted and golden. This will take 10 to 15 minutes. Now add the apples and sauté until they start to soften around the edges and get a bit of color as well, about 5 minutes.

Meanwhile, drain the chicken, reserving the apple cider for later. Toss the chicken pieces in the flour.

Remove the apples and onions from the pan. If you need to, add a drizzle of olive oil to the same pan. Over medium heat, lightly brown the chicken. You might have to do this in two batches.

When all the chicken is golden, add the apple cider vinegar and the reserved apple cider. Stir well, add the chicken stock, bring back to a simmer, and then pile the apples and onions on top (this is just vanity—the dish looks better this way).

Stick the pan into the oven for about 10 minutes or until the chicken is no longer pink.

Leftover Tip

The next day, cut the chicken into smaller pieces; if you need to moisten it, use a little chicken stock. Reheat and serve over egg noodles. If you want to be luxurious, stir in a little crème fraîche at the end.

SWEET CORN AND VEGETABLE "LASAGNA"

Layers of grits, cheese, tomato sauce, and vegetables get baked into a "lasagna."

This dish is all about simplicity and quick variations, so experiment with the concept and have some fun. Go ahead, improvise; don't follow the ingredients list but sauté whatever vegetables you have on hand, and if you like goat cheese or smoked mozzarella throw it in as well!

The number of servings can quickly be scaled up as needed by choosing a larger baking dish and just using more of the same ingredients, so while you are at it make some extra to keep in the freezer.

YOU NEED

For the Grits

3 cups milk

3 cups water

2 cups quick grits or polenta (not instant)

1 teaspoon salt

2 cups corn, fresh or defrosted frozen

½ cup grated Parmesan cheese

For the Filling

2 medium zucchinis, diced

1 teaspoon salt

Olive oil

2 cups chopped mushrooms

1 small red onion, chopped

3 cloves garlic, chopped

1 cup bottled roasted peppers, chopped and drained

1 tablespoon chopped fresh oregano

1 tablespoon chopped fresh basil

4 cups shredded mozzarella (or your favorite cheese)

4 cups tomato sauce, homemade (page 65) or your favorite store-bought

TO MAKE 10 SERVINGS

Start by making the filling: Toss the zucchini with a teaspoon of salt, put into a colander, and set aside.

Drizzle some olive oil into a large nonstick pan over high heat. Sauté the mushrooms until golden. Reduce the heat and add the onion, stirring until it's translucent.

RECIPES

Put the zucchini into a clean dishtowel and squeeeeze out the excess moisture so that they don't make the dish too wet. Add them to the pan along with the garlic, roasted peppers, and herbs. Let the vegetables gently cook for 10 minutes.

Meanwhile, make a pot of grits. Bring the milk and water just to a boil in a large saucepan. Slowly stream in the grits while whisking constantly. Stir in the salt and the corn and turn down the heat to medium low. Continue stirring until the grits thicken up. Stir in the Parmesan cheese. Remove from the heat.

Preheat your oven to 350 degrees.

Rub a little olive oil into the bottom of a baking dish, top with a layer of grits, then vegetables, then shredded cheese, a layer of sauce and grits, and on and on until you are out of ingredients. You want to end with sauce and cheese.

Cover the dish tightly with foil or a lid and bake until bubbling, about 35 minutes. Let the lasagna rest for a few minutes before serving.

Quick Tip

Instead of rummaging around in your spice drawer whenever you need salt, keep a bowl of it out, ready to grab whenever you need it. Kosher salt works great because it is easy to take pinches of.

TURKEY MEAT LOAF
The White Knight of the Week Night

This is the handsome dish that will rescue you someday. On a busy weeknight, throw it all together, slam the oven door shut, go do your thing for a while, then come back to the warm, comforting embrace of a kitchen with dinner in the oven. Mash some potatoes, mix a Caesar salad (page 124), and you'll have thrown together a dinner that will make you sigh and smile.

YOU NEED

For the Meat Loaf

1 medium onion, finely chopped

3 cloves garlic, minced

1½ cups bread crumbs

2 eggs

1¼ cups milk

1 teaspoon baking soda

2 tablespoons vinegar

½ cup ketchup

1½ teaspoons each salt and pepper

2 tablespoons chopped parsley

2½ pounds ground turkey (or chicken)

5–6 slices turkey or pork bacon (optional)

For the Glaze

1 cup ketchup

½ cup brown sugar

2 tablespoons Worcestershire sauce

1 teaspoon ground cumin

TO MAKE 6 SERVINGS

Preheat the oven to 350 degrees.

Mix all the meat loaf ingredients except the turkey and bacon in a large bowl, until they are well combined and mushy. The mixture will probably fizz excitedly, which is due to combining the baking soda and vinegar. Let it sit for 10 to 15 minutes, and then mix in the turkey until it is all well combined (it will be a wet mixture, to keep the loaf moist).

On an oiled baking pan, loosely form the turkey mix into a loaf. Or, if you are against the hang-loose, free-form look, plop the mix into a greased proper loaf pan. Drape the strips of bacon over the top of the loaf and tuck down the sides. Slide the meat loaf onto the middle rack of the oven and bake for about 50 minutes, or until it registers 170 degrees on a meat thermometer.

Meanwhile, combine the ingredients for the glaze in a small pot and bring to a boil for a minute or two. Twenty minutes before the meat loaf is done, pour the glaze over it evenly and return it to the oven.

Slice and serve with . . . mashed potatoes (page 46), of course!

Cook's Tips

Along with the turkey, add half a bag of defrosted frozen peas and ½ cup grated carrots or zucchini to the meat loaf mix. • If you want a "saucier" dinner, pour 3 cups of your favorite tomato sauce around the loaf before you bake it. Stir halfway through to incorporate the juices.

Leftover Tip

A crunchy roll, a slather of mustard, some crisp lettuce, and a slab of warm meat loaf. . . need I say more? • Cut a baguette into slices, spread with a bit of whole-grain mustard, top with a chunk of meat loaf, and put under the broiler until toasty. Drape with caramelized onions (page 69) and serve with a salad, little pickles, and more whole-grain mustard.

...⤜❦⤛...

LET'S PLAY!

Tell everyone one thing you complained about today. Round two: Name two other things you often complain about.

"A PERSON COOKING *is a person giving: even the simplest food is a gift."*—LAURIE COLWIN, author of *More Home Cooking*

"NEVER APOLOGIZE, *never explain."* —JULIA CHILD, chef

"JUST RENAME." —KIRSTIN

...⤜❦⤛...

SCRIBBLE AND STIR

Renowned as a writer and director—of romantic comedy films, best-selling books, articles, and blogs— **NORA EPHRON** *is best known to her friends as a consummate cook and ultimate hostess. Dinner at Nora's is a treasured affair not to be missed.*

"I would have to say that if we had a religion at all in our house, it was the family dinner. We all ate together—my parents and my three sisters—at least five nights a week, in the dining room. There was a sideboard, and my father carved the meat, and one of us helped with the vegetables and potatoes. The food was absolutely fantastic—over the years we had two great Southern cooks, and they could make ethereal yeast rolls and the flakiest piecrust you've ever had. The food was traditional American—pot roast, stews, roast beef, fried chicken, and always fish on Friday nights because (my mother said) Friday was the day when the fish was freshest because of the Catholics.

"Before dinner (which was at six thirty), we all met in the den, where my parents had a couple of drinks and there was a cut-glass dish filled with what are now known as crudités but were then known as celery sticks and carrots and black olives. Dinner was truly our time to be a family, and everyone (including the four of us) told stories about our day.

"I really do think that sharing food at a table is the way to friendship and family. A family is a group of people who eat the same thing for dinner. You don't have to serve 'great' meals. You can serve the simplest meals. The point is that it should be the event of the night.

"My dinners as a parent were much more informal than the ones I grew up with, but I did have the same rule my mother had—you don't have to finish it if you don't like it, but at least you have to taste it. The best thing I did with my kids was to sit down for dinner with them."

A Nice Big Pot of **CHILI CON BEANS**

Laurie and I have a difference of opinion when it comes to chili. I see it as cold-weather fare, something you serve to your friends for a casual get-together. You just leave the chili in a big pot on the stove, surrounded by a bunch of toppings. Everyone serves themselves and hangs out on the sofa in front of the fire.

Laurie, however, does not care if it is the hottest day of the year, and she especially likes to serve chili at large formal gatherings to people in tuxes and high heels. She does that for the same reason that I like serving it to small gatherings: because, as she says, "Everyone sharing food from one pot feels warm and cozy . . . like we are all one big family." Perhaps she is on to something, because chili always makes people happy and it is an easy vegetarian meal without anyone even noticing the meat is missing.

This makes about twelve servings—enough for a small crowd wearing tuxes or overalls.

YOU NEED

2 tablespoons olive oil

3 medium onions, chopped

1 red bell pepper, seeded and chopped

8 cloves garlic, minced

¼ cup chili powder (hot or mild, you pick)

2 tablespoons ground cumin

1 tablespoon ground coriander

½ teaspoon ground cinnamon

Stems from your cilantro, chopped (optional)

1 chipotle in adobo sauce, chopped (from the can; add more or less according to how spicy you want it)

1 28-ounce can crushed tomatoes (the fire-roasted ones if you can find them)

3 cups low-sodium vegetable broth or water

3 15-ounce cans black beans, rinsed and drained

3 15-ounce cans kidney beans, rinsed and drained (or 10 cups home-cooked beans of any color)

2 tablespoons brown sugar or maple syrup

2 tablespoons white wine vinegar

Salt and pepper to taste

Topping Suggestions

Shredded cheese

Chopped red onions or scallions

Tomato salsa

Tortilla chips—or try Sun Chips (they're sold in the first-ever compostable bag, yay!)

Chopped fresh cilantro

Low-fat sour cream or Greek yogurt

1–2 cups shredded cabbage, white or purple

Grilled corn, shucked

1–2 chopped avocados

Limes, cut in half for squeezing

Hot sauce

TO MAKE 12 SERVINGS

Heat a large pot over medium heat and drizzle in enough oil to cover the bottom. Add the onions and red bell pepper and sauté until onions are golden, about 8 minutes.

Add the garlic and spices and carefully sauté, stirring well so they do not burn, until heated and fragrant, about 1 or 2 minutes.

Add the cilantro stems, chipotle, tomatoes, 3 cups broth or water, and beans. Bring to a simmer.

Reduce the heat to medium low and cook, uncovered, until the chili thickens, stirring now and then, making sure you do not burn the bottom of the pot, about 40 minutes.

Stir in the brown sugar or syrup and the vinegar. Taste for seasonings. Serve the chili with the toppings on the side, and perhaps with some brown rice, a baked potato, and a big crunchy salad.

Cook's Tip

If you do burn the chili—try not to, but if you do (it has happened to me, too)—rename it Smoky Chili con Beans.

Leftover Tip

Leftover chili is great as filling in enchiladas or tacos, on top of baked potatoes, or labeled and saved deep in the freezer for another day.

SLOOOOOOW COOKER CURRY

Crock-Pot, slow cooker, genie chef hiding in your pantry: Whatever you call that pot, the magic part is that you just need to do a little prep the night before, or in the morning before you go to work. That evening when you come home and open the door, it will be to a house that smells warm and inviting, as if someone has been cooking all day long just for you.

YOU NEED

1 tablespoon vegetable oil

1 red onion, cut into wedges

5 cloves garlic, minced

1 tablespoon very finely minced fresh ginger

2 tablespoons curry powder, hot or mild

½ cinnamon stick

3 whole cardamom pods or ¼ teaspoon ground cardamom (optional)

1 14-ounce can good-quality crushed tomatoes

Salt and pepper to taste

1 pound small red potatoes, unpeeled, cut bite-size

1 whole organic chicken, 4–5 pounds, cut into 8 pieces, skin removed (you can get the butcher to do this for you)

1 cup Greek yogurt, whole or 2 percent

1 cup fresh or defrosted frozen peas

TO MAKE 6 SERVINGS

Heat up a large nonstick pan and drizzle in the oil. When it shimmers, add the onion and sauté until soft and golden. Add the garlic and spices, stir for 30 seconds, until fragrant, then stir in the tomatoes and bring to a simmer. Season with salt and pepper. (You can do this the night before: Chill the sauce, add the potatoes and chicken, and store in the fridge until you are ready to cook.)

Pull your slow cooker out from the garage, or wherever it lives. Rinse it out. Put the potatoes on the bottom, then top with the chicken and the tomato sauce you just made. Set the cooker to low for 6 to 8 hours. Half an hour before serving, fold in the yogurt and peas, and taste for seasonings . . . Does it need a little more salt? A pinch of curry?

Serve with basmati rice, naan bread, and a side of chutney.

Curry Without a Slow Cooker (Curry in a Hurry)
Follow the directions at left, but instead of using a pan, use a big, heavy-bottomed pot. Add the chicken and potatoes, spices and tomatoes and simmer for 40 minutes. Fold in the yogurt and peas, simmer for another 10 minutes, and serve.

GOOD THINGS COME
to Those Who Wait

JOSH VIERTEL *is the president of Slow Food USA, a nonprofit, global grassroots movement that links the pleasure of food with a commitment to community and the environment.*

LAURIE: What does this phrase *slow food* actually mean?

JOSH: Slow food is an idea—a way of living and a way of eating. It is the opposite of fast food. We started fast food; we have a responsibility to end it. Slow food helps you realize that your health, your kids' health, your community's health, and nature's health are all tied together—and food is the common thread.

LAURIE: Why is sitting down to a leisurely meal so important?

JOSH: It is part of what makes us human and where we learn to share and treat each other with respect. America has an honest food culture, and we should be proud of it. America is home-cooked food; church potlucks; growing your own greens; making biscuits from scratch; canning peaches for the winter. Slow food, home cooking, and eating around the table help us remember and teach our children the recipes they will cook for *their* children.

LAURIE: What do you want people to understand about the Slow Food movement?

JOSH: Every piece of food you eat has a story behind it. When you eat slow food, food that is home-cooked, from a local farm and in season, you choose to support a story that makes you proud.

ARROZ CON POLLO

The flavors of savory chicken, cumin, and vegetables are deeply buried in soft, comforting rice. It is the warm embrace of a Cuban mom all in one big pot. Serve it with a plate of avocado wedges, ripe juicy tomatoes, slivers of red onions, sprinkled with salt and lime. If you make enough for leftovers, you can transform the dish—with a few spices—into an Indian-flavored rice feast the next day.

YOU NEED

2 tablespoons olive oil

6 boneless, skinless organic chicken thighs, cut in half

4 skinless organic chicken drumsticks

Salt and pepper to taste

2 medium onions, chopped

1 red bell pepper, seeded and chopped

2 teaspoons cumin

3 cloves garlic, chopped

1 teaspoon chopped fresh oregano

1 15-ounce can chopped tomatoes, undrained

3 cups chicken broth, plus more if needed

1 cup wine (or stock)

1 teaspoon paprika

½ teaspoon turmeric

2 cups white rice

1 cup defrosted frozen or freshly shucked peas

For the Garnish

Cilantro

Toasted pumpkin seeds

Sour cream or Greek yogurt

Green pimiento olives

TO MAKE 6 SERVINGS

Heat the oil in a large casserole. Sprinkle the chicken pieces with a bit of salt and brown them, about 2 minutes per side. Transfer the chicken to a bowl and pour out all but 2 tablespoons of the fat.

To the casserole, add the onions and bell pepper, and cook over medium heat until soft, about 5 or 6 minutes. Add the cumin, garlic, and oregano and stir for a moment until fragrant. Now add the chopped tomatoes and return the chicken to the casserole. Stir well to coat the chicken with the tomato mixture.

Add the broth, wine, spices, and rice. Bring to a boil, reduce the heat, cover, and simmer for about 20 minutes. If the tomato-chicken mixture starts to dry out and the rice is still not quite done, add more broth. If it is too soupy, uncover during the last 5 minutes of cooking.

Just before it is done, stir in the peas. Season with salt and pepper. Garnish with cilantro, toasted pumpkin seeds, sour cream, and olives.

Leftover Tip

Today Arroz con Pollo, tomorrow Chicken Biryani: In a pot, heat enough olive oil to cover the bottom. Add whole cumin seeds, grated ginger, a pinch of cinnamon, and some curry powder and cook until fragrant—this will take less than 1 minute. Add the leftover rice and gently reheat. If you're so inclined, serve with raita (page 133) and mango chutney. Don't call it leftovers, call it Indian Rice Biryani.

RECIPES

GREEK MEATBALLS
in a Fragrant Tomato Sauce with Feta Cheese, Orzo, and a Greek Salad

Here is a gently exotic dish that is good to make on a Sunday afternoon while listening to a radio show. The meatballs are delicious all on their own—but baked in the tomato sauce, fragrant with spices, and topped with herbs and tangy feta cheese, visions of a festive, happy Greek family crowded around the dinner table will come to mind.

KIDS CAN

Measure the spices.
Help chop the salad.
Measure the ingredients for the dressing.
Shake, shake, shake the dressing.

YOU NEED

½ cup cold water

½ cup unseasoned bread crumbs

1 egg, lightly beaten

1 teaspoon salt

1 teaspoon pepper

1 teaspoon baking soda

1 small onion, finely chopped

½ teaspoon allspice

2 teaspoons ground cumin

¼ teaspoon ground cinnamon

3 tablespoons fresh lemon juice

2 tablespoons finely chopped fresh dill

2 tablespoons finely chopped fresh mint and/or parsley, plus more for garnish

2 pounds ground chicken or turkey

1 cup crumbled feta cheese

2 tablespoons olive oil

Fragrant Tomato Sauce (recipe at right, or you can cheat with your favorite store-bought kind, adding the spices you please)

TO MAKE 6 SERVINGS, WITH A FEW LEFTOVERS

In a big bowl, mix everything but the chicken, feta, olive oil, and tomato sauce. Stir until it is all mixed well together. Let it rest in the fridge for about 10 minutes, giving the bread crumbs time to absorb the liquids.

Add the ground chicken to the bowl and stir well.

Oil a large baking dish and put aside. With an ice cream scoop or a spoon, scoop out a bit of the chicken mixture; with wet hands, form into golf ball-size meatballs and place them in the baking pan.

After you have made all the meatballs, turn on the broiler and put the baking dish on the middle oven shelf. When they are starting to brown, gently flip them and broil the other side as well. This should take about 4 to 5 minutes a side.

Preheat the oven to 350 degrees.

Pour the Fragrant Tomato Sauce over the meatballs, and top with the crumbled feta cheese. Cover with a lid or foil and bake at 350 degrees for 30 minutes. Sprinkle with herbs and serve with orzo or quinoa tossed with olive oil, salt, and pepper.

FRAGRANT TOMATO SAUCE

2 tablespoons olive oil

1 medium onion, finely chopped

4 cloves garlic, finely chopped

2 28-ounce cans crushed tomatoes (Muir Glen or San Marzanos are good if you can find them)

½ teaspoon ground cardamom

1 cinnamon stick or ½ teaspoon ground cinnamon

1 teaspoon cumin

Pinch of cayenne

Salt and pepper to taste

TO MAKE 6 CUPS

Combine the olive oil, onion, and garlic in a medium pot. Gently heat until the onion is translucent and garlic is fragrant.

Stir in the remaining ingredients and heat to a gentle simmer. Simmer for about 15 minutes and taste for seasonings.

LET'S PLAY!

What qualities make a good student?
What qualities make a good teacher?

RECIPES

GREEK SALAD

You need not measure the ingredients in this salad; just add as much as you want of the vegetables you like.

YOU NEED

Handful of kalamata olives

Chopped vine-ripened tomatoes

Chopped romaine lettuce

Chopped cucumbers

Chopped seeded red bell peppers

Chopped celery

Sliced red onions

Feta cheese in cubes

A bit of fresh dill, mint, or parsley (all three would be great)

Toss with Greek vinaigrette.

GREEK VINAIGRETTE

YOU NEED

1 clove garlic, minced

⅓ cup good-quality red wine vinegar

⅔ cup olive oil

2 teaspoons minced fresh oregano or ½ teaspoon dried oregano

1 teaspoon salt

Pepper to taste

TO MAKE 1 CUPS

Put it all in a jar and shake, shake, shake.

Leftover Tip

Slip a warm meatball or two into a pita bread and top with leftover chopped Greek salad, or finely shredded lettuce, sliced cucumbers, and feta cheese. If you have Tahini Sauce (page 133), drizzle it on top.

MEATLESS MONDAYS

8

WHY EATING MORE VEGETARIAN DINNERS WILL
SAVE YOUR HEALTH, MONEY, AND THE EARTH

I had a eureka moment this year: *Eat less meat.* Okay, well maybe reading Jonathan Safran Foer's game-changing book, *Eating Animals,* had a little something to do with my lightning-bolt wake-up call. That was the straw that broke this camel's back. I devoured the book, and then placed it atop a few other favorites piled on my night-stand, including Mark Bittman's *Food Matters,* Michael Pollan's *The Omnivore's Dilemma,* Eric Schlosser's *Fast Food Nation,* John Robbins's *Diet for a New America,* and a must-watch DVD: *Food, Inc.*

All of these fueled my growing concern about the food I was feeding my kids. Then a well-timed two-hour lunch seated next to vegan advocate Kathy Freston, and a long conversation with Paul McCartney, who saw the "meatless light" a long time ago, sealed the deal. It was time to step out of denial and into conscious eating.

There is a growing arsenal of disturbing information about how our food is produced in this country, especially meat products, and it's not the way any parent would want it done. Sadly, much of our food has lost its integrity. The processing practices of our food system are harming our bodies and our planet—and unfortunately we're eating more of it than ever. Just look at the growth in diet-related health problems, life-threatening allergies, cancer rates, epidemics of obesity and diabetes—all of these are exploding in part because of what and how much we eat. But let's put all that aside for a moment and consider it this way:

Want to lose weight? Eat less meat.
Want to be more regular? Eat less meat.
Want your family to be healthier? Eat less meat.

Wait, there's more!
Want fewer chemicals in your food? Less meat!
Cleaner air? Less meat!
Protect drinking water and forests? Less meat!
Improve living conditions for animals? Less meat!
Want to help stop global warming? Animal agriculture is responsible for a shocking 51 percent of global greenhouse gas emissions. Eat less meat!

"We are not on the **SERENGETI HAVING TO RUN FROM THE LIONS,** *we don't need to eat that way anymore."* —JILLIAN MICHAELS, fitness trainer on *The Biggest Loser*

Contrary to what we were taught, we now know we have a choice. Eating meat *isn't* necessary—not for protein, not for our blood, not at all. Protein can be found in all kinds of foods, including cheese, beans, edamame, peas, tofu, nuts, quinoa, and lentils. According to the American Dietetic Association, a vegetarian diet is *at least* as healthy for every stage of life, from newborn to lactating motherhood to old age.

The overconsumption of meat is a relatively new problem. Americans now eat *150 times more* chicken than we did only eighty years ago. When our grandparents were our age, meat was harder to come by, and was considered a luxury. They didn't have steak every night. They had soups and pastas and vegetable stews. Meat was used to add flavor or as a side ingredient, more an embellishment than the center of attention. Today we are doing something that was unheard of not that long ago: eating meat for breakfast, lunch, and dinner. The average American is consuming about eight ounces of meat every single day—which is 45 percent more meat than the USDA even recommends!

So what to do and how to start? Becoming a vegetarian overnight is probably not feasible or desirable for most people. So why not start slower? How about . . . meatless on Mondays! That's an easy, simple step toward a healthier life. In fact, there's already a national movement to help inspire you (MeatlessMonday.com); a former Beatle advocating it (SupportMFM.org); and a prestigious university—Johns Hopkins Bloomberg School of Public Health—associated with it. What a perfect way to start the week: thinking about what is healthier for you and your family and making a small change with huge repercussions.

Talk about it at dinner. Here are some basic facts you can discuss to back up your family decision to start Meatless Mondays right away!

FACT: It is much healthier for you and your children to start eating less meat.

WHY: Because animal products are our main source of saturated fats, which contribute to high levels of chronic diseases like heart disease, stroke, diabetes, and cancer. Giving up meat once a week would reduce your saturated fat intake by 15 percent. We know obesity is a huge problem in the United States, and it's growing, just like our waistlines. Today 65 percent of the U.S. population is considered overweight. Eating less meat and reducing the fat in your family's meals could save your children from obesity, and all the diseases that go along with it, later in life.

FACT: The meat we generally consume is raised, processed, and transported in very unhealthful, inhumane ways that pose serious threats to public health.

WHY: More than 99 percent (that is not a typo!) of the meat purchased in supermarkets, cooked in homes, and consumed in American restaurants is grown on factory farms where animals are raised in miserable and unsanitary conditions, and fed foods their bodies are not naturally suited to digest. What's wrong with this picture? Unhealthy animals eat toxic chemicals, and then we eat the animals!

To make matters worse, animals on factory farms are being pumped full of antibiotics to make them grow faster and bigger. These are the same antibiotics we need for ourselves and our kids when we get sick. Ever wonder why our antibiotics are only good for a few years, then the bug develops resistance and we need to find new, much more expensive medicines? About eight times the amount of antibiotics that are fed to sick humans are fed to healthy animals. Many of our tried-and-true classes of antibiotics, such as those in tetracycline, are being fed by the ton to farm animals . . . who then pee them out into the mulch and mud . . . where bacteria develop resistance and then wash away into our streams, rivers, lakes, and bays. Shouldn't we be saving those medicines for people who need them? The World Health Organization and Centers for Disease Control think so, which is why they've long advocated for a moratorium on nontherapeutic antibiotic use on farms.

FACT: Eating meat hurts our health and our pocketbooks.

WHY: We all know that a steak costs more than broccoli at the supermarket, but what about the hidden costs of eating meat? There are more than seventy-six million foodborne illnesses reported a year in the United States (think about how many go unreported). According to a 1995 study, meat consumption costs the United States roughly $60 billion a year in medical costs. This calculation was made on the basis of the estimated contribution that eating meat makes to heart disease, high cholesterol, cancer, and foodborne illnesses.

FACT: Reducing the amount of meat your family eats is one of the most impactful things you can do to help the environment.

WHY: There are so many reasons for this, but since you probably need to start making dinner, I will give you just a few. Seventy percent of the world's farmland is currently involved in livestock production. Which means it is land that has been stripped of its trees. We really need those trees.

The "carbon footprint" of a hamburger is enormous because you have to include all the fuels that went into producing the fertilizer and pumping the irrigation water to grow the corn that fed the cow (even though that isn't their natural food source), as well as the greenhouse gas emissions that result from converting forestland to grazing land and from processing and transporting that burger . . . (My head is spinning, is yours?)

The Natural Resources Defense Council estimates that if all Americans eliminated just one quarter-pound serving of beef per week, the reduction in global warming pollution would be equivalent to taking four to six million cars off the road. Wow.

Factory farming relies heavily on chemical fertilizers, pesticides, antibiotics, and herbicides. The more meat we eat, the more factory farms have to produce, the worse the conditions get for the animals, the more degraded our environment gets, the bigger the impact on our health. It's a vicious cycle.

FACT: Going meatless on Mondays will help us save water.

WHY: The water needs of livestock are tremendous, far above those of vegetables or grains. An estimated eighteen to twenty-five hundred gallons of water go into producing a single pound of beef. Think about this: If you practice one year of Meatless Mondays, you would save about a ton of water—enough to fill up the bathtub twenty-two times *per week!*

This big problem doesn't require us to go to war with another country, spend trillions of dollars, elect a new government, or even find new values. We simply need some good old-fashioned common sense. We are eating too much meat, so let's start eating less. And when we do eat meat, let's buy the best quality we can afford (organic, grass-fed, pasture-raised).

While we are at it, let's not bother declaring ourselves anything. No labels required. This is not an all-or-nothing choice. Instead of becoming intimidated or paralyzed by some kind of ethical perfection, let's address the problems in front of us, and take whatever steps we can to fix them. As my friend Kathy Freston suggests, "Just lean into it," and start filling your loved ones' diets with delicious, bone-building, heart-helping, sustainable fruits, veggies, and grains.

Talk about it at family dinner. Everyone can come up with their own reason for eating less meat! In the pages ahead are some fabulous recipes to get you started.

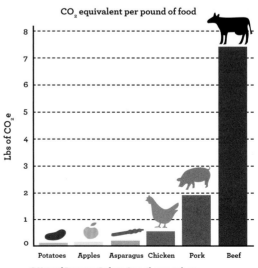

GLOBAL WARMING POLLUTION RELEASED BY PRODUCING YOUR FAVORITE FOODS

CO_2 equivalent per pound of food

© *Natural Resources Defense Council, www.nrdc.org*

OVERHEARD MUMBLINGS *from a dinner party shortly after the main course:* **"LAURIE, WE APPLAUD YOUR EFFORTS** *to go vegetarian, just not on the night we are here."* —STEVE MARTIN

OVERHEARD THAT SAME NIGHT *shortly after dessert:*
"When would it be appropriate to call in for some take-out food?" —MARTIN SHORT

MARK BITTMAN'S
Dinnertime Musings

MARK BITTMAN *has spent half his life sitting at tables, and the other half in front of a stove. This fact has provided him limitless material for his weekly* New York Times *column and his many cookbooks, including one of my favorites:* How to Cook Everything. *He is a flexitarian (someone who eats mostly plants, and just a little meat) and a minimalist (it doesn't take much to make tasty food) of the highest order. Mark believes we should all be eating less of certain things and more of others, and that conscious eating is something we should be teaching our kids.*

I think *The Joy of Cooking* is one of the best book titles of all time. It really sums it up. Cooking with your kids is a short-term joy with long-term benefits. You have to spend the time educating your kids about the kitchen, about food, eating right, about shopping, and the responsibilities of cleaning up. I used to say to my kids, "Cleaning up is part of dinner." You don't eat dinner and disappear. You eat dinner and part of the eating of dinner is making the house look good again. Otherwise the cook is going to be very unhappy, and that cook is me!

In my view, 80 percent of the stuff in stores is crap, and when I say 80 percent I mean 80 percent. You have to choose foods that have no ingredients because they *are* the ingredients.

In the old days, an orange was a common Christmas gift because they came all the way from Florida and that was a luxury.

Taking control of our food, knowing where it comes from, selecting it, and cooking it ourselves makes us more thoughtful. Sitting down to a meal with those we care about, instead of standing over a sink with a bowl of cereal, is an act of engagement rather than one of isolation.

I am eating 70 percent less meat than I used to. We just can't sustain the amount of meat we are demanding. On top of that, there is no way to treat animals right when we are killing billions of them a year in the United States alone!

We grew up being told that the more meat and dairy we ate, the healthier we would be. Nothing could be further from the truth. Plants promote good health. You eat more plants, you live longer.

In the past, every family had a cook; usually that was the mom. I had family dinner every night. I would go so far as to say I ate at home 340 nights out of the year. On the other hand, I grew up never eating a fresh vegetable. I didn't taste spinach until I was nineteen. It was canned fruit salad, Minute Rice, and salad with a dressing from the jar. I think my mom's bad cooking turned me into a cook.

Fast food isn't "bad" because it's fast—it's bad because of the crummy ingredients.

Food left closer to its natural state is more nutritious than food that has been refined to within an inch of its life.

Eating unprecedented quantities of animals that have been drugged and generally mistreated their entire lives isn't good for you or your kids.

"I'm not a vegetarian, I'm a
LESS-MEAT-ETARIAN."
—MARK BITTMAN

VEGETARIAN DISHES SO GOOD NO ONE WILL KNOW WHAT'S MISSING

CRISPY BLACK BEAN CAKES
with Guacamole, "Grilled" Corn, and Slaw

These bean cakes will make you a veggie believer. They are savory, soft on the inside, and crunchy on the outside. Piled on top of the corn with creamy guacamole and tangy crunchy slaw, it somehow seems like a fancy dish, even though the ingredients are simple.

YOU NEED

2–3 tablespoons olive oil

1 medium onion, chopped

4 cloves garlic, minced

2 tablespoons ground cumin, divided

1 4-ounce can mild fire-roasted green chiles (optional)

2 15-ounce cans refried black beans (if you cannot find refried black beans, use regular refried beans)

1 cup cornmeal

1 egg

2 tablespoons vinegar

1 teaspoon salt

½ teaspoon cayenne (optional)

1½ cups crispy rice cereal (any brand)

Guacamole (page 134)

Cabbage Slaw (recipe at right)

Salsa (page 133—or your favorite store-bought kind)

Fresh cilantro

TO MAKE 16 BEAN CAKES (ENOUGH FOR 6 SERVINGS WITH LEFTOVERS)

Heat up a medium-size skillet and drizzle in enough olive oil to cover the bottom. Sauté the onion until it's golden and soft. Add the garlic, 1 tablespoon cumin, and the green chiles; stir until fragrant and most of the moisture has evaporated. Dump into a large bowl.

To the onion mixture, add the black beans, cornmeal, egg, vinegar, salt, and cayenne. Stir well. If the mixture seems a little loose, add some more cornmeal. Let it rest in the fridge for about 15 minutes, or up to a day.

Preheat the oven to 350 degrees.

Mix the crispy rice cereal with 1 tablespoon olive oil and the remaining cumin and pour into a large, shallow bowl. Scoop up a heaping tablespoon of the bean mixture and plop it into the bowl of rice coating. Gently pat the bean cake down so the bottom gets covered in the coating, then flip, making sure the edges get covered as well, shaping it into a small, round, flat patty. They are delicate; you have to imagine you are holding a baby bird (that thought helps me get them right). Put on an oiled sheet pan and repeat with the remaining bean mixture.

At this point you have two choices. You can spray or drizzle the cakes with a little olive oil then stick the sheet pan in the oven for 30 minutes, and you will have tasty black bean cakes. Or to make them extra-crispy, you can sauté them in olive oil for about 2 minutes a side and finish them off in the oven. I think the extra crispiness is worth the effort.

Serve topped with guacamole, slaw, salsa, and fresh cilantro.

If you want to get tall and fancy when you serve this (it takes 3 extra minutes), put some "Grilled" Corn (page 108) on each plate, place a bean cake on top, plop on a spoon of guacamole, and heap the slaw on top of that as the crowning glory. Put a bit of salsa on each plate as well.

CABBAGE SLAW

YOU NEED

1 small white cabbage

1 large carrot

1 teaspoon salt

2 teaspoons sugar

¼ cup white vinegar

1 clove garlic, minced

1 tablespoon chopped fresh chives

2 tablespoons chopped fresh cilantro (optional)

TO MAKE ABOUT 3 CUPS

Cut the cabbage into thin strips. Grate the peeled carrot, or just keep peeling it with the peeler so you get thin strips. Toss the vegetables with the salt and sugar and let sit for 15 minutes.

Drain the cabbage and carrot well, and toss with the remaining ingredients.

"GRILLED" CORN

YOU NEED

5 ears corn (or 5 cups defrosted frozen corn)

½ red onion, chopped

2 tablespoons olive oil

1 teaspoon chili powder (optional)

Salt and pepper

Squeeze of lime

TO MAKE ABOUT 5 CUPS

Preheat the broiler, and oil a sheet pan.

Cut the corn kernels off the cob. Add the next four ingredients and toss. Spread the corn out on the sheet pan and put it on the top rack in the oven. Broil until the corn starts to sputter, some of it turning golden brown, 6 to 7 minutes. Take it out and season with the lime juice.

OVEN GRAINS, GREENS, AND CHEESE, PLEASE

This is a great, warm, comforting one-dish crowd pleaser. Cook it on a Saturday when you have family visiting, or a Tuesday just to make yourself happy. Make this into your very own family recipe! Use your favorite grain, or try a new one. The recipe suggests some greens and cheeses, but please do experiment with any you have on hand and love.

YOU NEED

2 tablespoons olive oil

2 medium onions, sliced

2 cloves garlic, chopped

2 cups sliced mushrooms

CHEAT SHEET FOR COOKING GRAINS

A few minutes before you think the grains are done, start checking them to make sure they don't get mushy.

1 cup	WATER in cups	COOKING minutes	YIELD in cups
QUINOA	2	15	2¾
AMARANTH	2	15–20	2½
PEARL BARLEY	3	50–60	3½
MILLET	2½	25–30	3½
WHEAT BERRIES	3	90–120	2½
SPELT	3	45–50	2½
BROWN RICE	2½	45	3

Salt and pepper

2 bunches kale, chopped

2 bunches Swiss chard, chopped

1 cup grated Parmesan cheese

1 egg, beaten

Squeeze of lemon

6 cups cooked, mild-tasting grains, like quinoa, barley, or wheat berries

6 cups Fragrant Tomato Sauce (page 98) or your favorite store-bought tomato sauce, plus extra to serve on the side

2 cups mixed cheeses, like a soft goat cheese, fresh mozzarella, and Fontina

TO MAKE 6 SERVINGS (PLUS LEFTOVERS)

Heat a large nonstick skillet over medium heat and drizzle in enough oil to cover the bottom. Sauté the onions, garlic, and mushrooms until they are soft and golden. Season with salt and pepper and dump them into a bowl.

In a large pot or pan with a lid, steam the greens until tender, 4 to 5 minutes (you might have to do this in a couple of batches). Put the cooked greens in a clean dishtowel or salad spinner and wring out all the excess water. Toss the greens with the Parmesan cheese and egg.

Season with a squeeze of lemon, salt, and pepper.

Preheat the oven to 400 degrees.

Now treat all the ingredients just like a lasagna. Put a layer of grains in your baking dish, top with tomato sauce, a layer of greens, the mushroom mixture, and a layer of the mixed cheeses . . . and so on until you finish with a layer of tomato sauce and cheese.

Top the dish with foil or a lid, stick it into the oven, and bake until bubbling, about 35 minutes. Then take off the lid and return the dish to the oven for 10 minutes.

Serve with extra tomato sauce and a simple green salad.

A BIG, HAPPY PLATTER OF ROASTED VEGETABLES

Maybe it's Sunday and you feel like you haven't had a very healthy food week, or maybe you are increasingly including vegetarian dinners into your week. Whatever the reason might be, once in a while it is lovely to spend some time preparing a feast of roasted vegetables.

Roasting vegetables is simple. Just add salt, pepper, a bit of oil, and a hot oven, and nearly every vegetable becomes an intensely delicious version of its former self. Their flavors have been mellowed and concentrated, with a sweetness that only roasting can bring out. To maximize the flavor of the vegetables, I cook them until the exteriors start to brown and caramelize and the insides are soft and tender. However, if you prefer them crunchy and al dente, do take them out earlier. Roast enough for plenty of leftovers to toss into salads, stuff into sandwiches, and blend into soups.

THE RECIPES

Have several sheet pans ready, either lightly oiled or covered with a piece of parchment paper to prevent sticking.

Preheat the oven to 450 degrees.

Vegetables That Roast in 20 Minutes or Less
Corn

Slice the kernels off the cobs with a sharp knife. Put them in a bowl and toss with olive oil and a bit of salt. Put on a sheet pan in a single layer and roast for 20 minutes or until the corn starts to brown.

You can also leave the husks on the corn, put the whole corn into the oven, and roast for 30 minutes. Now just pull off the husks and silk and serve. Done! How easy is that?

Quick Tip

Seasoning Suggestions: **After roasting, toss with a pat of butter and freshly chopped soft fragrant herbs like parsley, dill, chives, or basil. For a south-of-the-border dish, toss with chili powder, a squeeze of lime, and Parmesan cheese.**

Asparagus

Snap off the woody ends of asparagus. Toss with olive oil and salt. Put on a baking sheet in a single layer and roast for 10 to 15 minutes.

Seasoning Suggestions: **Before roasting, toss with chopped garlic, Parmesan cheese, or chopped fresh thyme. • After roasting, give them a squeeze of lemon or lime, or a drizzle of balsamic vinegar or Dijon vinaigrette, and a sprinkle of chopped fresh herbs.**

Kale

Believe it or not, kale is fantastic when you roast it! Take 1 bunch of kale and cut off the thick stems; drizzle it with olive oil, a sprinkling of salt, and perhaps some minced garlic. Rub the oil into the leaves so they are well covered. Arrange in a single layer on a baking sheet and roast, flipping the leaves and turning the sheets until the kale is crispy; it will take about 15 minutes. Squeeze on plenty of lemon juice and taste for salt and pepper.

Zucchini or Summer Squash

Halve and cut zucchini or squash into wedges. Toss the pieces with salt and a drizzle of olive oil. Roast for 15 to 20 minutes, flipping them halfway through.

Seasoning Suggestions: Before roasting, toss with Parmesan cheese, fresh chopped herbs or grated lemon zest, and chopped garlic or shallots. • *After roasting, squeeze on a little lemon juice or drizzle with balsamic vinegar or some Dijon vinaigrette.*

Vegetables That Roast for 20 to 30 Minutes

Peppers

Cut any color peppers into wedges, toss with a bit of olive oil, put on the baking sheet skin-side up, and roast until the skin is blistered and blackened—about 20 to 30 minutes. Transfer the peppers directly from the oven into a bowl, cover with plastic wrap or a tight-fitting lid, and let steam. Once the peppers are cool, uncover the bowl and peel off and discard the pepper skins.

Seasoning Suggestions: Before roasting, toss with a few tablespoons of hoisin sauce. • *After roasting, you can toss with chopped fresh herbs like mint, basil, or parsley; balsamic vinegar; or chopped pine nuts.*

Carrots

Peel and slice carrots into wedges or coins. Toss them with salt and pepper and a drizzle of olive oil. Roast for 20 minutes or until tender with golden caramelized edges.

Seasoning Suggestions: Before roasting, toss with any of the following: a teaspoon of ground cumin and/or coriander, fresh chopped herbs like thyme or rosemary, chopped garlic or shallots, or 1 to 2 tablespoons of maple syrup and a pinch of cinnamon. • *After roasting, drizzle with balsamic vinegar or some Dijon vinaigrette, or toss with a pat of butter and chopped parsley, dill, or basil.*

Cauliflower

Cut the cauliflower into slices from top to bottom (they don't really come out as slices, but don't worry about it). Toss with a few tablespoons of olive oil, salt, and pepper. Spread in a single layer on a baking sheet and roast until golden, about 30 minutes, flipping the cauliflower now and then.

Seasoning Suggestions: Before roasting, either toss with cumin, coriander, and minced garlic, onions, or toss with capers, raisins, sliced red onions, and parsley. • *After roasting, give it a squeeze of lemon, chopped fresh parsley, or grated Parmesan cheese.*

Brussels Sprouts

Cut off the brown ends and pull off any yellow outer leaves. Toss the brussels sprouts with olive oil, salt, and pepper. Pour them on a sheet pan and roast, shaking the pan now and then, until browned, about 30 to 40 minutes. Defrosted frozen brussels sprouts can also be used with great results!

Seasoning Suggestions: Before roasting, toss with grated garlic and a sprinkle of Parmesan cheese. • *After roasting, toss with a little balsamic vinegar, or a pat of butter and fresh chopped herbs, toasted hazelnuts, pine nuts, or walnuts, or grated zest from a lemon.*

DIJON VINAIGRETTE FOR ROASTED VEGETABLES

YOU NEED

½ cup red wine vinegar

¼ cup Dijon mustard

3 cloves garlic, minced

1 shallot, minced

1 tablespoon honey

1½ cups olive oil

Salt, pepper, and sugar to taste

TO MAKE 2½ CUPS

In a medium bowl, whisk together the vinegar, mustard, garlic, shallot, and honey. Slowly whisk in the olive oil to emulsify. Season to taste with salt, pepper, and sugar.

ROASTED RED PEPPER DRESSING

YOU NEED

½ cup olive oil

3 tablespoons red wine vinegar

2 tablespoons coarsely chopped roasted red bell pepper (either one you've just roasted or one from a jar)

1 clove garlic, smashed

½ teaspoon Dijon mustard

Pinch of sugar

Pinch of salt and freshly ground pepper

TO MAKE 1 CUP

Put all the ingredients into a blender and blend until smooth. Taste and adjust the seasonings.

VEGETABLE ENCHILADA PIE: No Fuss, Less Mess, but So Good Nonetheless

Great enchilada sauce + cheese = great enchiladas. It is that simple. So here is the recipe for a great but easy-to-make enchilada sauce. The enchiladas are quick since you stack the tortillas instead of roll them. And why don't we toss in some vegetables as healthy extras? As usual, the vegetables listed here are only suggestions; use whatever you have in your fridge or garden.

ENCHILADA SAUCE

YOU NEED

2 tablespoons olive oil

2 cups chopped onions

4 cloves garlic, minced

5 tablespoons chili powder, mild or hot

2 tablespoons cumin

1 shredded corn tortilla

1 28-ounce can diced tomatoes, drained (fire-roasted tomatoes are great for this)

2 tablespoons brown sugar or maple syrup

1 (spicy) or 2 (really spicy) chopped chipotle chiles from a can (optional)

1 cup water or stock

Salt and pepper to taste

TO MAKE 3½ CUPS

Heat a large pot over medium heat and drizzle in enough oil to cover the bottom. Sauté the onions until golden, then add the garlic, chili, cumin, and tortilla, stirring for a moment until fragrant.

Add the remaining ingredients and simmer for 20 minutes. (Now is a good time to start cooking the vegetables for the filling.) Put the sauce in a blender—you might need to do it in batches—and blend until smooth. Taste and adjust the seasonings. This can be made ahead and refrigerated or frozen.

FILLING

YOU NEED

2 tablespoons olive oil

1 medium onion, chopped

2 medium cloves garlic, chopped

2 cups shucked fresh corn or defrosted frozen corn

1 cup chopped zucchini

1 cup chopped asparagus

1 teaspoon dried oregano (optional)

3 cups canned black beans, drained very well

2 4-ounce cans mild chopped green chiles, drained very well (optional)

1 cup of your favorite salsa (if it is very watery, drain some of the liquid)

1 cup low-fat sour cream or plain Greek yogurt

About 14 corn tortillas, 5–6 inches each

3 cups shredded Mexican cheese or mozzarella

TO MAKE 6 SERVINGS

Heat a large nonstick skillet over medium heat and drizzle in enough oil to cover the bottom. Sauté the onion until golden, then add the garlic, stirring for a minute until fragrant.

Add the corn, zucchini, asparagus, and oregano. Sauté the vegetables until they are heated through but still crisp, about 3 to 4 minutes. Add the beans to the pan and put it aside.

In a bowl, mix the green chiles, salsa, and sour cream.

Preheat the oven to 400 degrees.

Cover the bottom of a medium-size baking dish with a thin layer of enchilada sauce, put a layer of tortillas on top, cover them with enchilada sauce, then vegetables, the sour cream mixture, cheese, another layer of tortillas . . . and keep going until you reach the top, ending with a layer of sauce.

Cover tightly with foil and bake in the oven for 30 minutes. Take off the foil, sprinkle with some cheese, and bake for 5 additional minutes.

Serve with guacamole (page 134), a salad—and enjoy.

...꧁⊶◈⊷꧂...

KIDS LOOOOOVE PESTO
On their pasta, of course, but also in their peas if you
please, a green drizzle in their soup is glorious, a
shmear on the sammy is better than mayo.
A spoonful of pesto makes the leftovers go down, in the
most delightful way.

GREEN LINGUINI with Pesto

*There are all sorts of ways to make pesto, starting with
opening a jar. But please don't do that! Pesto is very simple
to make yourself. It doesn't take long, and it will fill your
kitchen with the green smell of a summer herb garden.*

*This recipe uses a blender, but someday if you have
an extra ten minutes, try making it by hand, mixing all the
ingredients with a mortar and pestle. This is what Italian
grandmothers have been doing for centuries. It is definitely something you should get your kids to help you with.
After pounding a pestle up and down for ten minutes, they
might be so tired they will sit properly at the dinner table.*

HOMEMADE PESTO SAUCE

YOU NEED

¼ cup pine nuts, gently toasted (almonds work well, too)

2 medium cloves garlic

½ cup freshly grated Parmesan cheese

2 cups (lightly packed) basil leaves

⅔ cup extra-virgin olive oil

Salt and pepper to taste

TO MAKE 1 CUP

In a food processor or blender, pulse the pine nuts with
the garlic and Parmesan until finely chopped.

Add the basil and pulse until minced, turning off the
machine and scraping down the sides of the bowl every
now and then.

With the machine on, add the olive oil in a thin
stream and process until smooth. Taste and season with
salt and pepper.

LINGUINE

YOU NEED

1 pound linguini

Pat of butter (optional)

Freshly grated Parmesan cheese

TO MAKE 4–6 SERVINGS

Fill a large pot with water, and salt it so it tastes like the
sea. Bring it to a boil. Add 1 pound of linguini and cook
according to the package directions.

Throw the drained pasta and enough pesto to make
you happy into a large bowl; add a pat of butter, if you
like, to make it even more luxurious. Toss and serve with
freshly grated Parmesan cheese.

Butterfly PASTA WITH KALE

*Laurie taught me this recipe and it's one of her girls'
favorite comfort foods. Although we know that the pasta is
their favorite part, and they can be quite adept at fishing
it out from among the strands of kale, we also know that a
lot of greens end up in their tummies.*

YOU NEED

2 large bunches kale

1 pound farfalle pasta

3 tablespoons olive oil

6 cloves garlic, slivered

1½ cups sun-dried tomatoes from a jar, drained, rinsed,
and coarsely chopped

½ cup pine nuts, toasted

Salt and pepper or red pepper flakes

Freshly grated Parmesan cheese

TO MAKE 6 SERVINGS

Fill a large pot with water. Bring it to a boil, then salt it so
it tastes like the sea.

Remove the stems from the kale. Stack all the kale
leaves on top of one another, roll them into a fat cigar, and
slice it into thin slices. Or just chop, chop, chop it all—that
works, too.

RECIPES

RECIPES

Throw the kale into the pot for 4 minutes, then remove with a slotted spoon or tongs and drain well. Put the pasta into the same pot of water and cook according to the package directions.

While the pasta is boiling, drizzle a large pan with the olive oil, heat it over a medium flame until shimmering, add the garlic, and gently sauté it until golden and fragrant. Toss in the kale and the sun-dried tomatoes, cooking until the kale is tender and the sun-dried tomatoes are soft and bright.

When the pasta is done, drain it, reserving a few tablespoons of the cooking water.

In a large bowl, combine the pasta with the kale and remaining ingredients. If you want to moisten it a bit, use the reserved cooking water. Serve with a lovely mixed green salad.

Cook's Tip — *Add a can of drained white beans and a chopped, cooked Italian sausage or two and you have a great fall or winter dinner.*

Green Tip — *If you eat pasta often, or have little ones who do, throw a few extra servings of pasta into the pot, toss with olive oil, and keep in the fridge so you don't have to heat an entire pot of water to the boiling point every time you need some. Saving energy, water, and time!*

Caramelized SWEET POTATOES WITH QUINOA AND GREENS

I almost don't want to tell you how good for you this dish is. I am afraid you will shake your head and say, "Oh no, my kids won't eat that healthy"—but … will your kids eat sweet potatoes with marshmallows? Will they eat itty-bitty grains of pasta? If so, they will like these healthier versions.

Quinoa has become a delicious new staple in our lives. If you haven't tried it yet, you are in for a treat. It is a protein-rich seed that has a fluffy, creamy, slightly crunchy texture and a flavor not unlike pasta or couscous. One of the world's true super-foods, quinoa is a complete protein, containing all nine essential amino acids, and it's a great source of fiber, iron, and magnesium. It only takes fifteen quick minutes to cook, and is an easy, healthy alternative to rice or pasta.

YOU NEED

4 medium-size sweet potatoes

Salt and pepper

3 tablespoons olive oil, divided

1 chopped onion

2 cloves garlic, chopped

2 teaspoons peeled and chopped fresh ginger (optional)

1 tablespoon mild Indian curry powder (optional)

3 cups leafy greens such as kale, chard, or collards, cut in thin strips (or you could use 1 cup corn, peas, or edamame instead)

1½ cups quinoa

3 cups water or low-sodium chicken or vegetable stock

2 tablespoons olive oil, or a pat of butter

Squeeze of lemon

TO MAKE 4–6 SERVINGS

Peel the sweet potatoes and slice them ¼-inch thick. Toss them with the salt and 1 tablespoon of the olive oil. Place them on a well-oiled, nonstick baking sheet. Cover tightly with foil. Put into a cold oven (this is important, because the gradual rise in temperature helps bring out the sweet potato flavors).

Turn on the oven to 400 degrees. Bake for about 30 to 40 minutes. Since ovens bake at their own pace, I leave the amount of time up to you, but the potatoes should be a beautiful dark orange and very soft. Uncover and bake for about 20 more minutes, flipping them now and then, until they are caramelized on the outside, and soft and creamy on the inside.

In the meantime, heat 2 tablespoons olive oil in a medium pot and sauté the onion in it. Then add the garlic, ginger, and curry powder and sauté until sizzling and fragrant. Now add the greens and stir until wilted.

Put the quinoa in a fine-mesh strainer and rinse it thoroughly, until the water runs clear.

Add the quinoa to the pot of greens along with 3 cups stock or lightly salted water. Simmer under a lid until all the liquid is absorbed, about 15 minutes. Fluff the quinoa with a fork; season to taste. Add olive oil or a pat of butter if you like, and a squeeze of lemon is always good.

Put the quinoa on a platter, top with the sweet potatoes (if they are dark enough—almost burned—they taste like they are topped with marshmallows).

Serve with some mango chutney and raita (page 133).

More *Things to Do with* QUINOA

1. Put warm quinoa in a breakfast bowl with toasted walnuts, grated apples, a drizzle of maple syrup, and milk.

2. Toss a spoonful or two into your scrambled eggs.

3. Use quinoa in any dish you would make with couscous.

4. Toss cold, cooked quinoa in a salad to add extra crunch and protein.

5. Spanish-flavored quinoa: Sauté some onions and garlic; add ½ cup salsa and a pinch of cumin. Add 1 cup quinoa and 1½ cups water, and simmer for 15 minutes.

6. Instead of a "pasta bar" (page 65), have a "quinoa bar" with sauces and toppings to drizzle and dollop.

7. Make a quinoa "tabbouleh" with chopped kale, parsley, mint, and quinoa tossed with plenty of lemon juice, salt, and a drizzle of olive oil. Add feta and cucumbers to make it even better.

8. Use quinoa as the side dish whenever you would usually use rice (it is quicker and healthier).

9. Put a few tablespoons of quinoa into your soups to add some body and protein.

OMNIVORE'S DELIGHT

Never doubt a mom's impact. The son or daughter you are having family dinner with is taking mental notes, and someday will be waxing nostalgic about those wonderful hours spent sitting around the table. **MICHAEL POLLAN**'s *mother,* **CORKY POLLAN,** *can vouch for that. She should be proud—the family table she set nightly helped put her son on his path as one of the country's most important advocates of healthy eating.*

MICHAEL: First, my mom was committed to the idea of family dinner, and she enjoyed everything about it. There was a regular rotation of meals at our house—you could set the calendar by it. Mondays were flank steak or London broil, Tuesdays were Italian pasta and tomato sauce, Wednesdays were Chinese night, Thursday pepper steak, and on Friday, of course—baked chicken. I would say my mom was a huge influence on my interest in food. The other influence was my grandfather, who was in the produce business but started out selling potatoes on the Lower East Side of New York City, that day's version of the street pretzel. He was also a devoted gardener, and I learned a lot from him. I really became interested in where food comes from when I experienced growing it myself.

Were Michael's mom's memories the same as her son's? I asked Corky to consider whether or not Michael's best-selling books The Omnivore's Dilemma *and* In Defense of Food *had influenced her.*

CORKY: I was lucky when my kids were growing up because they were always very agreeable about food. There really wasn't anything I would serve that they wouldn't eat. Dinner was six sharp and everyone had to be there. I do remember we also had tons of junk food in the house for all the kids to eat. I think in a way it's why my kids have no eating issues. They rarely eat that stuff now because it wasn't a big deal.

As for his influence on me, he has completely affected the way I eat now. Because of his books, I don't eat beef at all, even though he still does! And I have a garden now. I grow vegetables. My favorite thing to grow is garlic. It's so easy, and the home-grown stuff tastes great!

RECIPES

TAL RONNEN
The Vegan Way

CHEF TAL RONNEN *is a celebrated vegan chef who has surprised and won over many a carnivore—most notably Oprah Winfrey—with his delicious meatless recipes. He is the author of* The Conscious Cook.

LAURIE: What exactly does vegan mean and why do so few people practice it?

TAL: Vegan means eating everything in the world except animal products. Eating vegetarian has oftentimes been presented as an "all or nothing" option, which has caused people to resist it outright. What I recommend to people is to eat green a couple of times per week. That way you let yourself, your family, and everyone else at the table in on all of the benefits of vegan without making a drastic change. Over time, you may find you want to make the switch permanent. People often say they feel better eating this way once they've tried it a night or two a week, and that's really the message I'd like to get across: Give it a try, and see if you feel better.

LAURIE: What about prep time?

TAL: In the old days, ninety minutes was not a lot of time to prepare a family meal. Today you look at all the cookbooks and they're all thirty-minute meals. **I think we should step away from the mentality that taking the time to cook is necessarily a bad thing.** It's true that many nights a week, you just don't have the time to make more than a thirty-minute meal. But for the days or nights you do, an extra half hour in prep time can open up a whole world of culinary adventure.

LAURIE: What were your family dinners like growing up?

TAL: Both my parents worked full-time, but good food from a variety of cultures was very important to them. They made eating well a priority, even if it was takeout. So while I was eating every type of cuisine by the time I was five, I didn't have the experience of spending time in the kitchen with my grandmother, watching her cook. It wasn't until I was a teenager and I saw some of my family's friends spending all day Sunday cooking dinner together that I became jealous that I didn't have that experience. That was really one of the big reasons that I wanted to learn to cook.

LAURIE: So where did the vegetarian and vegan twist come in?

TAL: I noticed that people ate a lot of meat in this country, and I wanted to change the perception that eating meat for protein was healthy. Here we tend to think that protein equals animal protein. Everywhere else in the world it doesn't. In South America, for example, people get their protein largely from whole grains. In Mexico and India, it often comes from legumes. Asia gets much of its protein from soy. These cultures aren't exclusively vegetarian, but meat has always been an accent on their plates.

LAURIE: What is step one to going vegetarian or vegan?

TAL: Step one is gradually reducing meat consumption. Try new things. Try quinoa, it's amazing. Try Gardein—a protein made from a variety of vegetable and whole-grain proteins. It's a great replacement for chicken or beef and can be easily swapped into your favorite recipes.

"The best way to **INTRODUCE NEW FOODS** *to kids is* **NEVER TO MENTION IT."** —MARIO BATALI, chef and author, *Molto Gusto: Easy Italian Cooking*

LEMON HERB GRILLED GARDEIN SCALLOPINI
with Romaine, Orange, and Jicama Salad
BY TAL RONNEN

GARDEIN SCALLOPINI

YOU NEED

1 pack Gardein Frozen Scallopini (available in most supermarkets)

2 tablespoons fresh rosemary leaves

4 cloves garlic, roughly chopped

Zest and juice of 1 lemon

2 tablespoons fresh thyme

1 teaspoon extra-virgin olive oil

1 teaspoon salt

1 teaspoon black pepper

1 teaspoon agave nectar (or honey)

TO MAKE 6 SERVINGS

Place all ingredients (except for the Scallopini) in a food processor and process until blended.

Rub each side of the Scallopini with the mixture and grill for 4 minutes on each side.

Slice and serve over the Romaine, Orange, and Jicama Salad.

Green Tip

Gardein, a new substitute for chicken, is made from soy, wheat, and peas and is a great source of protein.

LET'S PLAY!

NAME TWO THINGS
Everyone name two things that make you laugh.

ROMAINE, ORANGE, AND JICAMA SALAD

YOU NEED

2 heads romaine lettuce, washed and ripped into small pieces

3 green onions, thinly sliced

2 oranges, peeled and diced

½ red pepper, diced

½ yellow pepper, diced

½ jicama, julienned

HERB VINAIGRETTE

YOU NEED

1 small shallot, finely chopped

2 cloves garlic, finely chopped

1 tablespoon chopped fresh parsley

1 tablespoon chopped fresh basil

¼ cup white wine vinegar

1 teaspoon agave nectar (or honey)

6 tablespoons olive oil

Salt and pepper to taste

TO MAKE 6 SERVINGS

In large bowl, combine the romaine, green onions, oranges, peppers, and jicama. Toss well and set aside.

In a food processor, combine the shallots, garlic, parsley, basil, vinegar, and agave. Pulse while slowly adding the oil. Season with salt and pepper.

Toss the dressing with the salad ingredients and serve with the sliced Gardein Scallopini.

RECITE TONIGHT

I WAVE GOOD-BYE WHEN BUTTER FLIES
(AN EXCERPT)

It makes me sad when lettuce leaves,
I laugh when dinner rolls,
I wonder if the kitchen sinks
And if a salad bowls.

—*Jack Prelutsky*

RECIPES

KIDS
IN THE KITCHEN
9

RECIPES KIDS CAN MAKE THAT THEIR
FRIENDS AND FAMILY WILL LOVE

COOKING WITH KIDS!

Plan for your kids to help you on days when you have patience and time. It does take longer to cook with kids in the kitchen: They do ask a lot of questions, and they will undoubtedly make a fantastic mess. So be sure to be prepared, forgiving, and in a festive mood. Here are a few more suggestions for success.

- Pick your own twenty-second hand-washing song (like "Happy Birthday"), and make it a ritual to sing it while washing your hands with plenty of soap and warm water.

- Give your child his or her very own apron. Put yours on, too.

- Repeat your safety talk on sharp knives and hot stoves.

- Let the kids help pick the menu. Start with simple recipes featuring ingredients that they like.

- Have everything out and ready before you start. It is much easier if all your ingredients and utensils are laid out on the counter. If your kids are little, chop and measure the ingredients in advance, and put them in little bowls on a tray.

- Create a kid-friendly work space. If the counter is too tall, bring in a step stool for them to stand on, or perhaps try working at the kitchen table—it may be the perfect counter height for a little person.

- Have fun! Put on some music, wear your fancy cooking hats, roll up your sleeves, and dig in. When you approach cooking as creative and fun-filled, your child won't think of cooking as a "chore," and neither will you!

- Talk about the ingredients: Where do the potatoes come from? How do they grow? If you have herbs on the windowsill or vegetables in the garden, let the kids do the picking. If you have time to go to the market together, great!

- Taste the food, a lot! Listen to your kids' opinions. What does a raw carrot taste like compared with when it is cooked? Does this tomato sauce need a little more salt? Dip a lettuce leaf into the salad dressing and decide together if you need more oil or vinegar.

- Put the kids in charge of making sure all the compostables end up in the compost, recyclables in the right bins, and finding alternatives to using plastic wrap and foil.

- Be delighted in the results, no matter what! Kids thrive on success, so sprinkle the meal with compliments and drizzle with love.

The immediate reward will be a dinner that your kids are excited about. Kids love to taste their own creations . . . so not only is cooking with kids fun for everyone, but it helps them to eat better, too! The future reward will be the day you come home and sit down for a home-cooked meal made entirely by your own home-grown chef.

NOODLEPANPIE with Broccoli and Cheese: A Recipe for Tweens, and Little Kids with Big Helpers

Noodlepanpie is crunchy on the outside, noodley soft on the inside, with an oozy cheesy heart. You won't stop eating it until it is all gone, gone, gone.

YOU NEED

1 pound spaghetti noodles, or a big bowl of plain leftover noodles

1 head broccoli, torn apart into little pieces

1 cup Parmesan cheese, plus more for sprinkling

2 tablespoons olive oil

2 cups of your favorite shredded cheese (like mozzarella, cheddar, or Jack)

Salt and pepper

1 big helper person

TO MAKE 6 SERVINGS

Fill a big pot of water and put enough salt in it that it tastes like the sea. Have your big helper put the pot on the stove and bring it to a boil.

Add the noodles to the pot and stir them right away; cook them for as many minutes as the noodle package tells you to, then throw in the broccoli and cook for 3 minutes more. Overcooking the noodles a bit will help them stick together. Ask your big helper to take the noodles and broccoli off the stove and drain them well. Toss the noodles with the Parmesan cheese.

Heat a medium-size nonstick pan on the stove over medium heat, drizzle 2 tablespoons of olive oil into it, and put half of the noodles in the pan. Flatten them, then top with the cheese and finish with the other half of the noodles. Let the noodle pie gently fry for about 10 minutes. You might need to add a little more olive oil.

When it is golden underneath, have your helper flip it like a big pancake. The easiest way to do this is to spray or oil the pan's lid (or a large plate) flip the noodles onto it, and then slide them back into the pan. Cook until golden and crunchy on the outside and gooey and cheesy on the inside.

Veggie Tip

If broccoli isn't your favorite vegetable, you can use cooked peas, spinach, asparagus, shredded zucchini or carrots, or any other veggie that will make you happy.

Asian Tip

You can easily transform this into an Asian-flavored dish by omitting the cheese, tossing just the boiled noodles with 1 egg beaten with a teaspoon of toasted sesame oil, some grated ginger, and 1 tablespoon each soy sauce and chopped green onions. Then follow the rest of the recipe at left. Serve with hoisin sauce on the side.

DISCOVER ARTICHOKES

Whoever first looked at the artichoke and said, "I am going to eat that pokey thistle," was very brave and we are very grateful, because it's a vegetable kids will quickly learn to like. Why? Perhaps because it is scary looking or perhaps because it is a utensil for dip or perhaps because it is entertaining to eat. Whatever the reason, don't be scared of this tasty vegetable any longer. Here is how to tackle it, steam it, eat it, and a few dips to enjoy it with.

HOW TO STEAM AN ARTICHOKE

In a large pot, bring a few inches of salted water to a simmer. If you want to get fancy, you can add a bay leaf, some lemon slices, and a garlic clove.

At this point, you could just dump the artichokes into the pot, but if you want them to look a little nicer, trim the stem and the top by a ½ inch. It is easiest to do this with a serrated bread knife. Cut all the pokey tips off the leaves with a pair of kitchen shears.

Put the artichokes into the pot and—depending on how large they are—steam covered for 30 to 45 minutes. At some point, you might need to add a little more water. When you can easily pull a leaf free, they are done.

Picking Tip

The artichoke season is March through May. It is the flower bud of a beautiful purple thistle. When you pick one at the market, make sure that it is heavy for its size, dark green, with tightly closed petals.

SERVE WITH NOTHING AT ALL OR...

Faux Aioli

Mix 1 cup mayonnaise with 1 or 2 minced garlic cloves, 1 tablespoon tasty olive oil, 1 tablespoon lemon juice, and 1 tablespoon Dijon mustard.

Lemony Herb Vinaigrette

Whisk ¼ cup lemon juice and ½ teaspoon salt in a small bowl. Gradually whisk in ¾ cup olive oil. Just before serving, stir in some chopped herbs.

Creamy Horseradish Dip

Combine ½ cup Greek yogurt with 2 (or more to taste) tablespoons cream-style horseradish sauce, the zest of ½ lemon, and salt and pepper to taste.

Balsamic Vinaigrette

Combine ¼ cup balsamic vinegar with ½ teaspoon salt, 1 chopped garlic clove, and 1 tablespoon Dijon mustard. Whisk in ¾ cup good-quality olive oil.

Plain Ol' Melted Butter

Perhaps with a chopped clove of garlic, a bit of salt, and a squeeze of lemon.

HOW TO EAT AN ARTICHOKE

Pull off each leaf one by one, dipping the bottom light green part into a dipping sauce. Gently nibble or scrape off the bottom of the leaf by putting the leaf in your mouth, closing your teeth on it, and pulling the leaf outward. Throw the remainder into the compost. When you get to the heart portion, ask a grown-up to scoop out all the fuzzy stuff for you—then make sure you get it back, because it's the best part!

"AS SOON AS MY KIDS STARTED TO EAT *solid food, I realized that they should eat what we were eating and* **I SLOWLY STARTED TO INTRODUCE THEM TO THE FOODS I LOVED.** *In the name of palate education, their steamed vegetables and brown rice gave way to the subtle flavors of green chiles and cumin and eventually the heat of the red pepper. This led my son Noah, age five, to exclaim,* **'YOU KNOW, DAD, I THINK I'M A SPICY GUY!'"** —GARY, dad of Noah and Jules

CAESAR PITA PIZZA PIES

Have a pita pizza party for your best friend—or your whole family! The best part is that you get to pick your own toppings . . . you can even put a Caesar salad on top of the pizza, making it a crunchy, munchy Caesar pita pizza pie.

YOU NEED

For the Pita Pizzas

6 pita breads

Olive oil

1½ cups tomato sauce (page 65) or your favorite jarred pizza sauce

2 cups shredded mozzarella cheese

Optional Toppings

Pepperoni

Chopped tomatoes

Thinly sliced onions

Sliced mushrooms

TO MAKE 6 SMALL PIZZAS

Preheat your oven to 450 degrees.

Put a baking sheet on the bottom rack of your oven. Brush both sides of the pitas with olive oil, then spread the tops with tomato sauce and sprinkle with the mozzarella and any topping you please.

Using pot holders, take the baking sheet out of the oven and gently place your pizzas on it (you might need a grown-up to help you with this). Bake for 10 to 12 minutes or until you think they are perfect.

CAESAR SALAD

YOU NEED

2 heads romaine lettuce, inner leaves best, torn into bite-size pieces

Bunch of croutons

½ cup Parmesan cheese

For the Dressing

2 cloves garlic, minced

1 teaspoon Worcestershire sauce

3 tablespoons mayonnaise

¼ cup fresh lemon juice

2 tablespoons grated Parmesan cheese

1 tablespoon Dijon mustard

½ cup olive oil

Salt and pepper to taste

TO MAKE 6 SERVINGS

Put all the salad dressing ingredients into a large bowl and whisk, whisk, whisk until smooth.

Now take a lettuce leaf, dip it into the dressing, and see how it tastes. Does it need more salt? Or lemon? Make it taste exactly how you like it best, then toss with the lettuce, croutons, and cheese.

Cook's Tip

It's easy to make your own croutons! All you need is some bread, cut into cubes, tossed with a bit of olive oil, sprinkled with salt and pepper, and perhaps some minced garlic and Parmesan cheese, too. Spread onto a sheet pan and bake in a 400-degree oven for about 15 minutes. Ta-da, done.

A Grand Family-Size TURKEY, APPLE, AND CHEESE PANINI (GRILLED SANDWICH)

A gigantic sandwich! Crunchy on the outside, cheesy and tasty on the inside. It is already squished flat so it is perfect for a picnic or a trip to the zoo. Just cut it into wedges and wrap it tight.

This version includes cheddar cheese, turkey, and tangy apples—but if you can imagine a better one, make it!

YOU NEED

1 large ciabatta bread, or any flat, crusty loaf of bread, sliced open

Some Dijon mustard and mayonnaise, for spreading

8 slices sharp cheddar (about 8 ounces)

8 slices roast turkey from your deli

1–2 tasty apples, cored and thinly sliced

Olive oil

...⋯⋯⋯⋯...

PANINI POSSIBILITIES ARE ENDLESS!

How about a . . .

- Ham and cheese panini.
- Nutella and banana if you please panini.
- Bacon, cheddar, and tomato panini.
- Grilled chicken, fresh tomato, pesto, and mozzarella panini.
- Everything-in-your-fridge panini.
- Pail of garden vegetables without snails panini.
- Peanut butter and jam thank you Mam panini.
- Meatball and fettuccini panini.

You could eat a panini every day of your life, and never eat the same one twice.

TO MAKE 4–6 SERVINGS

If you have a panini press, preheat it.

Spread the inside of the ciabatta with Dijon mustard and mayonnaise. Layer one side of ciabatta with 4 slices of cheddar, the turkey and apple slices, and then the remaining cheddar. Top with the other half of ciabatta. Brush the top and bottom of the sandwich with olive oil.

You might need some grown-up help with the next part:

Heat up a nonstick pan over a medium flame and drizzle it with olive oil so the bottom is covered. Place the panini on it and balance a weight on top of the sandwich. You can use something like a heavy skillet, a foil-wrapped brick, or a teakettle filled with water. Press down on the weight and grill 3 to 4 minutes on first side. Then flip the sandwich, put the weight back, and continue cooking until it's golden and the cheese is melted, about 3 to 4 minutes.

If you are using a panini press, grill according to its instructions.

Cut the panini into pieces and serve with a side of mustard, a salad, and some pickles.

Easy Cheesy **DINNER FRITTATA**

Eggs for dinner! Or lunch, or a brunch by the sea. You crack a bunch of eggs and cook them with some filling. I say asparagus, potatoes, and cheese, but you can say anything you please—maybe tomatoes, mozzarella, and pesto, maybe corn and peas.

Just start cooking the filling first, and when it is done add the eggs, and right before you put the frittata under the broiler, sprinkle it with cheese.

YOU NEED

For the Frittata

8 organic, free-range eggs

2 tablespoons grated Parmesan cheese

¼ teaspoon salt and a pinch of pepper

For the Filling

2 tablespoons butter or olive oil

2 tablespoons diced red onion

½ cup diced potatoes

½ cup chopped asparagus

½ cup cubed mozzarella, Gruyère, or Fontina

1 tablespoon chopped soft herbs like basil, dill, or parsley

Cook's Tip

To make individual baby frittatas, preheat the oven to 425 degrees. Sauté the filling and let it cool for a moment. Fold the filling and the cheese into the beaten eggs. Pour into personal-size buttered ramekins and bake until set, 10 to 12 minutes.

TO MAKE 4–6 SERVINGS

Preheat the oven to its broil setting.

In a medium-size bowl, using a fork, whisk together the eggs, Parmesan, salt, and pepper. Set aside.

Heat a medium-size, nonstick, oven-safe pan over medium-high heat. Add the butter and let it melt. Add the onion, potatoes, and asparagus to the pan and sauté for 8 minutes or until the potatoes are soft.

Pour the eggs into the pan and reduce the heat to medium-low. Stir with a rubber spatula once. Cook for 4 to 5 minutes or until the egg mixture is starting to set (thicken). Top with the mozzarella cubes.

Place the pan into the oven and broil for 3 to 4 minutes, until lightly browned and fluffy. Remove from the pan and cut into wedges. Garnish with herbs.

Big Kids, Small Kitchen:

THE TWENTY-SOMETHING

Family Table, by Phoebe Lapine

Once upon a time, my parents provided for every meal. Now, when my refrigerator stands empty because I am either too poor or too harried to fill it, I look at this period as the Golden Age of young adulthood. Then I remember—I'm only twenty-three, that Golden Age is elapsing right now—and I close the refrigerator door to go meet my friends for a meal.

My family didn't have a strict dinnertime ritual growing up. Home cooking was frequent, but when my mother's time ran short, the meal turned into takeout, the dining room table to a couch with *Jeopardy!* on in the background. Some meals were long, others spent in silence. But no matter which room of our small New York City apartment we migrated to, at the end of a long day, we were always together.

Since college, I've returned to a love of cooking and savoring meals (with friends at the center of them), but this time with a new job, new budget, and new coffee table—which, being from a thrift store, is not so new. For a while it seemed I would never recapture the communal eating of college or the intimate dinners of my childhood. And then one day in late July 2008, my friend Cara started "Magazine Club." Our monthly meeting takes away all the pressure of having to finish a novel in time. With this club, everyone arrives with an article and a dish it inspired—and focuses on the regularly scheduled hanging out and group eating, the most important elements.

For us food-obsessed quarter-lifers, cooking is cathartic. But the friend part embodies what we remember loving about our childhood meals: the familiarity of the flavors, the comfort of the company, the uncompromised attention to reaching over a shared platter, at the table or on a couch, and digging in.

PEA NUTTY NOODLES

Dear Kid, you know what the best part of cooking dinner is? Apart from not having to do the dishes (as that would not be fair)?

It is a secret grown-ups haven't told you yet ... After you have made the sauce, get out some little spoons and taste a tiny bit of it. What do you think? Is it salty enough? If not, add a little salt. Does it need a little more honey? How about adding a little chili sauce and making it a tiny bit spicy, or adding a little more and making it very spicy (but only if you promise to eat every little bit)? Then add a squeeze of lime; how does it taste now? See, that's what's so cool about cooking dinner yourself—you get to make it taste exactly the way you like it best.

PARENTS CAN

Clean their rooms.
Boil the pasta.
Set the table.
Wash their hands.

YOU NEED

For the Peanut Sauce

1 pound of your favorite shaped pasta

1 cup peanut butter

½ cup soy sauce

⅔ cup warm water

3 tablespoons chopped fresh ginger

2 cloves garlic, chopped

1 tablespoon toasted sesame oil

1 tablespoon honey

3 tablespoons white (rice or wine) vinegar

Garnishes: *Pick and Choose
Any You Please and as Much as You Want*

Chopped peanuts

Diced cucumbers

Diced apples

Sliced scallions

Limes, cut into quarters

Sliced cabbage

Asian chili sauce, if you are brave

Chopped fresh cilantro or mint

Shredded carrots

TO MAKE 6 SERVINGS

Pick out the garnishes you want to serve with the noodles and chop, dice, and slice them. Put them in little bowls.

Ask your parents, nicely, to boil the pasta until it is al dente (not too mushy). Remind them gently that the pasta water should have enough salt to taste like the sea. When it is done, have them quickly rinse the pasta in cold water. Thank them for helping you.

Now mix all the ingredients for the peanut sauce together in a big bowl with a big spoon. You will have to stir, stir, stir until it is all mixed together and smooth (or you could get a parent to mix it all in a blender).

Taste the sauce ... is it perfect? When it is, toss in the pasta and pour into a pile on a big platter or bowl. Put the little bowls of garnishes around the platter, and yell *diiiiinner!*

Oh, Mama, It's
EDAMAME

Are you ready for this news flash? Edamame—otherwise known as baby soybeans—is as good a source of protein as meat or eggs! Nicknamed the "wonder vegetable," edamame is the only veggie that contains all nine essential amino acids. News flash number two: Kids love it!

Although savored for years internationally, edamame is fairly new to the U.S. market. It's now found in the frozen food section of most supermarkets. You can buy them in the pod (so much fun to suck out of their shells!) or shelled for easy adding to salads or grains. Fresh edamame are much harder to come by, and that's why growing them provides the ultimate bonanza. Edamame is the perfect plant to grow with your kids because you can just count the days until they pop up their green heads. The ones you grow yourself taste fantastic.

Fun to grow, fun to pick, fun to eat. Grab them right from the freezer and pop into some boiling water; when they float to the top, they are done. Serve the pods in a bowl with a sprinkling of salt or a side of low-sodium soy sauce, or toss the beans with brown rice and chopped scallions for a quick, nutritiously complete lunch or side dish. Yum!

The ABCs of Afternoon
SNACKS AND TEA

Well-timed, planned, and nutritious snacks help ensure that your child has the energy to do homework and run around outside, as well as to arrive for dinner in good humor and with a good appetite. Simple, healthy after-school snacks that require dipping, spreading, and flavor combining can be prepared ahead of time and left in the fridge. Make some of them sweet, some of them savory, some of them crunchy, and all with a goodly amount of healthy thrown in. Just as important, gather chairs or stools around the snacks, light a candle or two, and dig in together. You will no doubt hear stories about teachers, friends, and foes.

WHOLE WHEAT CRACKERS, CHEESE, AND SLICED APPLES Dip the apples and the cheese into honey or caramel. Serve with hot or cold apple juice.

GRAHAM CRACKERS AND PEANUT BUTTER Add a crock of honey to spread on top.

PRETZELS AND CELERY STICKS WITH MUSTARD AND CHIVE CREAM CHEESE Serve with hot apple cider.

SLICED ORGANIC TURKEY WITH SLICED CHEESE You can use large lettuce leaves to wrap up your slices, or wrap them around pretzels. Add some Dijon mustard and Thousand Island dressing to dip the wraps in, and serve with herbal tea—iced or hot.

FRESH STRAWBERRIES Dip them in vanilla yogurt and a little brown sugar, and serve with chamomile tea.

PITA CHIPS, CELERY, AND CARROTS And perhaps a bell pepper and a cucumber, too! Use some hummus (page 133) and tzatziki (page 133) for dipping. Serve with mint or spiced tea.

CRUNCHY CELERY STICKS WITH TOPS LEFT ON You can add some carrots, also peeled and left whole (with their tops on, too). Dip into peanut sauce (page 137), and serve with Asian crackers and decaf jasmine tea.

CUBES OF FRESH WATERMELON Dip a cube of watermelon in some crushed pumpkin seeds, then pop it in your mouth with a cube of feta cheese and a fresh mint leaf—yum! Serve with mint tea.

PERFECT PARFAIT Layer vanilla yogurt and sliced fruit in a tall glass. Top with a sprinkle of granola.

SNACK KEBABS Put cubes of low-fat cheese and grapes on pretzel sticks.

BERRY CONES Fill ice cream cones with chopped strawberries tossed with honey; top with vanilla yogurt.

"I LIKE CHILDREN,
if they're properly cooked."
—W. C. FIELDS, comedian

"We need to see the experience of cooking as less of a chore and more as an **OPPORTUNITY FOR ENGAGEMENT** *in the pleasures of life with your children and with your friends."* —DAN BARBER, executive chef and co-owner, Blue Hill, Blue Hill at Stone Barns, and Blue Hill Farm

LET'S PLAY

LIKES AND DISLIKES: *You need paper, pens*
Ask everyone to write down three of their likes and three of their dislikes on scrap paper. Help the younger ones by writing for them. Try to come up with things that won't be too obvious to your group. Read the cards one at a time and have everyone try to guess which family member the information belongs to.

LET'S PLAY

Everyone relate a memory from kindergarten.

DIP-INTOS: NUTRITIOUS DIPS You Can Make for Your Kids

HOMEMADE ONION DIP

YOU NEED

2 tablespoons olive oil

1½ cups diced onions

2 cloves garlic

¼ teaspoon kosher salt

1½ cups Greek yogurt (or low-fat sour cream)

1 teaspoon Worcestershire sauce

1 tablespoon chopped chives

Salt and pepper

TO MAKE 2 CUPS

In a large nonstick pan drizzled with the olive oil, sauté the onions and garlic over low heat until they are soft and caramelized, about 30 minutes. Remove from the heat and set aside to cool.

Mix the rest of the ingredients, and add the cooled onions. Season with salt and pepper.

Refrigerate for at least 1 hour before serving.

"As soon as I was old enough to peer over the worktops, I was **FASCINATED BY WHAT WENT ON IN THE KITCHEN.** *It seemed such a cool place,* **EVERYONE WORKING TOGETHER TO MAKE THIS LOVELY STUFF** *and having a laugh doing it."*

—JAMIE OLIVER, chef and author of *Jamie's Food Revolution: Rediscover How to Cook Simple, Delicious, Affordable Meals*

OUTWARD BOUND
The Great Restaurant Adventure

Is it still a family dinner if you're eating in a restaurant? Yes! Eating out is fun and relaxing when it's a special treat for everyone. It's a good time to experience new foods and cultures, and the perfect time to show off the manners you have practiced at home. But restaurant dining is only a success if everyone is happy, including other diners!

Also keep in mind that in restaurants, most "kid meals" are much higher in calories and fat than whatever you would normally prepare at home, thanks in part to the ubiquitous fries and soda. If possible, avoid the kid meals altogether. Try ordering off the main menu, or ask for an extra plate and share everyone's larger meal with the little ones.

Here are a few more things to consider when eating in restaurants. Those who should know—restaurateurs and their staffs—helped us compile this list of suggestions.

- Keep the kids at the table. Restaurants can be dangerous places, with hot dishes flying out of the kitchen, broken glass on the floors, and waiters and busboys racing back and forth.

- Order your young children's food first. Bring crackers or fruit in your bag for them to munch on while they wait.

- Always bring a distraction for your young gang such as a pad of paper and pencils, word games, or cards. While you're waiting for the meal to arrive, start asking fun questions. Friends of mine never go to a restaurant without a deck of cards. Gin rummy and hearts are now an integral part of their family fun together.

- Bring your own (BPA-free) sippy cups to reduce young children's spills (and disposable cups and straws). The hardworking busboys will thank you.

- Manners, manners, manners. Yours especially! Your kids will be watching (and learning) how you treat the wait staff, handle delays, deal with mistakes, and inquire about the check.

- Take a walk, outside. If young children start screaming, head outside to calm them down. Screaming kids are the quickest way to ruin everyone's dinner.

"Children are eating more **UNHEALTHY FOODS** *today and in ever larger sizes."*

—ROBERT WOOD JOHNSON FOUNDATION

FRESH TOMATO SALSA

YOU NEED

½ small jalapeño chile, seeded and deveined, minced (optional)

¼ small red onion

1 small clove garlic, minced

Small handful of chopped fresh cilantro leaves (about 2 tablespoons)

¼ teaspoon salt

Juice of ½ lime

2 ripe medium tomatoes, cut into chunks

TO MAKE ABOUT 1½ CUPS

Pulse all the ingredients except the tomatoes in a food processor until minced. Add the tomatoes and pulse until roughly chopped, about two 1-second pulses.

Or, if you want to do it by hand, finely dice the onions and tomatoes, then throw in the remaining ingredients.

HUMMUS/TAHINI SAUCE

YOU NEED

¼ cup tahini

2 tablespoons olive oil

1 small clove garlic

¼ cup fresh lemon juice

¼ cup water, or the liquid drained from the beans

1 15-ounce can organic chickpeas (garbanzos), drained

Salt

Optional toppings: parsley, olive oil, paprika, and cumin

TO MAKE 1½ CUPS

Put the tahini, olive oil, garlic, lemon juice, and water into a blender and blend away until it's frothy, white, and creamy. This is tahini sauce, and it can be used as a dip as well.

Take a handful of chickpeas and blend into the tahini sauce until smooth. Continue to blend in chickpeas a little at a time until the hummus has thickened, but isn't too thick, and is still pale. Add salt to taste.

Swirl the hummus into a shallow bowl, make a little well in the center, drizzle with olive oil, and sprinkle with spices.

Edamamus

Follow the recipe above but replace the chickpeas with 1½ cups of defrosted frozen edamame (soybeans).

GREEK TZATZIKI OR INDIAN RAITA

YOU NEED

½ medium hothouse cucumber or 3 small Persian cucumbers, peeled, seeded, and diced fine

1 cup Greek yogurt (regular or 2 percent)

1 tablespoon fresh lemon juice

1 small clove garlic, minced

1 tablespoon finely chopped fresh mint leaves or dill

Salt and pepper to taste

TO MAKE 1½ CUPS

Put the cucumber in a clean dishcloth or cheesecloth and squeeeeze out the moisture (this is important to avoid a runny tzatziki).

Combine the cucumber, Greek yogurt, lemon juice, garlic, and herbs. Season with salt and pepper to taste.

INDIAN RAITA

Add ½ teaspoon toasted cumin seeds, cayenne to taste, and chopped tomatoes and cilantro if you like. Omit the dill.

LET'S PLAY

Ask Mom and Dad:

Did they go to their high school prom?

With whom?

What fantastic outfits did they wear?

GUACAMOLE

YOU NEED

3 large, ripe Haas avocados

1 tablespoon chopped fresh cilantro or oregano

1 clove garlic, minced

2 tablespoons chopped red onion

Salt

Squeeze of lime

TO MAKE ABOUT 2 CUPS

Put the first four ingredients in a bowl and mash with a fork until smooth and creamy. Taste and add salt and lime until you think it is perfect.

TOASTED SESAME AIOLI

YOU NEED

½ cup light mayonnaise

1½ tablespoons Asian toasted sesame oil

2 teaspoons soy sauce

2 teaspoons fresh lime juice

½ teaspoon minced fresh ginger

1 clove garlic, minced

TO MAKE ⅔ CUP

In a small bowl, stir all the ingredients together.

HONEY MUSTARD SAUCE

YOU NEED

½ cup mild Dijon mustard

½ cup honey

2 tablespoons mayonnaise

1 clove garlic, grated

Salt and pepper to taste

TO MAKE ABOUT 1 CUP

Mix all the first four ingredients in a small bowl and season with salt and pepper to taste.

...⚬⚬⚬...

Tonight's Dinner Is

TOMORROW'S LUNCH

Since packing your child's lunch for school the next day is often an after-dinner ritual, it's fair game to sneak in a little green advice about the joys of waste-free lunches!

If you consider that there are about fifty-three million school-aged kids in America, that's a heck of a lot of juice boxes needlessly filling up the trash. Making your kids' lunch boxes free of throwaways will teach your children the value of reusing and save you money. Consider this: A lunch with the basic disposable items in it generally costs $4.02 per day, versus $2.65 for a waste-free lunch. That translates to a savings of about $246.60 per child per year (WasteFreeLunches.org).

Here is the big payoff for your child: **If every student adopted a waste-free lunch, more than three and a half billion pounds of trash would be kept out of our landfills each year.** That is something your child can be very proud of helping to accomplish!

- Do use "reusables" like fabric lunch bags, thermoses, and reusable containers. By choosing containers made out of high-quality materials, such as stainless steel and cloth, you can reduce your child's exposure to harmful chemicals found in plastics like phthalates and BPA as well as lead in older lunch boxes.
- Do pack water in stainless-steel water bottles. Good-bye juice boxes, good-bye extra sugar!
- Do buy healthy snacks (nuts, whole wheat crackers) in bulk and pack them in reusable containers.
- Do pack whole fruits—no need for packaging.
- Do tuck a cloth napkin in your kid's lunch box, perhaps one in a fun cotton or linen print.
- Do use stainless-steel or bamboo reusable utensils.

- Don't use plastic bags—but if you do, rinse and reuse them.
- Don't buy individually wrapped snacks, meals, or desserts—they are expensive, often loaded with fats, sugars, and preservatives, and use excessive packaging.
- Don't use disposable utensils, straws, and napkins.

RECIPES

Family Dinner

FIELD TRIPS

Continue the family fun by taking your gang on a food adventure. Pack your compass, a couple of canvas bags, and your wallet. It's time for some sightseeing with a delish twist! Why not make it a once-a-month ritual to explore a new food market or ethnic restaurant? Here are some family field trip ideas.

THE GROCERY STORE. If members of your family don't go shopping with you routinely, it's time for them to start. Everyone can and should experience the time it takes to shop for, pay for, and bring home groceries.

A LOCAL FARMER'S MARKET. The best way to purchase the freshest, in-season food and support your local farmers is also the best way to learn about fresh food—farmers love to share what they know.

THE FARM. Lots of small farm operations have visiting hours and "pick your own" days. From apples to pumpkins to berries to corn, it's a great way to show your kids where dinner comes from!

ETHNIC GROCERY STORES. Stores specializing in a particular culture's cuisine are eye-opening trips for the family. You and your kids will be amazed and inspired by all the foods and products you have never seen before. Don't forget to ask the proprietor how to use unfamiliar ingredients—they, like farmers, want to share their passion and knowledge.

ETHNIC NEIGHBORHOODS like Little Italy, Little India, Japan Town, Chinatown, Koreatown. Most larger cities have such community neighborhoods, and they are chock-full of markets and restaurants, many of them family-owned. Have lunch or dinner and taste authentic ethnic food perfectly cooked according to ancient traditions.

COOKING CLASS AS A FAMILY, either at a local cooking school or in your home (some teachers come right to your kitchen). Friends and family make great teachers, too! Ask them to teach a class.

FISH MARKET. See what fresh really looks and smells like (it doesn't smell "fishy")!

RESTAURANT SUPPLY STORE. Let your kids each pick out something inexpensive but exciting to use, like new measuring cups or mini spoons.

COMMUNITY GARDEN PROJECT. Take a tour, attend a plant sale or seed-saving swap, or sign up as a volunteer. See what your neighborhood gardeners are growing.

SOUP KITCHEN, SHELTER, OR FOOD PANTRY. Volunteer as a family at a church or Salvation Army program. It's a profoundly moving way to show your kids how they can have a real impact on other people's lives and, at the same time, show them the reality too many people face on a daily basis, most with dignity and courage. One in four children are going to sleep hungry in America. Need is up and food donations are down. This field trip will work wonders building up those gratitude muscles.

RECIPES

Green Tip

2.8 billion juice boxes end up in landfills every year. • An eight-ounce box of apple juice contains thirty grams of sugar and zero grams of fiber. A normal-size apple contains eighteen grams of sugar and three grams of fiber.

LET'S PLAY

CAR TALK
Ask your parents to describe
the first car they ever owned.

"A mind that is **STRETCHED BY A NEW EXPERIENCE** *can never go back to its old dimensions."* —OLIVER WENDELL HOLMES, poet, physician, and essayist

CHAN LUU'S TOFU SUMMER ROLLS WITH PEANUT SAUCE

*Our friend **Chan Luu** from Nhatrang, Vietnam, contributed this beautiful salad rolled up in a rice paper noodle wrapper. Make it in advance, or bring the rice paper noodles and vegetables to the table and let everyone make their own salad roll.*

"The majority of Vietnamese are Buddhists, and so is my family," Chan Luu says. "Throughout my childhood, at least once a month my mother prepared vegetarian offerings to God—a practice we believe cleanses our body and soul. This is one of those dishes and one of my favorites." Fresh herbs are the core ingredients in Vietnamese cooking. The bursting flavors of every bite will make a great fresh lunch or dinner any day.

TOFU SUMMER ROLLS

YOU NEED

1 package firm tofu, drained

1 tablespoon vegetable oil

1 package round Vietnamese rice paper noodles (can be found in the Asian section of most gourmet markets), about 8–9 inches in diameter

1 small bag (5–6 ounces) mixed baby lettuce (preferably spicy mix)

Thin slices of cucumber (2 slices per roll)

Julienned or shredded carrot (about 1 tablespoon per roll)

Fried shallots (can be found in most Asian markets)

1 bunch fresh mint

1 bunch fresh basil

1 bunch fresh cilantro

1 bunch garlic chives (or regular chives)

TO MAKE 6–8 ROLLS

Preheat the oven to 350 degrees.

Pat the tofu dry using a paper towel, and then coat the tofu with 1 tablespoon of vegetable oil. On a nonstick baking pan, bake the tofu until the outside layer is golden and crispy, about 20 to 30 minutes. Remove from the oven and let it completely cool, then cut it into thin slices.

Prepare a clean surface on your kitchen counter. Have ready a bowl of warm water and a clean kitchen towel.

Dip one of the rice paper noodles into the water very quickly. Let the water drip off the rice paper, and then lay it on the kitchen counter. To avoid too much water—which could make the rice paper soggy—use the kitchen towel to remove any excess water.

On the corner nearest to you, about 1 inch above the edge of the rice paper, start layering some mixed lettuce, tofu, 2 slices of cucumber, a pinch of carrot, a pinch of shallot, 2 mint leaves, 2 basil leaves, some cilantro, and some garlic chives. Pick up that end of the rice paper, fold it over the vegetables, then start rolling (away from you), slightly pressing as you roll so that your roll will be tight when it's finished. Be sure to let the tip of the garlic chives show through at the end.

PEANUT SAUCE

YOU NEED

1 tablespoon vegetable oil

1 clove garlic, crushed

2 tablespoons hoisin sauce

3 tablespoons peanut butter

1 cup water

Pinch of cayenne (optional)

1 teaspoon chopped roasted peanuts

TO MAKE 1¼ CUPS

Pour the vegetable oil into a small cooking pot. Over medium heat, fry the garlic until it's golden. Mix in the hoisin, peanut butter, and 1 cup of water. Reduce the heat and stir until everything is well combined and the consistency of heavy cream (if it's too thick, add some water). Sprinkle in a pinch of cayenne pepper. Garnish the sauce with crushed peanuts on top and serve at room temperature with Tofu Summer Rolls.

FUN FACTS

Two peanut farmers have been elected president of the United States—Thomas Jefferson and Jimmy Carter.

It takes about 540 peanuts to make a twelve-ounce jar of peanut butter.

"THINK OF YOUR KIDS' MEALS AS A RAINBOW, *literally a variety of colors on their plate or in their lunch box. As long as they aren't artificial colors* **YOU WILL BE GIVING THEM A NATURALLY BALANCED MEAL."** —KRISTEN TOBEY, co-founder of Revolution Foods, private supplier of school lunches

RECIPES

FOR SICKLY DAYS
or *Tricky Days*

When the World Is a Little Too Tough, and for Nights When the Sandman Has Lost His Way

MILK AND HONEY Warm a cup of milk and add enough honey to sweeten it.

VANILLA MILK Mix 1 cup of warm milk, 1 tablespoon of honey, and a dash of vanilla.

A LITTLE SOOTHING RICE SOUP Mix 3 cups of chicken or vegetable broth, 3 tablespoons white rice, and perhaps a teaspoon of chopped fresh garlic and healing ginger. Simmer for 20 minutes until the rice is soft and silky.

HOT LEMONADE Squeeze a goodly amount of lemon juice into a cup of hot water. Add honey to sweeten.

THE ABCs OF FEELING BETTER Cook a pot of alphabet pasta; add butter, salt, and toss lovingly.

A SNACK TO GET YOU BACK ON TRACK Toast a piece of bread. Butter it and, as the butter melts, sweetly slather it with honey and sprinkle with cinnamon. Or top the toast with peanut butter, sliced bananas, and a drizzle of honey.

HONEY IS HEALING

The ancient Egyptians used honey to treat cuts and burns.

A spoonful of honey can quiet children's nighttime coughs and help them— and their parents—sleep better.

For a sore throat, let a teaspoon of honey melt in the back of the mouth and trickle down the throat. This will ease inflamed raw tissues.

JAMIE OLIVER'S BIG WISH

CHEF JAMIE OLIVER *is on a mission, and we are going with him! He is the worldwide best-selling author of eleven cookbooks and beloved star of nine international television shows. But he's not stopping there. Jamie has a wish and it involves everyone. He wants every child to learn about food, where it comes from, and how to make it healthy and delicious.*

LAURIE: What are the top five things you think every teenager should know how to cook?

JAMIE: I think it's important that they learn a variety of meals where they use different cooking skills. Here is my list:

- A simple stir-fry to get them used to the idea of chopping, fast frying, and paying attention to what's going on in the pan.
- A great basic pasta dish like a spaghetti Bolognese so they can master the art of creating a really rich, lovely sauce and boiling pasta to perfection.
- A good basic salad—so they can make a tasty and healthy plate of food out of a few basic (and cheap) raw ingredients—and a really quick homemade dressing.
- A good roast dinner, so they can learn how to cook meat properly in the oven. Roast dinners are also brilliant because you've got to be organized to bring all the elements of the meal—the meat, the gravy, and the vegetables—together hot, steaming, and beautiful at the same time.
- A really hearty, simple stew so they have another cheap family meal in their repertoire and understand that slow cooking on a low heat can turn even the toughest bit of meat into something soft, sticky, and full of flavor.

LAURIE: What was your family dinner like growing up?

JAMIE: It was *always* 'round a table, together. Me, my dad and my mum, and my sister. My parents were big believers in the whole family eating together and so am I, but that's been lost today. Too many kids eating in front of the TV or the computer while Mum and Dad do something else. Dinner was always a good time to talk about what was going on at school, with friends and all that. My favorite "food love memory" has always been Mum's roast chicken with all the trimmings on a Sunday.

YOUR

GREEN TABLE

Why Your Choices Matter

10

How fantastic for all of us that the kitchen is *the* best room in the house to teach and to practice basic green values. Really, there is no easier way to embrace these goals than preparing for and enjoying family dinner.

But before I get all excited talking about my favorite topic, we need to embark on a small rescue mission for the word *green* itself. Five innocent little letters that have come into serious overuse in the last few years. Please don't hold that against them.

Green *is* a good, kind word meant to invoke so much more than its simple, verdant definition. It's a value system, a consciousness, a way of thinking, and a way of living. I believe it is one of the key values we all want to teach our children, and it's a concept that should permeate everything we do in the kitchen—shopping, cooking, eating, cleaning—without paralyzing us in the process. Being green is not about perfection, which is downright impossible anyway.

It is about connecting the dots so we understand where things come from and what impacts result from our use of them. It means making informed choices, reducing waste,

buying local, and even growing a little bit ourselves—salad greens in a pot, herbs or tomatoes on a windowsill or balcony. It's also about reducing your family's meat consumption because it's healthier for them and for the planet.

Thinking green is a conscious choice we make to try to live a sustainable life (to sustain: keep in existence, maintain), implementing changes when and where possible and adding more, incrementally, over time. It's an attitude and a gratitude adjustment. Believe me, once you get started you won't be able to stop! You will be amazed at all the ways you'll find to incorporate the concept easily into your kitchen routines, and how much happier you will be as a result. I'll even go so far as predicting you will feel a kind of euphoria once you've started down this path. It just feels better to be a good steward of yourself, your family, your home, and your planet.

"UNLESS SOMEONE LIKE YOU CARES A WHOLE AWFUL LOT, *nothing's going to get better. It's not."* —DR. SEUSS

Here's a way you can experience what I'm talking about this very evening while you are making dinner. Try this simple three-day kitchen experiment: Out of everything that you normally toss in the trash, put those items that can decompose into a big bowl or bucket instead.

COMPOSTING 101

Eggshells

Fruit rinds

Corn husks

Bottoms of your broccoli

Tops of your carrots

Old rice

Avocado skins

Onion skins

Tea bags

Coffee grounds

Brown wilted lettuce

Asparagus bottoms

The chips that fell onto the floor

First, you will not believe how much you routinely throw away (and seeing is believing!). Some of it is food scraps, but an awful lot of it is food waste, a result of buying too much. (The Environmental Protection Agency estimates that Americans generate roughly 30 million tons of food waste per year!)

Second, you'll start to realize that all those discards normally filling up a plastic garbage bag could instead be on the way to an important "second life" as compost—what gardeners call "black gold"—a great soil builder that could be enriching your yard or window boxes full of veggies and flowers. After taking a good hard look at what you collected after just three days, can you imagine the amount of food that would be in your bucket after a week? After a month?

Consider composting at home. There are lots of Web sites to help you get started (howtocompost.org). This could easily become one of the best science experiments your kids have ever done.

Post a list of biodegradable items on your fridge for the whole family to see (visit SimpleSteps.org for more suggestions) and ask everyone to help collect scraps. Warning: Your kids are really going to get into this! They genuinely want to be greener. They are learning about it at school and will be proud to practice it at home. Just watch their commitment grow! Soon they will reprimand you when they see something tossed in the garbage that they know doesn't belong there. (I swear it wasn't me who threw out that banana peel!)

This simple green act—questioning what gets thrown away—is a valuable lesson your family will apply to other aspects of their lives. It will happen naturally because everyone's eyes have been opened. That is one of the great rewards of green thinking. It gets into your head and then into your heart, and from there it's just a short trip to under your skin. Green thinking will start to direct you—like having your very own green guardian angel—to make better, healthier choices, to waste less, to appreciate more.

Green Tip

Save your egg cartons and bring them back to the farmer's market or your school for art projects.

EVERYTHING OLD IS NEW AGAIN

The values of thinking green are the values upon which our ancestors raised their families. Most Americans practiced green living before it had any label, out of both necessity and a sense of frugality that had to do with the "Waste not, want not" philosophy once ingrained into the American spirit. In the "old days," resources were limited, expensive, and difficult to come by, and it was patriotic to use them in the most efficient ways possible. Believe it or not, being green was, and remains, a truly "conservative" value.

Despite the way we are living now, there isn't an endless supply of anything—not even clean water or clean air—and it doesn't get more basic than that. Sheryl Crow, a fellow eco-warrior, learned much of her green consciousness from her mother, Bernice, who was an obsessive recycler and reuser. Her mom laughed when I asked her about it. "I think I was just cheap," she said. "We didn't have much money and that's what you did without thinking about it. You never wasted anything."

...⟨≈⊙≈⟩...

The average household throws away 14
percent of its food purchases.

Back in the day, foods and other staples weren't overprocessed and overpackaged, either. Every kind of food wasn't available anywhere, anytime. Seasons actually meant something and dictated what you could or couldn't eat. Late summer was a time for corn and tomatoes, and winter was for special treats like navel oranges and cranberries. Many families grew their own basics (carrots, squash, peppers, potatoes, and so on) and canned or pickled the extras. When you ran out, that was that. Looking back, was it such an "inconvenience" to have to wait for June to come around until you could buy strawberries again?

The waiting actually made things taste better. How delicious that first bite each spring of a sun-baked strawberry tasted after a long cold winter; or the first bite of summer's sweet corn ("Knee-high by the fourth of July" was the farmer's expression). Now all this food is available all year long, shipped from all over the world at a tremendous cost to the environment and our health, not to mention our beloved rituals and our taste buds.

This "everything, everywhere, anytime" food system is cheating us out of a seminal and sensual experience! It's tampering with the integrity of our food and our rituals! The comment "my food travels more than I do" sums that up perfectly. It's mind blowing that the food we eat every day journeys, on average, fifteen hundred miles. Even before it is loaded on that fossil-fuel-burning, CO2-spewing truck, ship, plane, or train, our food is sprayed in the field with

"IN THE 1930s, ALL FOOD WAS ORGANIC."

—GARY HIRSCHBERG, president and CEO, Stonyfield Farm

toxic petroleum-based chemicals; fertilized with more toxic petroleum-based chemicals (all of which run into and pollute our waterways); picked before it's ripe; and processed and stored in a warehouse (not adding anything to its nutritional value or freshness). Or it might be produced on a factory farm—one of the worst contributions to twenty-first-century food production. Then it's overpackaged in layers of cardboard, Styrofoam, and plastic, and loaded onto vehicles for transport—often for days or even weeks—to supermarkets across the country.

Grapes are a good example. Every year 270 million pounds arrive in California, most of them shipped from Chile. Their fifty-nine-hundred-mile journey in ships and trucks releases seven thousand tons of global warming pollution each year and three hundred tons of soot- and smog-forming pollutants. That's enough air pollution to cause hundreds of asthma attacks in urban Los Angeles. And what about all the chemicals those grapes were sprayed with? We are eating those along with the grapes.

Every step of the way, the modern industrialized process of supplying food to families decreases its original nutritional content (hey, that's not what I thought I was paying for!) and contributes to polluting our land, water, and bodies. A lose–lose situation if ever there was one. It's not sustainable, and it's not healthy on any level. Do we really need grapes year-round? I smell a family dinner discussion!

WATER, WATER EVERYWHERE . . .
But What Happens to All Those Bottles?

Another simple example of the impact of your choices at home is water. Quenching thirst with water is a habit your kids learn from you at the table. We want them drinking it, we want them choosing it over soda or high-calorie energy drinks, and even over most juices. A whopping 7 percent of an average American's calories come from soda (10 percent for children and teenagers). Those unhealthy calories are contributing to today's obesity epidemic.

What's So Bad About BPA?

We keep reading about the evils of BPA, but what the heck is it really? And how do we avoid it? Bisphenol A (BPA) is a chemical that can enter our bodies through food and drink. It is known to leach from hard (shatterproof) plastic containers such as baby bottles, reusable plastic water bottles, and sippy cups. BPA mimics estrogen in the body. Studies have shown serious effects including reproductive problems, altered behavior patterns, and even an increased risk of obesity and diabetes. In addition to its use in hard plastics, BPA is also used to line food cans (say it ain't so!) that hold everything from vegetables to baked beans, beer, infant formula, and soft drinks. Studies have shown that the chemical can leach out of these containers and contaminate the food. Until BPA is banned from food products, the healthiest thing to do, when possible, is to choose BPA-free plastics or products in glass containers.

We also want them to drink water the old-fashioned way, out of a glass. I know that sounds kind of radical, but there was a time when the idea of "buying" water was laughed at. Unfortunately, brilliant marketing and billion-dollar ad campaigns have turned bottled water into the "convenient" first choice for many people (beware that word *convenient*—it's often not). As a result we now have an entire generation of kids who are completely unfamiliar with the better, less expensive alternative: water from the kitchen tap.

...ᴄᴏᴏᴏ...

The United States goes through a hundred billion plastic shopping bags every year. An estimated twelve million barrels of oil is required to make that many plastic bags.

So here is my point: We need to understand the impact of that choice and then decide how many plastic water bottles we really want to go through each day. Americans buy twenty-five billion single-serve plastic water bottles a year, according to the Container Recycling Institute. If that includes you and your family, you're spending loads of money. The Earth Policy Institute (EPI) estimates that per person, the average family of four spends about $1,095 a year on bottled water—that's $4,380 total! If you don't like the taste of your tap water or want to purify it, why not buy a simple inexpensive filter that fits on your faucet?

Financially, buying water is about as crazy as buying air to breathe. We've gotten so used to this habit that it's become the new normal and we have completely lost track of the simpler, cheaper way of drinking water. Even worse, most of those billions of plastic bottles eventually end up in landfills and oceans, where they will take up space for close to a thousand years while trying their hardest to biodegrade, but never quite succeeding. Very few water bottles end up getting recycled. Two and a half million plastic bottles are thrown away every *hour*, so you can do the math on that one.

We also have to account for the fact that plastic bottles are made from oil, a very costly and scarce resource: About a million and a half barrels per year are devoted to satisfying America's bottled water habit, according to the Earth Policy Institute.

And as with all environmental issues, there is also a health component. While many people think the water they buy in a bottle is healthier and cleaner than tap, that is not necessarily true. New research concludes that the plastic bottle or jug that holds the water may actually be leaching toxic chemicals into it. Moreover, according to the congressional General Accountability Office (GAO), some water sold in plastic bottles is even *less* safe than tap water because it may be contaminated by chemicals during processing. Contrary to popular belief, bottled water does

not have to meet the same rigorous safety standards as tap water, so it might contain contaminants at levels that you wouldn't find in tap water. Drinking from plastic is a twenty-first-century habit that we may someday regret.

The subject of bottled water would make for a great family discussion at your next dinner. Once you talk over the facts, see if your family wants to commit to reducing its plastic bottle purchases. My family switched over a few years ago to stainless-steel reusable bottles with wide mouths that make drinking from and cleaning them easy. They are on our nightstands, in the gym bag, and waiting, filled up and cold, in the fridge. We haven't eliminated plastic bottles completely from our lives, but we've drastically reduced them. (Remember: Don't let the perfect be the enemy of the good.) Several Los Angeles schools have instituted their own policies and stopped selling plastic water bottles on campus, thereby substantially increasing the number of reusable bottles brought from home by students.

Okay—I'm done, and I'm showing serious restraint here because there is a heck of a lot I haven't covered, but it really amazes me how intricately connected all these environmental issues are with the family table—how our food is processed, what we buy and when, what we eat and how much we waste. As parents, our task is to consider all these issues so that we raise thinking, caring, mindful children. We have to set the table, metaphorically speaking. That's the best way for our kids to learn. We have to reinforce it every night we can, in our own kitchens. What an awesome opportunity, what a great challenge, what a beautiful learning experience for everyone.

V IS FOR VICTORY

During the 1940s, the U.S. government did a very smart thing: It called on its citizens to help our brave soldiers fighting the war in Europe. How? Simply by stepping into their own backyards, grabbing a shovel, and planting a vegetable garden.

Food was scarce and prices high during both world wars. The government turned to the public for help and asked the country to start growing their own food. Thus "victory gardens" were born!

Millions of people heard the call, and vegetable gardens began popping up everywhere. As a way to lower food costs, it worked better than anyone imagined. **By the end of the war, there were some twenty million backyard gardens producing ten million pounds of fresh fruit and vegetables each year. That amounted to an astonishing 40 percent of the fresh produce consumed in the United States at the time.** Growing your own vegetables was viewed nationwide as an honorable way to serve your country. Gardening became a family pastime and a national morale booster.

Today we have plenty of reasons to reignite that good old-fashioned victory garden patriotism. Economic pressures and concerns over food safety are just two reasons. Tackling obesity and food-related health problems, recapturing how our food is grown, cutting back on processing, rising hunger rates, and improving healthy eating overall offer a few more. Whatever the reason that inspires us individually, and as a country, we desperately need a new victory garden movement sweeping across the lawns of America!

The White House felt it, too, and did something that hadn't been done in decades: They tore up some grass and poured the compost on. **The Obamas planted the first vegetable garden on the White House grounds since Eleanor Roosevelt's victory garden during World War II.**

"The garden was something I always thought about," **Michelle Obama** explained at the time. "Like most busy moms, and working families, I would find it difficult to feed my family in a healthy way, quickly. I decided to change our diet. And it was really simple things like adding more fruits and vegetables, trying to sit down as a family and prepare a meal a couple of times a week, eating out a little less, eliminating processed and sugary foods as much as possible. And I saw some really immediate results with just those minor changes . . . The garden is a part of that. It is a really important introduction to what I hope will be a new way that our country thinks about food."

Let's get digging. V is for Victory!

AN APPLE A DAY

When you bring a doctor's prescription to the drugstore and the pharmacist hands it right back to you with a confused look on his face, you know something strange is going on. That's because the prescription in question is for a corn, tomato, and cilantro salad, and it can only be filled at your local farmer's or produce market.

DR. PRESTON MARING writes these kinds of directives every day, because he believes that **what people eat is the major ingredient in their personal health.** He is so passionate about the importance of fresh, seasonal food that he did something completely unique—he started a farmer's market at the hospital where he works, the Kaiser Permanente East Bay Medical Center in Oakland, California. Dr. Maring decided fresh food would be a lot more useful to his patients than the typical hospital gift shop's trinkets and toys. "When about 35 percent by weight of all the food eaten in the United States is either fast food or pizza, it makes sense for health care providers and medical care programs to start looking for ways to make a big difference," he says.

This big idea helped his entire community, bringing everyone together: the farmers by providing customers for their produce, and the patients by giving them easy access to fresh local ingredients. "One of my patients started shopping at the market every Friday after a lifetime of eating fast foods. She saw real and significant changes in her weight and health. I'm just your basic doctor, but I am on a mission to try to change the health of lots of people," he says. It's working: Today there are more than thirty-two farmer's markets affiliated with Kaiser Permanente medical facilities across the country.

Since starting the farmer's market, the doctor himself has become an avid cook and now offers a recipe a week to anyone who needs some inspiration (kp.org/farmersmarketrecipes).

"I see a lot of patients and I have become convinced that a sharp chef's knife, two cutting boards—one for meat, one for vegetables—and a salad spinner are the most important public health tools there could be," Dr. Maring says. Doctor knows best!

GREEN ANGEL CHALLENGE: Twenty-five More Things You Can Do

Now that you are starting to compost and reduce your water bottle purchases, here are a few more ways to up those green credentials. These are all easy things you can do to become more self-sufficient, reduce the amount of waste your family produces, eat healthier, save money, and teach your kids respect for the land that provides us with so much.

- Support your local farmer's market. Make it a regular family field trip.

- Buy organic when possible (see sidebar at right).

- Be a nag! Bug your grocer to carry more organic produce (if it's in season, of course) and pasture-raised meat.

- Turn your stale bread into bread crumbs or croutons, toss uneaten vegetables and cheese rinds into soup, save chicken or turkey bones and make stock. (Pour it into ice cube trays and freeze the cubes so you have just the right amount when you need it.)

- Complain to the store manager when organic items you want to buy are overpackaged. I found organic zucchini last week that was plastic-wrapped within an inch of its life, nestled in a Styrofoam tray. Ugh!

- Follow the Michael Pollan rule . . . the first five ingredients need to be recognizable as food. If your grandmother wouldn't recognize the ingredients, leave it on the shelf.

- Try to stay away from "individual" portions—they cost more on every level.

"I have discovered that **EATING SIMPLE FOOD** *made from simple ingredients is the* **TRUEST WAY TO LOVE YOURSELF** *and those around you."* —MARIEL HEMINGWAY, actress, author of *Mariel's Kitchen: Simple Ingredients for a Delicious and Satisfying Life*

- Make enough food for leftovers. (Some things even taste better the second time around.)

- Say no to plastic bags! Bring your own bags (keep a bunch in your car) and don't put things in smaller produce bags that don't need it, like apples, asparagus, or celery. Bagging everything is so forever ago.

- Don't buy more than you really need. This requires pre-planning and list making, but it's worth it. So much money and food goes down the drain because we overbuy.

- Get to know your local food bank, and support it. A recent national report states that food bank donations are down 9 percent, but demand is up 20 percent.

...·e·ↄ)i(ⲉ·e·...

IN A SIMPLE BOX OF BLUEBERRIES
After being washed, a box of blueberries was tested by the USDA, and an astonishing forty-three different pesticides were detected.

...·e·ↄ)i(ⲉ·e·...

THIRTEEN
FRUITS AND VEGGIES
You Should Try to Buy Organic

Because it's always better to minimize exposure to toxic chemicals, it's a really good idea to choose organic foods like milk and produce when you can.

Conventionally grown food may silently sneak antibiotics, pesticides, or hormones into your home and onto your child's plate. There is a growing consensus in the scientific community (and among concerned moms!) that even small doses of pesticides and other chemicals can have adverse effects on health. On top of that, it's just common sense. We aren't interested in feeding our kids chemicals, thank you very much.

WHAT YOU REALLY WANT TO BUY ORGANIC
(because they tend to have the highest pesticide residue)

Apples	Peaches
Celery	Pears
Cherries	Carrots
Grapes	Kale
Lettuce	Strawberries
Nectarines	Bell peppers
	Blueberries

Download the Environmental Working Group's wallet-size guide to organic produce at FoodNews.org—there's even an iPhone app!

"As the garden grows, **SO GROWS THE GARDENER."** —ANONYMOUS

- Replace your Teflon cookware with better nonchemical choices like stainless steel, copper, and cast iron.
- Grow a windowsill salad bar and herb garden!
- Join a fruit and vegetable co-op or CSA (which stands for "Community Supported Agriculture"). This is a group of people who join together and pay a set weekly or monthly fee to have whatever is fresh delivered to their door.
- Do an overhaul of your cleaning supplies and make your own (see page 151), or buy supplies that do not contain toxic chemicals.
- Only run your dishwasher when it is completely full— and run it in the early morning or overnight when there's less demand on the energy grid. Let things air-dry when possible.
- Use recycled paper products. Buying paper towels and napkins made from hundred-year-old trees makes no sense. Choose post-consumer recycled paper products. Reduce the number of paper plates and plastic you use. Rinse and reuse take-out containers.
- Start a new habit: Use cloth napkins during meals and dishcloths to dry your hands instead of reaching for paper towels. Hide those paper towels.
- Ask the butcher in your supermarket where the meat comes from. Ask for organic, grass-fed beef. Buy and cook less meat.
- Don't buy soda. Make that a treat when you go to parties.
- When ready, replace old appliances with energy-efficient ones.
- Start a no-waste lunch policy at your kids' school.
- Start reducing your disposables. Make a family list at dinner of everything that the family uses once or twice that could be replaced with a nondisposable. This will be an eye-opening activity. (Two billion disposable razors are thrown away every year. Maybe we can do better.)
- Say no to Styrofoam. Don't buy it for your home or office. Twenty-five billion Styrofoam cups are thrown away every year! There are earth-friendly alternatives available everywhere now.
- Curb your faucet. Rinse your dishes and produce in a bowl or basin, not under running water. Use the water you washed the produce with to water your plants.

TO WRAP OR NOT TO WRAP . . .
That Is the Question!

I started thinking about the amount of plastic wrap we were using in the kitchen when I began to notice that everyone in my house had what I would call a plastic problem. Actually it was more serious than that, it was an addiction—heretofore undiagnosed—to plastic wrap, the classic kitchen staple that conveniently covers food but ends up living in landfills forever. Plastic doesn't biodegrade: Every single piece used to cover a bowl, going back to its invention around 1957, still exists!

Where was I? Oh, yes. As we were all cleaning up after dinner, I watched my kids and my sister wrap leftovers—and then, to my horror, wrap them again, and again. Clearly an intervention was needed and alternatives considered. Tupperware works, although we had plenty of bottoms but not enough tops that fit them. (Sound familiar? Kind of tired of that old problem!) Tupperware is plastic, too, but at least it can be used for years and years. Start trying to completely eliminate plastic from your life and you will soon reel from frustration. (By the way, when did they start adding those plastic nozzles to every carton of milk or juice?)

Looking for ways to become "plastic wrap reducers," we started using glass bowls with plates placed on top as lids, and that works nicely for some things. Increasing our beloved Ball Jar allotment was already in the works. Those see-through jars make finding leftovers, salad dressings, and sauces really easy—and have the added bonus of being chemical-free.

Kirstin was working hard on her own plastic problem, one day at a time. The moment I knew we were all out of the woods was the day she showed up with her very own solution . . . shower caps! They were still plastic, yep, but they could be used over and over again. They work great on almost all sizes of bowls and containers, including all that lidless Tupperware clogging the cupboards! They keep things fresh in the fridge or on the counter (never microwave with it, of course). They even come in fun bright colors, will amuse your friends and relatives, and are as cheap as a bag of chips. This might be the craziest idea in this book but I promise you, it works!

...∞∙∞...

Make Your Own

CLEANING PRODUCTS
By Ed Begley Jr.

It's fairly common knowledge that I have a line of nontoxic household cleaners (called Begley's Best, in case you haven't heard). I'm here today, like any good pitchman, to charm, beg, coerce, and implore you to give nontoxic cleaning a chance. If you do, I promise that you'll have a clean house, help protect your personal environment, *and* save some money.

Here's the kicker: I'm *not* here to pitch a single one of my products. Instead, I want to encourage you to make your own.

And if you do, *you'll really* save some dough and lower your carbon footprint by saving a trip to the store. Why? Because you probably already have all the basic ingredients needed to make your very own line in the comfort of your home, including the empty spray bottles or jars to hold the concoctions (please wash them out first).

Here are the simple recipes. Give them a try—you won't be disappointed.

GLASS AND SURFACE CLEANER

2 cups white distilled vinegar

2 cups water

Swirl together in a spray bottle, then apply as you would any glass cleaner. Wipe with a clean, soft cloth.

HOUSEHOLD CLEANSER

2 cups baking soda

1 cup liquid castile soap (available at drugstores)

4 teaspoons vegetable glycerin (available in health food and drugstores)

Mix in a bowl and keep in a jar. Apply with a damp cellulose sponge or clean lint-free rag. Wipe with a damp sponge.

DRAIN OPENER

1 cup baking soda

1 cup vinegar

Pour the baking soda down the drain and follow with the vinegar. Cover the drain and let it sit for at least 30 minutes. Flush with a kettle full of boiling water.

GROWING VEGETABLES
By Dominique Browning

I have never been very good at growing vegetables. I want to do it. I try to do it. I try really hard. Every spring I buy small tomato plants, along with carrot, beet, string bean, and zucchini seeds, and I plant them dutifully in a patch of earth near the flower beds so that I can keep an eye on things. All starts well. I fuss, I hover, I water, I murmur. But every summer, without fail, something goes wrong. Trouble comes when I least expect it . . . well, why should life among vegetables be any different from life among humans? Just as I'm fantasizing about my mozzarella and tomato salads, just as I'm beginning to plan my ratatouille, the rabbits decide to throw a party, or the slugs and snails have an orgy.

Last spring, I gave up. What I'm really good at growing is herbs. So rather than let the brussels sprouts break my heart yet again, I doubled up on basil, mint, sage, rosemary, thyme, verbena, comfrey, and chamomile. I enlarged a bed right next to the kitchen door, so that the bunnies would have to knock if they wanted a snack. And I discovered some remarkable things.

First, children of all ages love herbs. There is nothing more satisfying than asking a young man, the kind of young man who normally can't tell a rose from a hydrangea, to go out and snip a few stalks of basil for the salad. The promise of dinner will put his learning curve on fast-forward.

Second, herbs are fantastic for hot baths—a few sprigs of lavender in the evening's tub will help you sleep; a few sprigs of rosemary in the morning bath will put a spring in your step.

Third, an herb garden will inspire you to master the art of infusions: Verbena steeped in hot water will help you fight your child's cold; a tea of rosemary or mint at the end of dinner aids digestion. And the whole family can participate in mixing and serving concoctions from the garden. Herbal infusions are the perfect end to a family dinner.

As for the vegetables: Last winter, I had tossed the remains of a delicious roasted squash dish onto an old compost pile, in a far corner of the garden. Several months later, I noticed a curious vine sprawled across the top of the pile. It was covered with beautiful yellow flowers. I forgot about it until this fall, when I discovered that I had a gorgeous crop of acorn squash crowning my compost. Maybe raising vegetables is like raising children. It's when you don't know what you're doing, when you don't plan or push or prod, that the most amazing things happen.

DINNER GUEST RECIPE
SUMMER CORN, TOMATO, AND CILANTRO SALAD

BY DR. PRESTON MARING

Make this recipe when the first fresh corn of the season becomes available. Once when I made this, I got so excited that I forgot to cook the corn. Turns out the raw, fresh, young kernels were crunchy, sweet, and perfect as is.

YOU NEED

4 ears fresh corn, husked

1 pint cherry tomatoes, stemmed and halved

½ red onion, diced

⅓ cup chopped cilantro

Juice of ½ lemon

1 tablespoon red wine vinegar

2 tablespoons olive oil

Salt and freshly ground pepper

Salad greens (optional)

TO MAKE 4 SERVINGS

Mix everything together. Mound on top of fresh salad greens. Serve. Marvel at what you created.

A PANTRY ON YOUR PATIO

Even with the growing awareness of how beneficial it is to grow some of our own food, a lot of us think that it's only possible for people with a lot of space. That's not true!

This summer on a small patio and with a few containers, dirt, and seeds, we grew a salad of baby greens in nineteen days! And not just one salad, either; we kept picking from that container for weeks. Our little tomato plant produced eighty-nine tomatoes (yes, we counted)! And not once did we have to buy overpriced herbs in a plastic container, because they were happily growing in a box outside.

"It's bizarre that the **PRODUCE MANAGER** *is more important to my children's health than the pediatrician."* —MERYL STREEP, actress

"Eating **VEGETABLES YOU GROW YOURSELF** *is the single* **GREENEST THING** *you can do."*

—MICHAEL POLLAN, author of *The Omnivore's Dilemma*

PLANTS WANT TO GROW!

That is what they are bursting inside their little seed shells to do. All they need is a little bit of help from you.

STEP 1. Read the seed package! It will tell you exactly how your seeds like to live.

STEP 2. Get some containers. You can use a traditional planting pot, but how about being playful and recycling some of that old stuff lying around—buckets, boots, and big old pots?

STEP 3. Make sure there are a couple of drainage holes in the bottom of each container, throw in a handful of gravel or pottery shards to help water drain out, and top with rich earth bought from a garden center or borrowed from a neighbor's yard (with permission, of course).

STEP 4. Pat in your seeds, remember to keep the soil moist, and give them plenty of sunlight.

STEP 5. Be amazed, delighted, and filled with satisfaction! The food *you* grow will be the best you ever taste.

Green Tip

Ask the people at your plant store what will grow best in your containers. Chances are they will be plants with cutesy, bubbly names like tiny, mini, thumb, dwarf, tot, baby . . .

LET'S PLAY!

BROCCOLI MOMENT

At some point during dinner, exclaim "Broccoli moment!" Everyone grabs a piece of broccoli, holds it up, counts 1, 2, 3, and everyone together munches down. Not sure why, but for the little ones it works like a charm! (This moment can be dedicated to any vegetable you are serving.)

"*I think* **EVERYBODY SHOULD HAVE A LITTLE GARDEN.** *No matter where you live, having green things growing around you changes how you feel.*"—OPRAH WINFREY

TABLE TALK

11

CREATIVE IDEAS TO EXPAND MINDS, BUILD VOCABULARIES,
AND KEEP FAMILY CONVERSATION FLOWING

Dinner is as much about digestible conversation as it is about delicious food. Yet many people find this aspect of a meal harder to do than whipping up the main course. If that's you, take comfort—you're not alone. As strange as it may sound, not everyone knows how to talk to one another. One of the more common replies people give when asked about their childhood dinners is, "No one spoke; we just ate."

As basic an effort as talking is, if you have ever sat at a table with people who don't do it, five minutes can seem like an eternity. Hearing "Pass the potatoes" becomes a cause for celebration. No wonder so many people turn on the television!

Don't assume I had it easier than anyone else just because I had a professional comedian at my table. Believe it or not, my ex-husband wasn't very good at table talk, and there were many nights when I kicked him (gently of course) under the table to remind him to engage. He didn't have dinner conversation role models growing up, either. His own childhood family dinners were about yelling, *not* talking, and meals were about refueling, not socializing. I'm guessing "Savor your food, Larry," was probably not a sentence he ever heard in his small Brooklyn kitchen.

And of course, in my family, I wouldn't exactly call what went on talking, either . . . it was more like tiptoeing around sensitive subjects, accidentally wading into the wrong territory, lots of arguing, and then tears. There were also those miserable awkward years from eleven to thirteen when all we talked about at dinner was how accident-prone I was. I must have knocked over that glass of milk a hundred times! The expression "Don't cry over spilled milk" wasn't coined in my house. Spilled milk was a perfect reason to cry!

"LISTENING *is the art by which we* *use empathy to* REACH ACROSS THE SPACE BETWEEN US. *Passive attention is not enough."*

—MICHAEL P. NICHOLS, author of *The Lost Art of Listening*

DEIPNOSOPHIST:
Noun. A person skilled in table talk.

My own personal experience tells me that pleasant, lively banter in the form of *one conversation*, with everyone participating, is not always easy to do—especially when exhaustion sets in at the end of the day. Let's face it, most of us are in need of conversation first aid!

One of the great benefits of family dinner is the opportunity it provides to teach our children how to carry on a conversation. Basic skills like listening, waiting your turn to speak, and not interrupting others are all modeled and learned at the table. A friend reminiscing about her family dinners wistfully said to me, "I loved our dinners because I really felt listened to."

A common thread of family dinners among previous generations was the expectation that everyone came to the table ready to talk and share. I heard this repeatedly from people I interviewed for this book. Being a good conversationalist is a skill that will serve your kids well their entire lives, but it requires practice.

If you take away meals, there aren't a lot of other opportunities in the day to practice, especially for teenagers. They are in danger of losing their conversation skills altogether thanks to their number one choice for communication: text messaging. This popular form of talking is actually anti-conversation, preferring instead to encourage shortcuts, abbreviations, and code-like spelling. One parent told me he communicates with his kids by text message inside his own house. ("It's the easiest way to reach them!")

"WE KIND OF BLEW IT WHEN OUR DAUGHTER HIT ADOLES- CENCE. *She got so surly and uncommunicative that in an act of self-preservation,* **WE STOPPED SITTING AT THE TABLE** *and started eating in front of the TV. If I had thought to play games at the table, I think we could have gotten through that stage better."* —SARAH, mom of one daughter

Another parent complained that conversation at her table is an opportunity for her daughter not to communicate. "My thirteen-year-old doesn't want to talk to me and seems offended by my desire to talk to her."

Table talk games are your solution! No more "How was your day?" . . . "Fine," followed by silence. These games will loosen everyone up and get your gang talking, guaranteed.

Remind your group that it's everyone's responsibility to be a good dinner guest. (Hey, there's no free lunch . . . I mean dinner!) A positive attitude and a participatory spirit are enough to get the ball rolling, and if you don't have either, start anyway. Chances are good that the silent grumps will jump in if they see you having fun. Persevere. It took awhile to make this great food; you want the experience of dinner to last. Good conversation will help extend the time your family is engaged, sometimes long after the last bite.

Some of these ideas are just for warm-up, some are to get everyone thinking, and some offer a chance to teach a little bit. That's the beauty of the captive audience: It gives you the perfect opportunity to sneak some learning in without anyone even noticing (and if they don't notice, they can't object!). As long as you make it fun, you can pretty much get away with anything—even reviewing SAT test words, or memorizing the presidents of the United States in chronological order.

"Don't take **EYE ROLLING** *as an insult. Think of it this way: At least they are listening."* —WENDY MOGEL, PhD, author of *The Blessing of a Skinned Knee*

AS YOUR VOCABULARY EXPANDS, So Does Your World

When playing a new word game, put everyone at ease by defining the word and giving an example. You want everyone to participate and not feel like they are going to be judged, ridiculed, or teased (so no judging, ridiculing, or teasing). Toss some easy ones to the kids at the table who might need extra encouragement. Ask direct questions; call on people by name. Be the leader.

Another tip: Know your crowd. Not every word game works for every group. What my teenager will play now at the table has shifted since she hit the oh-so-pleasant "I refuse to cooperate" age of fifteen. Younger kids are generally game for everything and will amaze you with how quickly they catch on. Set them up for success by adapting the game to their abilities and interests. Call on them first. They can hardly wait to get started!

With a few variations and modifications, these games can work for all ages. You can also play many of them in restaurants—where they can help put an end to antsy-pants squirming while young ones wait for their food to arrive. These games and conversation starters work wonders to equalize the playing field—no one person can monopolize the conversation or recede quietly into the background.

A really wonderful bonus to playing these kinds of verbal games is the amazing responses your children come up with that you didn't anticipate. What a great way to encourage them to think, reflect, learn, and express! Sharing a meal is fun. That's the take-away lesson these games will provide.

Getting-to-Know-You GAMES

You think you know your group really well? Don't be so sure. Try these games and I guarantee, you will all learn something new about one another!

Pet Peeves and Idiosyncrasies

Pet Peeves and Idiosyncrasies is a favorite game at the David household; we never get tired of playing it (perhaps because we have so many of both!). It's also a great icebreaker with new guests.

First of all, pet peeves and idiosyncrasies are very different although they are commonly confused. It's fun to have your family debate the subtle difference. Ask each person to name a pet peeve and one of their idiosyncrasies (you can do them as separate rounds, together, or one-a-night). My daughter Romy wants me to include her pet peeve here but I hope it won't confuse you because this one actually crosses the line between the two: She doesn't like it when people make dents in their pile of ketchup on their plate. If they dip a fry in it, she feels they should smooth it out afterward to get rid of the holes. I will let you decide that one, but feel free to challenge respondents if you think a pet peeve is really an idiosyncrasy. Our friend Bella's pet peeve is dogs that lick her face. What is yours?

Addendum: If your family has a good sense of humor and they aren't sensitive types, you could also play a version of this game where you name one another's idiosyncrasies and pet peeves (believe me, they know more of your quirks than you do!). Of course, this version is for advanced (thick-skinned) players only!

Limitations and Virtues

I like this one because it really makes everyone think and it gives you insights into the responder. First, provide an explanation of what a limitation is and what a virtue is. Then the self-reflection begins. If I was playing this round, I might say: "One limitation I have is that I can't carry a tune—I'm completely tone-deaf." Everyone at the table who knows me would at this point voice their hearty agreement, and then my sister would tell an embarrassing story about

when I was twelve, which most of the table would enjoy immensely even though they have heard it many times before. This is the goal of table games, to lead everyone to great family stories and good conversations.

For a virtue, my answer would be: "I always make an effort to carry my own reusable bags when I go shopping." Everyone would groan and roll their eyes—but ultimately agree that this is indeed a fine virtue!

My Special Talent Is

Here's a way to reveal something you're good at that no one else knows about. For example, my special talent is that I am really good at making delicious, unusual sandwiches from whatever happens to be in the fridge. I think this is a really handy skill to have in life! Another friend might reveal that she is accomplished at applying false eyelashes. Your neighbor might have been a jump rope champion in elementary school. You never know what you'll learn with this game!

Something I Like About Myself

Self-explanatory. Play this quick game with your little ones.

What I Know About You or What I Like About You

There are two ways to play this one. You can pick one featured person at the table, and have everyone tell one thing they know about him or her. After you go around the table, you pick the next person. Or you can answer the question based on who is sitting next to you so that each person is passing the ball to the person to the left or right. If you want, you can use a spoon, or the saltshaker, or any fun item that you can pass around to the next speaker. This will help little ones keep track of whose turn it is and build excitement for the moment that spoon is in their little hands. For example, I am sitting next to Cazzie who is sitting next to Bella who is sitting next to Alex who is sitting next to Ben.

I start by saying, "I know that Cazzie got high scores on her world civ exam." I pass the spoon to Cazzie, and she looks at Bella and says, "I know that Bella got stung by a bee yesterday and didn't even cry." Cazzie passes the spoon to Bella, who looks at Alex and says, "I know that Alex loves Legos," and so on. This simple game teaches your gang so much. Along with just being fun, your kids learn to listen to one another without interrupting, to patiently wait for their turn, to come up with positive things to say about one another, and to make the most of their moment in the sun.

Start clockwise (explain what that means) and then reverse it (counterclockwise—teach them that, too). If the game is working and you want to do a bonus round, have the leader pick someone from the table in their head and say something they know about the person. The group has to guess who they are talking about.

I Remember When . . .

Everyone completes the sentence. Decide whether the sentence will be something about yourself, or something about another person at the table. As in, "I remember when I couldn't stop hiccuping in class." Or, "I remember when Mom locked the keys in the car." This game is really fun with siblings. We played last night and it's funny how my sister has completely different memories than I do—or in some cases, no memory at all! I said that I remember when she locked me in the garage when I was eight and she, strangely, had no idea what I was talking about.

Would You Rather . . .

Would you rather be really good at one thing or just okay at a lot of things?

Would you rather listen to an opera on the radio or watch golf on TV?

Would you rather prepare Thanksgiving dinner or clean all of the dishes?

Would you rather go bowling or shopping for pants?

Would you rather sit next to a brilliant person at dinner who smelled bad, or a boring person who smelled fantastic?

Would you rather jump in a cold pool or do an extra hour of homework?

Have your group come up with more Would You Rathers!

Name Change

Taking turns around the table, everyone says what they would call themselves if they could change their names today. (It's a good question in general: Do you like your name?) Bonus round: Go around the table and let each person rename the person sitting next to them.

CONVERSATION-STARTER QUESTIONS

Here is a list of classic (and not-so-classic) questions to get the fun started at your dinner table. One question a night might be all you need. If no one volunteers to go first, then you jump in to set the example. Make sure everyone has a chance—but if a conversation erupts, let it go on! The point of this is to get the talking ball rolling, not to play Twenty Questions. One question might be all it takes.

- What was your high for today and what was your low?
- Tell me one thing that made you happy today (or one thing that makes you happy in general).
- Name something you are afraid of. Okay, true story: It was a holiday dinner and I tossed this question out to those at the table. My twenty-four-year-old niece Amy volunteered first and announced that she had never told anyone before, but she had a terrible fear of . . . sponges. She couldn't use them, she couldn't touch them, and she

"PEOPLE AREN'T NECESSARILY PRESENT WHEN THEY TALK TO YOU. *We are losing the capacity for normal conversation.*"

—SUSAN STIFFELMAN, author of *Parenting Without Power Struggles*

couldn't be near them. I am not exaggerating when I tell you that the table fell into a stunned silence for a few seconds and then everyone burst out laughing. I'm laughing again just retelling this episode here! Romy, my twelve-year-old at the time, topped it when she asked a serious follow-up question: "Can you eat sponge cake?" Moral of the story: You never know what new things you will learn about your own family!

- Name a fear you would like to conquer.
- Name three places where you would never go.
- Name three things you would want to have on a deserted island. (And it can't be anything that needs charging! That's the beauty of a deserted island!)
- Come up with a family motto or mission statement: for example, "Work hard, be kind"; "Leave the world a better place than you found it"; "Never drink coffee after three."
- Name some things you take for granted.
- Finish the sentence: *Thank you for . . .*
- What is your perfect birthday dinner? Your perfect birthday day?
- Name all the pets you have had. (This is a great way for kids to hear about your pets growing up!)

"If you **ACCEPT A DINNER INVITATION** *you have the* **MORAL OBLIGATION** *to be* **AMUSING."**

—WALLIS SIMPSON, Duchess of Windsor

- Name something that causes you anxiety or makes you nervous.
- Describe your dream vacation. Give lots of details.
- Name two things you do to help you relax.
- What is the grossest thing you have ever eaten?
- What will be obsolete in the future? (Obsolete: no longer around in the future.)
- How is middle school different from elementary school?
- Who has been in a school play? Do you remember any lines from it?
- Who is nicer in high school: boys or girls?
- Have you ever been the victim of peer pressure? Give an example. (It would be great if a parent goes first, describing what this means and providing an example from his or her own experience.) Have you ever been a bully?
- What is your best feature? What is your worst?
- What are you more courageous about today than you were two years ago?
- Parents, were you ever grounded? Details, please.
- Parents, tell your kids all the places you have traveled.
- If you could speak an animal language for a day, which would you pick?
- Which sport in the Olympics would you wish to excel in?
- Fill in the blank: *I wish . . .*
- If you had free lessons for a year, what would you like to learn?
- Do you have a recurring dream? Describe it.
- Name some clues that tell you it's spring, fall, summer, or winter.

I Never

This is a game of elimination; your five fingers are the only equipment necessary. Go around the table and say something you have never done. For example, I have never eaten a tomato. If anyone else at the table has eaten a tomato, they raise one finger. The next person goes . . . "I never watched an episode of *M*A*S*H*." Your statements need to be truthful and reasonable (for example, if you are a guy, you can't say, "I never had a baby"). When all five fingers are raised, you are out. The object is to come up with enough common things that you're never done but others surely have and by doing so you knock others out. The person with the fewest fingers raised wins. This game will be frequently interrupted by requests for explanations, stories, and so on. That is a good thing; let it roll.

WORD GAMES

A Simile, a Metaphor, and an Oxymoron

This is a fun game to play when your kids are learning grammar in school and offers a great brushup for the adults who probably have fond memories of the English teacher who taught it to them. That's another idea: Tell your kids stories about your favorite or least favorite teachers. (See, Mom and Dad had to go through it, too!)

Define a simile and a metaphor, and then everyone comes up with one and decides which it is. Oxymorons are fun to think up, too. Give them a few examples and keep adding to your list. Be creative, use your imagination, have fun.

SIMILE

Noun. A figure of speech likening one thing to another by the use of *like, as,* et cetera. Example: Tears flowed like wine.

METAPHOR

Noun. A figure of speech in which one thing is spoken of as if it were another. Example: All the world's a stage.

OXYMORON

Noun. A figure of speech in which contradictory ideas or terms are combined. Example: thunderous silence.

Large shrimp	Rolling stop
Clearly confused	Good grief
Alone together	Sweet tart
Deafening silence	Old news
Seriously funny	Living dead
Pretty ugly	Hot chili
Freezer burn	Student teacher
Working holiday	

Spell It (Young or Old)

Pick a word out of the dictionary and go around the table asking everyone to spell it. If the first person gets it wrong, go to the next person. Choose words appropriate for your age group. The key to this being fun is your family members' ability to spell some words correctly. The best part of the game is the pride on their faces when they get one right.

Spell It, Define It, Use It (Tweens and Up)

Pick a word out of the dictionary, have them spell it, then define it, then use it in a sentence. If they get any section wrong, go to the next person.

SAT Words You Should Know

This is a great one because everyone at the table will learn or relearn new words. There are lots of books (see Resources) out there that you can keep right on your table and pick up at any point during dinner when you need a little conversation starter. I still remember certain words

I learned for that scary high school test like: obstinate . . . stubborn; ominous . . . foreboding; omniscient . . . all-knowing. And that is just the O's! It's funny how kids absorb things. My daughter was thick into the third book of the Twilight series when she screamed from her room that she recognized a word from our dinner the previous night. Okay, I have to admit it, that was a little satisfying! Try some tonight:

SALIENT . . . striking, obvious
APATHY . . . indifference
RUMINATE . . . to ponder
COPIOUS . . . abundant
NEBULOUS . . . hazy
SANGUINE . . . possessing a positive attitude
QUAGMIRE . . . predicament
ACERBIC . . . harsh, bitter
EMINENT . . . prominent, noted
TACITURN . . . habitually untalkative

Category Word Games/Picnic

Pick a category and everyone lists one thing from that category. Go around as many times as is entertaining. For example, the category is summer. I say watermelon, the next person says flip-flops, the next person says beach blanket, and so on. The classic version of this is to play it as a memory game. The person repeats the answers before theirs and then adds their own. We use this game a lot in restaurants waiting for food.

Picnic is another fun variation on this game. The first person starts by saying, "I'm going on a picnic and I am bringing salami." The next person says, "I'm going on a picnic and I'm bringing salami and crusty bread," and around the table you go. Trust me—it soon gets hard *and* makes your mouth water! Next thing you know, you'll be planning a picnic!

Ten Questions

Yep, just like Twenty Questions but ten fewer! Vegetable, Animal, or Mineral? The kids can take turns guessing what's on your mind and learn how to ask a yes or no question.

Stinky Pinkies

This is a great game just for the name itself! Basically, it's a guessing game using rhyming synonyms (one of two or more words that have the same or nearly the same meaning). You give the first two words (column one) as the clue and everyone else guesses the match (column two). With a little help on the first one, the rest will come easily and everyone will feel clever and smart.

ANGRY BOY	MAD LAD
HAPPY FATHER	GLAD DAD
LEFTOVER GLUE	WASTE PASTE
SUGARY SNACK	SWEET TREAT
ILL HEN	SICK CHICK
POLICE STORE	COP SHOP
INSECT'S TROUSERS	ANT'S PANTS
RABBIT SEAT	HARE CHAIR
QUICK EXPLOSION	FAST BLAST
COZY CARPET	SNUG RUG
ARTIFICIAL RATTLER	FAKE SNAKE
STINKERS BED	SKUNK BUNK
JUNK MONEY	TRASH CASH
FUNNY CAT	WITTY KITTY
MONSTER MOVIE	CREATURE FEATURE

GAMES FOR YOUNG CHILDREN

The Favorite Game

Write topics on small pieces of paper, fold them, and place in a bowl in the center of the table. Take turns picking one out and going around the table saying what your favorite is (have a parent read the category if the youngest can't read). Topics can include (but are not limited to): movies, teachers, school subjects, ice cream flavors, colors, numbers, vacation destinations, music, TV shows, fruits, desserts.

What Fruit, Animal, Flower, or Tree Am I?

Go around the table and have everyone say which one of these things they would be and why, one subject at a time. For example, "If I was an animal, I would be a rabbit."

When I Grow Up

Going around the room, each child says what they want to be and why. For instance, "I want to be an astronaut so I can look at the earth from above and find life on another planet."

Alphabet Game

Pick a letter and have everyone come up with a word that starts with that letter. Add categories to make it more challenging. For example: animals that begin with the letter B.

Once Upon a Time

Start a story out loud and go around the table adding to it. Decide if you'll go around once or many times. The last person it comes to finishes the story and has the fun of saying, "The end." Here are some suggested beginnings:

- "It was a dark and stormy night . . ."
- "A dog barked in the distance . . ."
- "She carried her plate to the kitchen counter . . ."
- "It was so hot you could fry an egg on the sidewalk . . ."
- "The old man said a final good-bye to his dog . . ."

Telephone

An oldie but goody—and maybe a game you never thought to play at dinner. Start the game by whispering a multipart story into one person's ear. The more details, names, and plot twists, the better. That person then whispers the story into the next person's ear and so on until the last person tells the story they heard out loud. It will likely be very different—and much funnier—than the original story.

My Mom Doesn't Like Peas

The person who knows the trick of this game asks everyone at the table, each one in turn: "Our mom doesn't like P's; what can you give her instead?"

The first one may answer "Sugar" and that will suit her, but the next one might say "Potatoes," and that will not do, because the letter P is in that word.

The catch to this is that everyone thinks the vegetable "peas" is the subject to stay away from instead of just the letter P. Even after everybody has discovered the trick it will be difficult to think of words, and any players who fail to answer before 5 is counted are out. "My Grandma Doesn't Like Tea (T)" is played in the same way.

BOOKS to Keep Kids Guessing and Learning

There are lots of books available on common expressions, trivia, and fun facts, and all are a hostess's or busy parent's dream. I generally use these books at the table for fun little moments of learning, to cover awkward silences, or just for a laugh. Five minutes of snippets from one of these books and everyone is relaxed and chatting away!

The Dictionary of Word Origins
by Jordan Almond

This handy little book lists the history of words, expressions, and clichés we commonly use. Reading a few at the table gets people loosened up, makes them laugh, makes them think, and maybe even sets your conversation off in a direction you wouldn't have expected. Why do we "toast" people on special occasions? Well, this book can tell you. The "toast" was once literally in the glass. The custom was to place a small piece of toast in the bottom of the glass as a delicacy. When you drained your glass while drinking to a person, you drank this bit of "toast." Try that one on your group tonight!

The Mega Book of Useless Information
by Noel Botham

I found this book fascinating and not useless at all. You never know when some crazy fact will come in handy, at the very least for good dinner conversation. This particular book is chock-full of categories like "The Things People

Say," "Laws Old and New," "Crazy Customs and Traditions," "Rude Facts" (a kid fave), pages of famous insults and the people who said them, and much more. You can turn any page into a guessing game or multiple-choice quiz, or just read it straight through! Pass it around the table to include everyone. Examples include:

- Sheep can survive up to two weeks buried in snowdrifts. (Who knew?)
- People who are lying to you tend to look up and to the left. (Be on the lookout for this.)
- In Hawaii, all residents may be fined as a result of not owning a boat. (So don't take up residency without at least a canoe.)

The New Book of Lists
by David Wallechinsky and Amy Wallace

More than eight million copies of this classic whopper have been sold worldwide. There is so much fun info inside, your kids will be grown by the time you go through it all. Some favorite topics include:

- Twenty-four actors who turned down great roles and what they were. Did you know that Robert Redford turned down the role of the son Ben in The Graduate? The role made an instant star of Dustin Hoffman in 1967.
- New neuroses. For example, Cellyell—loud talking on cell phones in public places by people with the neurotic need to invade their own privacy.
- Nine body parts you didn't know had names, like lunnule, the white crescent-shaped mark at the base of a fingernail.

The Road to Success Is Paved with Failure
by Joey Green

I love telling stories to my kids about people who faced rejection only to overcome it and prove everyone wrong. These kinds of tales will help fortify them when they go out into the world and have to deal with some inevitable rejection themselves.

- Theodore Roosevelt ran in 1886 as the Republican candidate for mayor of New York City . . . and lost.
- Dr. Seuss's first book was rejected by twenty-seven publishing houses.

READ

AROUND THE TABLE

~ 12 ~

FROM NEWS TO POETRY—INSPIRATION IS YOUR DINNER GUEST

Family dinner offers the perfect time for some meaningful discussion about the day's news from around the corner or around the globe and a chance to delve into big-picture questions, ethics, and values.

GETTING STARTED: NEWSPAPERS

You don't need to go any farther than today's newspaper, local or national. So many prominent public figures I interviewed for this book made a point of telling me how their political views and social advocacy interests were formed during the nightly discussion of current events at the family dinner table.

News on the Internet is fast and easy, but nothing can replace the smacking down on the table of the good old-fashioned folded newspaper for accentuating a point! (I can still hear my dad doing it!) Not to mention highlighting a paragraph, hanging it on the refrigerator, watching the edges yellow and curl. I think it will be a sad day if the paper, in its current physical form, becomes an icon of the past. Calling all parents and grandparents who know the value of the ink on your fingertips to come to the rescue. Bring back the newspaper as a front-and-center honored guest at family dinner! Spend a few minutes perusing your favorite paper, finding articles that you think your group

will be interested in. Read an excerpt at dinner, pose a question, and off you go. One small example from my table: If your teens are waving their driver's permits at you (a truly horrible rite of passage I wouldn't wish on any parent!), bring to the table one of the many articles about the dangers of texting and driving. Discuss that one ad nauseam!

Scouring the Paper

When looking for stories that reinforce your values, you might be surprised by my next suggestion: Check out the obituaries. Every day there are moving tributes to people's long lives, hard work, and courage. You wouldn't believe how many inspiring stories you will find about individuals you've never heard of who have accomplished great things.

"Family dinner opened for me an **INTEREST IN THE WORLD.** *Every meal I got to hear my parents and siblings discussing cultural and political affairs that I don't think I would have been exposed to if not at dinner. For me it* **SHAPED MY IDEAS FOR MY FUTURE."**

—RABBI DAVID SAPERSTEIN, director, **Religious Action Center of Reform Judaism**

"I think you've got to **CHALLENGE YOUR KIDS,** *and the dinner table is the perfect place. It's a controlled atmosphere, you're there for forty-five minutes to an hour, and you can talk and really* **COMMUNICATE YOUR IDEALS** *to your children."* —PASTOR TRI ROBINSON, Vineyard Boise Church, Boise, Idaho, author of *Saving God's Green Earth*

Here's a perfect example: I know you've heard of Jackie Robinson, but have you heard of a gentleman by the name of Bill Powell? I hadn't, either, until I read his obituary in *The New York Times*. He did for racial barriers in golf what Robinson did *a year later* for baseball! An avid golfer since his caddying days beginning at the age of nine, as an adult he was refused tee time by the golf courses near where he lived (PGA by-laws barred nonwhites from membership until 1961). Did he give up and drop his passion? Heck no, he did something about it! He became the only African-American to build, own, and operate a golf course in America! His motto: "Stand firm. Never give up. Never give in. Believe in yourself, even when others don't."

So, a few ground rules, or should I say goals for discussing news items:

- Everyone has to listen to others' opinions or views without interruption (at least try).
- No one can allow the conversation to devolve by hurling insults or making fun of another person's position.
- Understand that the "right answer" might not exist or a conclusion may not materialize by the end of the meal—it's great when the discussion can be ongoing.
- It's your choice whether you want to wade into controversial topics. My view is, if not now, then when? Any opportunity to spread a little life wisdom is an opportunity we should grab.

"EVERY NIGHT AT DINNER,
I heard about how my parents and their friends were trying to make the world a better place. To this day, I think my sister and I strive to carry on that tradition." —JENNIFER, Washington, DC

DINNER DISCUSSION TOPICS and Moral Dilemmas

Discussing and debating moral dilemmas is a good way to teach your kids deductive thinking and to get a read on where they stand on issues. Of course, it's also a perfect opportunity to insert some parental guidance on how to deal with tough decisions. They will be faced with many of their own dilemmas in life—they probably are already grappling with some—so we want to prepare them to think critically and find their own voice.

I think the old adage of never discussing politics or religion at dinner should be retired along with "Children should be seen and not heard." Debate is healthy, disagreements a part of life, and we want our kids to hear opposing viewpoints and practice responding in a mature manner. Someday I want to hear my kids say "I respectfully disagree" when they do. That will be my parenting high for the week!

Here are some discussion topics:

- The high school dropout rate is huge. What do you think of this idea for new legislation: You have to finish high school in order to get a driver's license before the age of twenty-one. What are the pros and cons?
- Should schools continue to schedule after-school activities during dinnertime?
- Should we drill for oil off our coasts? Why or why not?
- Should talking on a cell phone or texting while driving be illegal in every state? If so, what should the punishment be?
- Which is worse: finding a bottle of alcohol in your child's backpack, or finding marijuana there? (That was a question my daughter asked me. We talked about that one for a week!)

- What do you do if a friend's parent shows up to drive you home from a party but you can tell he or she has been drinking?

- What is the proper etiquette for cell phones and texting in restaurants? If you are in someone's car as a passenger? How about using iPods on buses or trains when others can hear them?

- Should movie stars have the characters they play in films smoke cigarettes? Does it glamorize or make cool something that is harmful to your health? Or does it add to a character's personality and to the story line?

- The number of people voting in America is at an all-time low. What do you think of this idea for new legislation: You will automatically be registered to vote when you get your driver's license. What are the pros and cons?

- Should community service be required of everyone for one year between high school and college?

- If you accept an invitation and a better offer comes along, is it okay to cancel the first one?

- Should your school principal have the right to randomly search lockers if he or she suspects that some students may have brought weapons or drugs on campus?

- If someone tells you a secret and you promise not to tell before hearing it, and it turns out that it could hurt another person, do you break your silence?

- You get a good look at a woman with a young child stealing some baby food from a grocery store. The police ask you for a description. Do you provide it?

- Do you tell on a friend (to their parents or to the school) if you know they're doing drugs?

- Do you give money to homeless people if there is a chance they might buy alcohol with it?

- Is it okay to pretend to be someone else, using their Facebook or IM account?

- You're on your way to an important job interview with not a second to spare, and just as you're about to walk into the office building, you see an old lady drop her groceries on the sidewalk. Helping her collect them will make you late. Do you help her or keep going?

- If you had the chance to read people's minds, would you? What are the pros and cons?

- You see a schoolmate being bullied, but you don't know her well. Do you step in and help?

Family Dinners Build

LANGUAGE SKILLS

The research is in! Children who do well on school achievement tests are the ones who eat meals and snacks with their families (achievement levels are not affected by whether mothers worked or didn't work outside the home). Those who eat dinner with their families four or more times a week are more likely to score better than those who have dinner three or fewer times a week. What's happening at dinner? Longer conversations! Here are some tips.

- **When having conversations at dinner,** discuss people's motivations for what they say or do, including your own. ("What were they thinking?") Understanding others' perspective helps kids develop empathy and avoid conflicts.

- **Talk up to kids.** Expose kids to new words used in sentences.

- **Have extended conversations** with your kids at the table about issues you care about. Longer conversations provide kids with a chance to think, hear new words, and expand their own conversation skills.

"The difference between knowing 3,000 words and knowing 15,000 words when you arrive at kindergarten is enormous. **USING GROWN-UP WORDS WITH CHILDREN** *as they enter the toddler and preschool years* **HELPS THEM LEARN."** —ELLEN GALINSKY, president of the Families and Work Institute and author of *Mind in the Making*

DINNER WITH A PURPOSE

Talking to **ROBERT F. KENNEDY JR.** *about what his family dinners were like growing up was a rare look back at a unique family's valued dinnertime ritual. His memories were vivid, warm, and admiring. And also incredulous. How did his mother do it every night, he wondered out loud, with all those kids?*

LAURIE: You had very formal dinners growing up. What were they like?

BOBBY: We had to be on time for dinner, it was at six usually. The very young kids who were not considered old enough to participate in adult conversations, those under seven, before the age of reason, were put at a smaller table. We had to have our nails cleaned with a brush, we had to have our hair combed, and when the dinner bell was rung, we had to get to the table right away. If we didn't show up, we'd be in big trouble.

My mother sat at one end of the table and my father at the other. He came home for dinner whenever he could; and then sometimes he'd go back to work.

My mother was a constant, she was always there and she insisted there be a single conversation. She didn't want to sit at a table where there were many conversations going on. For Sunday dinner, we had to be prepared to discuss current events. On Saturdays, we would write down three stories from the newspaper. We all had notebooks to do this in. Or we might get called on to recite a short biography of a prominent figure. For Sundays, each of us also had to have a poem memorized.

My father loved ballad poetry like Rudyard Kipling or Alfred, Lord Tennyson or Longfellow. We all memorized poems like Tennyson's "Ulysses," "The Charge of the Light Brigade," Kipling's "Gunga Din," "The Cremation of Sam McGee" or "The Midnight Ride of Paul Revere," which was my grandmother's favorite. I bet you could ask any of my brothers and sisters today and they could recite those as well as many others. We also played a lot of games at the table: spelling games, a game called Ghost, and Botticelli.

LAURIE: You had to write biographies? How did you do it without Google?

BOBBY: We had books back then. They're becoming forgotten today. We had well-worn encyclopedias, the Britannica and Compton's encyclopedias in the house. Those provided source material for a lot of my biographies. But we also had lots of other books: children's history books, and books about the lives of the saints, that kind of thing, so we would do biographies, mainly of historical figures, or if we were feeling particularly pious we could do one of the saints.

LAURIE: There were a lot of kids at that table spanning a lot of different ages. What was the discipline like?

BOBBY: I really don't understand how they did it. Having my own family has amplified my admiration for my parents. I don't know how my mother had the discipline to do it night after night. It was such an important part of our family life. It was kind of the one constant: We were all expected at the dinner table, we were all expected to participate, and we were all expected to perform.

There were many times when very famous people came to dinner; we often shared the table with sports figures or political figures or cultural figures of the day. But we were always included in the conversation and we were expected to say something smart, not to be silly or stupid, but to participate. I think that was really important in developing kids who had a broader view of the world.

LAURIE: Do you credit your family dinners for turning you into an advocate for environmental justice?

BOBBY: Yes, that ritual, the dinner table ritual, was where we learned a lot about what was going on in the world, and about what was right and wrong, how to conduct ourselves and how to talk and how to speak, how to interact. I think it gave all of us very useful conversing skills.

LAURIE: How many of your childhood rituals do you do today as a parent?

BOBBY: I try as best I can to replicate our family dinners, sometimes with piddling success. We make the kids turn off all

the screens and sit through all of dinner, we bless our meal, we all eat at the same time, no one gets up without being excused, but it's really hard, and there are so many distractions. It's a struggle oftentimes to hold them there. But you've got to do it.

LAURIE: What was your favorite part of family dinner growing up?

BOBBY: At dessert every night my father would usually eat chocolate cake with ice cream, which was his favorite, and he would tell us a historical story. He would tell us about what he was doing at the Justice Department, about his civil rights cases, or later he'd ask us questions about how we felt about the Vietnam War, or drugs, about all the issues of the day. Then he would usually tell us a story about history. He was a really good military historian and he would tell us about many of the battles that changed history. That was always my favorite part of dinner.

"My father always played a **DINNER GAME WITH US WE CALLED THE GLOBE GAME.** I used to be terrified I would be called on to recite the capitals of every state. I had performance anxiety at age eight! But looking back, I think it **GAVE ME A WANDERLUST TO SEE THE WORLD."**

—CAROLINE M., mom of three boys

"Poetry helps us to realize that **HUMAN BEINGS ARE MORE ALIKE THAN WE ARE UNALIKE."** —DR. MAYA ANGELOU, poet, author, and educator

POEMS TO PONDER

Way back when, a long time ago, children were expected to memorize and recite poetry. Dinners in the 1920s might feature—along with pan-broiled chops, mashed potatoes, and creamed peas—the reciting of poetry for guests' amusement by the host's enchanting eight- or nine-year-old child. Shakespeare, Wordsworth, or Longfellow might be on the menu. The standards for schools at the time made sure children were well prepared for such occasions. In fact, public schools expected first graders to memorize "The Land of Nod" by Robert Louis Stevenson and "Hoppity" by A. A. Milne, among many others. Poetry was cherished as an important part of a child's education.

Shakespeare himself was "a product of a memorizing culture in which huge chunks of literature were learned by heart," writes historian Michael Wood about our greatest playwright. In Wood's words, "poetry is among the most exciting gifts a young person can receive."

What a shame that we have long since dropped this tradition in our homes and schools, and gone from a culture that memorized everything to one that memorizes nothing, not even important telephone numbers (speaking for myself at the very least)!

Mary Ann Hoberman thinks so, too, and as one of America's first children's poet laureates (I know, I didn't know we had one, either), she urges everyone to discover the pure joy of committing a poem to memory. "When you memorize a poem, it truly becomes 'yours,'" she explains. "Nothing is more satisfying than 'getting it by heart' and you will know that poem far more deeply and completely when you have read it out loud a number of times."

Poetry for the dinner table, memorized or just read, is the perfect way to recapture this charming and confidence-building tradition.

So what's stopping us modern-day parents? Let's bring this lovely ritual back. To that end, I asked my good friend Paul Cummins—who wore a headmaster's hat in Los Angeles for twenty-five years, founded three schools, worked to restore the arts to public school curriculum, and began

...❦...

Every day take time to start
To learn a little poem by heart.

—Mary Ann Hoberman

several much-needed after-school programs—why he thinks we need to bring poetry back to the table.

"Poetry is so important because it teaches children the magical qualities of language. It shows you that words do more than give information; they transport us over the tops of mountains and across wide seas," he replied, poetically of course.

Okay, that cinches it. If you have young ones at home, get started! Little ones will be the most receptive to this idea, as their brains are still elastic and open. You will revel in the speed with which they devour and repeat a ditty. What a fantastic surprise this will be for the grandparents at Sunday dinner! The glorious, thundering applause will be heard throughout the neighborhood, and the beaming, prideful smile on your child's face will be all the dessert you need.

THE POWER OF POETRY
For Families

A Conversation with Dr. Maya Angelou

MAYA ANGELOU, *award-winning author and poet, is one of the world's literary treasures. She moves and inspires people with the beauty of her words and the melodic cadence of her voice.*

LAURIE: Can you explain to me what the power of poetry is?

DR. ANGELOU: I can, by telling you a recent story. My son, my only born child, has a number of physical challenges. He was in Miami at the Jackson Memorial Hospital, which specializes in spinal cord injuries, and he was about to have I guess about his sixth operation on his spine. The operation was a success and I came home back to North Carolina after about a week. He phoned me a few days later and asked me, "Mom, do you remember the poem 'Invictus'?" I said, "Of course," but what I really remembered was teaching him 'Invictus' when he was about eight years old and seeing this little black boy walking around the house in Los Angeles with his chest stuck out like a partridge saying:

> *Out of the night that covers me,*
> *Black as the Pit from pole to pole.*

And I said yes, I remembered. He asked, Would I recite it? So I said yes. And when I finished, he said, "Thanks, Mom, but you forgot a verse." And he reminded me of the verse I had forgotten, and then he asked if I would say the whole poem with him in my cadence? And I said yes.

> *It matters not how strait the gate,*
> *How charged with punishments the scroll.*
> *I am the master of my fate:*
> *I am the captain of my soul.*

And when I finished that he said, "Thanks, Mom, they just finished removing over a hundred stitches out of my back. Love you, bye!"

That, Laurie, is the power of poetry.

INVICTUS

Out of the night that covers me,
Black as the Pit from pole to pole,
I thank whatever gods may be
For my unconquerable soul.

In the fell clutch of circumstance
I have not winced nor cried aloud.
Under the bludgeoning of chance
My head is bloody, but unbowed.

Beyond this place of wrath and tears
Looms but the Horror of the shade,
And yet the menace of the years
Finds, and shall find, me unafraid.

It matters not how strait the gate,
How charged with punishments the scroll.
I am the master of my fate:
I am the captain of my soul.

—William Ernest Henley

Paul Cummins's Five Dinner Table Poems to Read, Memorize, and Talk About

- "The Shooting of Dan McGrew" by Robert Service. A wonderful story, good for reading and memorizing passages. Good reading on a dark and windy night.
- "The Highwayman" by Alfred Noyes. My daughter Emily's favorite poem when she was eight—a love story and a tale of adventure. A romantic tale.
- "Stopping by Woods on a Snowy Evening" by Robert Frost. The interlocking rhymes, the mood, the repetition of the last line—all create magic.
- "Jabberwocky" by Lewis Carroll. A delightful nonsense poem that actually tells an adventure story—a brilliant use of invented words.
- Nursery Rhymes. Some of the children's nursery rhymes are for all ages and have an element of the mysterious to them, for example:

> I do not like thee, Doctor Fell,
> The reason why I cannot tell;
> But this I know, and know full well,
> I do not like thee, Doctor Fell.

Dr. Maya Angelou's Six Poems or Poets Everyone Should Read

"At some point when you're alone or facing an empty house with no nurture in it, or facing a fearful tomorrow, you need to be able to pull something up out of your mind. The computer may not work, the phone may have gone dead. You need to have something," explains Dr. Angelou.

- "If" by Rudyard Kipling
- Poems by Paul Laurence Dunbar
- Poems by James Weldon Johnson
- "The Bells" by Edgar Allan Poe
- "Annabel Lee" by Edgar Allan Poe
- "The Raven" by Edgar Allan Poe

BILLY COLLINS
Former Poet Laureate of the United States (2001–2003)

"I was first exposed to poetry by my mother, who had memorized hundreds of lines of poetry as a schoolgirl in rural Canada. My mother had so much poetry in her head that she had lines ready for just about any occasion, whether someone was late or the weather was turning cold. Because of her, I came to think of poetry as a part of everyday life, not an exotic or elitist activity. I think the way to bring poetry into the lives of children is to treat it not as literature but as a pleasure that comes from hearing and saying our language at its best.

"One of my favorites is "The Owl" by Edward Thomas. It is a beautiful poem about gratitude that should be read at every table. I've read it so often at mine that my friends start throwing dinner rolls at me!"

THE OWL

> Downhill I came, hungry, and yet not starved;
> Cold, yet had heat within me that was proof
> Against the North wind; tired, yet so that rest
> Had seemed the sweetest thing under a roof.
>
> Then at the inn I had food, fire, and rest,
> Knowing how hungry, cold, and tired was I.
> All of the night was quite barred out except
> An owl's cry, a most melancholy cry
> Shaken out long and clear upon the hill,
> No merry note, nor cause of merriment,
> But one telling me plain what I escaped
> And others could not, that night, as in I went.
>
> And salted was my food, and my repose,
> Salted and sobered, too, by the bird's voice
> Speaking for all who lay under the stars,
> Soldiers and poor, unable to rejoice.
>
> —Edward Thomas

Three Poems for Your Little Ones to Recite Tonight at Dinner

By Daniel Waters, *former poet laureate of West Tisbury, Massachusetts*

CORN ON THE COB
*From left to right,
We munch across
And afterwards
Need dental floss.*

·

LAUNDRY DAY
*Nothing smells as clean and fine
As fresh-washed linens on the line,
All rinsed and wrung and tightly pinned
To catch their share of sun and wind.*

·

CHICKADEE'S LAMENT
*Of all the discomforts
Inflicted by fall,
The ice in the birdbath
Is cruelest of all.*

....

Recite Tonight a Favorite Classic

DUST OF SNOW
*The way a crow
Shook down on me
The dust of snow
From a hemlock tree
Has given my heart
A change of mood
And saved some part
Of a day I had rued.*

—Robert Frost

...ᦰ◈ᦰ...
RECITE TONIGHT

Moses supposes his toeses are roses,
But Moses supposes erroneously;
For nobody's toeses are posies of roses
As Moses supposes his toeses to be.

—*Anonymous*

EXCERPTS FOR THE TABLE

For more inspiration, I often look to published speeches of accomplished men and women—and one of the best places to find words that encourage, move, and enthuse are college commencement addresses. No need to wait for one of your kids to graduate from college to hear and discuss a character-building commencement address. Every June, *The New York Times* and other newspapers run highlights from all the great speeches delivered at universities across the country. They are chock-full of advice, insights, and powerful tales of struggle and success. It is an honor to be chosen to deliver a commencement address, and honorees labor long and hard on their comments—why not share their valuable lessons at the table? Here are a few excerpts to pass around. The best part: Every June there's a whole new batch to choose from!

....

Larry Page, *Google Co-Founder, University of Michigan, 2009*

I had one of those dreams when I was 23. When I suddenly woke up, I was thinking, What if we could download the whole Web and just keep the links? And I grabbed a pen and started writing. Sometimes it is important to wake up and stop dreaming. I spent the middle of that night scribbling out the details and convincing myself it would work. The optimism of youth is often underrated. Amazingly, I had no thought of building a search engine. The idea wasn't even on the radar. But much later, we happened upon a better way of ranking Web pages to make a really great search engine, and Google was born. When a really great dream shows up, grab it.

"TOO OFTEN WE GIVE CHILDREN ANSWERS *to remember rather than problems to solve."* —ROGER LEWIN, PhD, anthropologist and science writer

Robert M. Gates, *U.S. Secretary of Defense, United States Military Academy, 2009*

During the Revolution, a man in civilian clothes rode past a redoubt being repaired. The commander was shouting orders but not helping. When the rider asked why, the supervisor of the work detail retorted, "Sir, I am a corporal." The stranger apologized, dismounted, and helped repair the redoubt. When he was done, he turned toward the supervisor and said, "Mr. Corporal, next time you have a job like this, and not enough men to do it, go to your commander in chief, and I will come and help you again." Too late, the corporal recognized George Washington. The power of example in leadership.

Tavis Smiley, *Radio and Television Talk-Show Host, Rutgers University, 2007*

The tragedy of life does not lie, young folk, in not reaching your goal. The tragedy lies in having no goal to reach. It is not a calamity to die with dreams unfulfilled, but it is a calamity not to dream. It is not a disaster to not be able to capture your ideals, but it is a disaster to have no ideals to capture. It is not a disgrace to not be able to reach all the stars, but it is a disgrace to have no stars to reach for.

Kamala D. Harris, *San Francisco District Attorney, San Francisco State University, 2007*

As you grow in your career, you may hit another barrier—the limits that others set for you. A ceiling on what you can accomplish and who you can be. That happened to me. When I decided to run for district attorney, it was considered a man's job even here in San Francisco. No woman had ever been elected district attorney in San Francisco. No person of color had ever been elected district attorney in San Francisco.

I remember the day I got my first poll results back. I was sitting in a small conference room, a little nervous, but very hopeful. Then I read them. I was at 6 percent. And that wasn't good. So I was told what you all have probably heard in your life, and that you will certainly hear in your future. I

was told that I should wait my turn. I was told that I should give up. I was told that I had no chance.

Well, I didn't listen. And I'm telling you, don't you listen, either. Don't listen when they tell you that you can't do it.

Tom Hanks, *Actor and Producer, Vassar College, 2005*

Smart folks concocted a computer simulation of gridlock to determine how many cars should be taken off the road to turn a completely jammed and stilled highway into a free-flowing one. The results were startling. Four cars needed to be removed . . . four cars out of each one hundred . . . Call it the Power of Four . . . If merely four people out of a hundred can make gridlock go away by choosing not to use their car, imagine the other changes that can be wrought just by four of us out of a hundred. Take a hundred musicians in a depressed port city in Northern England, choose John, Paul, George, and Ringo and you have "Hey Jude." Take a hundred computer geeks in Redmond, Washington, send ninety-six of them home and the remainder is called Microsoft. Take the Power of Four and apply it to any and every area of your concern. Politics: Four votes swung from one hundred into another hundred is the difference between gaining control and losing clout. Culture: two ticket buyers out of fifty can make a small, odd film profitable. Economics: by boycotting a product 1 consumer out of 25 can move that product to the back of the shelf, and eventually off it altogether.

Four out of one hundred is minuscule and yet can be the great lever of the tipping point.

James Fallows, *Author, Ursinus College, 2008*

In the end, we are our habits, so take time developing good ones . . . Some of these are obvious. No joke, don't smoke! Also, don't type IMs [instant messages] while you drive. Get in the habit of sports and exercise—by your tenth reunion, you'll know who has and hasn't, and you'll know even more each subsequent one.

Get in the habit of being happy. We all have problems, which we can't control; what we can control is how we look at them. Get in the habit of being excited. It's a great big world, with no excuse for being bored. It's fun to have feuds and enemies—I've had my share—but break the habit of nursing grudges.

Here's one tip: Always write angry letters to your enemies, but never mail them . . . Take every chance to tell your spouse, when you have one, and your children that you love them. When in doubt, phone your mom.

HUFFINGTON POST'S
Family Dinner Downloads

Although one of the most important rules about family dinners is "No technology at the table," some rules are meant to be occasionally broken—especially if it's for a good cause! And what could be a better cause than inspiring great family dinner conversations?

That's why we're partnering with The Huffington Post to bring you **Family Dinner Downloads.**

Once a week, HuffPost's editors will select and highlight one of the most compelling news stories of the week—stories that are sure to spark an interesting discussion among the whole family. These stories might be about a serious issue in the news or a fun, lighthearted one—but they will always be presented in an age-appropriate manner, and will always promote lively dinnertime conversations about core values like honesty, respect, courage, fairness, and justice.

The family can gather around the laptop or smartphone—or pass around a printout—and check out the Family Dinner Download of the Week, which will end with a question or two that will get everyone thinking and sharing their thoughts, feelings, and opinions. It's a great way to learn how your kids see the world, and to let them discover how you see things, too.

All you have to do is go to **www.huffingtonpost.com** and click to the "Family Dinner Downloads" page. There you will find the latest conversation-starting story—a new one available every Friday at 5 PM ET, just in time for dinner—as well as an archive of all the previous Family Dinner Downloads. Great new discussion topics, every week, all year long!

GRANDPARENTS
and the Extended Family
~ 13 ~

WORDS OF WISDOM

"A GRANDMOTHER is a sprinkling of parent, a dash of teacher, and a dollop of a best friend." —ANONYMOUS

THREE CHEERS FOR GRANDPARENTS and the Extended Family!

How is this for an incredible statistic: There are seventy million grandparents living in America today. Grandparents are one of the largest and fastest-growing segments of the U.S. population, and they are no slouches. Today's Grammy and Pops are well educated, wealthier, and younger than previous generations (the average first-time grandparent is forty-seven!).

If you are lucky enough to have these members of your extended family alive and well—and accessible—you are truly blessed. Sunday dinner at Grandma and Grandpa's is not to be missed, what with all those great cooking aromas and the smells of homemade pies and cookies. And even if your grandparents don't bake from scratch, you know time with them will be nutritious and delicious anyway, filled with unconditional love and attention!

When people start recounting memories of grandparents, smiles take over, and Memory Lane is paved with joy. Grandparents, aunts, and uncles are a gift to any family. They are the walking, breathing encyclopedias of your family history. That history helps define who you are and where you came from. Yet lately we aren't taking full advantage of our relatives' vast family knowledge. According to Ancestry.com, the largest family history Web site, many of us lack basic information about our personal histories—things like our mother's maiden name, relatives' military history, or

"Being a grandparent is a **TOTALLY DIFFERENT KIND OF LOVE.** *It's love without the responsibility and somehow because of that it is incredibly rewarding."*

—BARBARA, grandmother of five

what their early jobs were. "A lot of kids don't connect to their history because they are not sitting down together at the table. The family dinner is the number one place where most of this information usually gets passed on," says Lou Szucs, a vice president at the site.

Talking about family history at the table is no idle chatter. Researchers have found that the sharing of personal history is much more important than we may realize—it's yet another tool to build self-esteem and resilience in your child. The astute research team at Emory University's Center for Myth and Ritual in American Life (MARIAL) has been studying this issue and says that passing along family history builds character in children and a sense of a world beyond one's immediate surroundings.

Their findings show that if you pass on the family lore, your kids will be:

• Less prone to engage in negative activities.
• Active members of the family, helping it to function better.
• More resilient in the face of usual and unusual life stresses.

Not a bad outcome from a weekly visit to Grandma's for Sunday dinner! Emory professor Marshall Duke says that family stories give kids an important context for their lives. "It teaches them that there is more than just their few years. There are people who came before them; there are people who are connected to them, experiences that belong to them because they belong to their family's story. These narratives give us a sense of consistency and continuity, and even when things are bad, Grandpa will tell you "it was bad before and we got through it."

Relationships with extended family are important attachments for children of all ages. (Hey, some of them have been around long enough to remember victory gardens and can tell us what life was like before cell phones!) So along with grandparents, invite aunts, uncles, cousins, and old family friends for dinner—make it a ritual where kids can hear all the embarrassing stories about you that you would never tell yourself. Everyone will laugh out loud. It will be history in the making.

"Having grandchildren is the **VINDICATION OF EVERYTHING ONE HAS DONE** *as a parent. When we see our children passing on our values to another generation, we know we have been successful."* —MARY RUTH DAVIS

SOULFUL COOKING
with Bryant Terry

CHEF BRYANT TERRY *is the author of* Vegan Soul Kitchen: Fresh, Healthy, and Creative African-American Cuisine. *His interest in cooking, farming, and community health can be traced back to his childhood in Memphis, Tennessee, where his grandparents first taught him to grow, prepare, and appreciate good food.*

LAURIE: Tell me about your grandparents.

BRYANT: Both sets of my grandparents were a huge influence on me. They came from rural Mississippi. The agrarian knowledge that they had, and the desire to grow their own food, was so strong. Both sets of my grandparents grew tons of food in their backyard, and tended fruit trees in the front yard, including pear, peach, and nectarine. Every available inch of the yard was used to grow food. They grew so much that my grandfather would give it away to neighbors and church members.

LAURIE: What are some of your food memories from their kitchens?

BRYANT: One of my favorite foods that my maternal grandmother used to make was her fried pie. Most people would call them a turnover, but she called it a fried pie. She would stew the pears from her trees and then stuff them inside the dough, which she also made by hand, and then fry them. That was just the best treat that we could have.

She also had a seemingly never-ending pot of greens cooking on the stove. It was a mélange of collards and turnips, maybe some mustard greens. I just loved eating those greens. We often ate them with her homemade chow-chow. She had this huge pantry where she kept all of her preserves and pickles and chutneys because that's what they would eat for the leaner months. We would spoon that over the greens and sop the juices up with corn bread.

LAURIE: How would you describe the food you cook?

BRYANT: I use the terms *African-American cuisine* and *soul food* interchangeably. The cuisine has constantly evolved and changed throughout history. It's not just the obvious comfort foods like deep-fried fatty meats, sugary desserts. That's certainly a part of it, but people need to widen their notion of what soul food is. Even soul food restaurants have confused what is authentic soul food; they've been convinced it's fried chicken and macaroni and cheese. That is a very narrow understanding of it. Just two generations ago, my grandparents were growing their own food and cooking everything fresh and in season. Who's to say what they were cooking and eating wasn't authentically African-American cuisine? Ironically, what they were cooking is the same type of food that any of my haute cuisine chef friends are cooking: farm to table food, fresh, local, seasonal, sustainable food. It's the same thing.

I worry that we risk losing so much knowledge and connection to our ethnic backgrounds. When I think about family and food, I think about my grandparents' connections to the land and how important it is to pass down these recipes, traditions, and stories. Without that, our generation will lose a big part of what it means to be a family living in America. We have to hold on dearly to those memories and honor the knowledge that came before us.

"MY GRANDMOTHER ALWAYS SAID, *you cannot know where you are going if you don't know where you came from. Boy was she right."* —BRYANT TERRY, chef

DINNER GUEST RECIPE
ROASTED TURNIPS AND SHALLOTS SOUP with Turnip Greens

BY BRYANT TERRY

YOU NEED

2 bunches young turnips with greens

3 medium shallots, peeled and cut into ½-inch pieces

3 teaspoons extra-virgin olive oil, divided

Fine sea salt

⅛ teaspoon cayenne pepper

3 cloves garlic, minced

6 cups vegetable stock

1 tablespoon minced fresh thyme

White pepper

TO MAKE 4–6 SERVINGS

Preheat the oven to 400 degrees.

Trim the roots from the turnips and cut into ½-inch pieces. In a medium bowl, toss the turnip pieces and shallots with 1 teaspoon of the oil, ¼ teaspoon of the salt, and the cayenne. Spread them in a parchment-lined baking dish and roast for 1 hour, stirring every 15 minutes for even browning.

While the turnips are roasting, trim and discard the tough stems from the greens. Chop them into bite-size pieces, rinse well, and drain. Combine 2 teaspoons of olive oil and the garlic in a large saucepan over medium heat. Sauté for 1½ minutes, until fragrant, then add the greens and ¼ teaspoon salt. Sauté the greens until tender, stirring occasionally, about 5 minutes. Add the vegetable stock to the saucepan and set aside.

When the turnips and shallots are done roasting, transfer them to the saucepan. Add the thyme. Bring to a boil, then reduce to a simmer and cook for 5 minutes. Add white pepper and additional salt to taste. Serve hot.

"THERE IS NO PLACE LIKE HOME, *except Grandma's.*"

—ANONYMOUS

...⋙⊙⋘...

BRYANT TERRY'S FAVORITE CDs TO LISTEN TO WHILE YOU'RE MAKING THIS RECIPE!

The Best of Cannonball Adderley: The Capitol Years

Inspiration Information 3 by Mulatu Astatke and the Heliocentrics

Filles de Kilimanjaro by Miles Davis

Cesária by Cesária Évora

We Insist!: Max Roach's Freedom Now Suite by Abbey Lincoln and Max Roach

...⋙⊙⋘...

DO YOU KNOW?

Need help serving up your family history? Devised by the **MARIAL CENTER** at Emory University, the "Do You Know" game will get the family narrative flowing! Parents, toss a few of these questions out during dinner the next time your extended family is at the table—or answer them yourself and fill in the family history blanks for everyone. Savor the memories and stories. You can even assign family members as "keepers of the legends" for safekeeping and passing on. You will be amazed at what everyone thinks they know but doesn't! You will be doubly amazed at how much your kids love learning about you!

- Do you know how your parents met? Where they grew up?

- Do you know how your grandparents met?

- Do you know what was going on in the world when you were born?

- Do you know the source of your name?

- Do you know which person in your family you look most like? Act like?

- Do you know the national background of your family (English, German, Russian, et cetera)?

- When did the family emigrate to this country? How did they arrive?

- Do you know some of the jobs that your parents had when they were young?

- Do you know some of the things that happened to your mom and dad when they were at school? What were their best subjects or their worst?

RECIPES

AUNT ISABELLE'S ICEBOX COOKIES

BY JILL HANSEN

Aunt Isabelle loved to feed people. Her saying was, "If you go away hungry from my kitchen, it's your own fault." She grew all her own vegetables on her fifty-acre farm, passed the love of farming on to her extended family, and was still weeding her garden on her ninety-fifth birthday. Aunt Isabelle's kitchen, warmed by the woodstove, was a sanctuary for everyone who knew her. You could count on it and the never-diminishing tin of her signature Icebox Cookies!

YOU NEED

2 cups brown sugar

1 cup (2 sticks) butter

2 eggs

1 teaspoon baking soda

1 teaspoon salt

$3\frac{1}{2}$ cups flour

1 teaspoon baking powder

2 teaspoons vanilla

1 cup chopped walnuts

TO MAKE 3 DOZEN

Combine the sugar and butter until creamy, then add in the eggs and beat again.

Combine all the dry ingredients except the nuts. Gradually add into this the sugar-and-egg mixture until a dough is formed. Then add the vanilla and nuts.

Roll the dough into 2 rolls about 2 inches in diameter, then wrap and store them in the "icebox" overnight.

Slice the dough very thinly, approximately ¼-inch thick, and bake at 350 degrees on an ungreased cookie sheet for 9 minutes or until golden brown on the bottom.

RECIPES

GRANDMA HELEN'S APPLE CAKE

BY CAROL PETERS

My mother, Helen Warshawsky Kubel, was born in 1909 to a poor Jewish family on the outskirts of Warsaw, where she, her parents, and her six siblings lived in a single-room house with a stove in the center of the room. Great food was cooked on that stove.

Apple cake was one of her specialties. She never measured. During one visit home, I stood at her side, and as she began scooping flour with her hand, I transferred the handfuls to a cup (she didn't own a measuring cup, so I used a coffee cup). I did the same with the apples. I wrote down this treasured recipe and it's delicious every time!

YOU NEED

1½ cups sugar, divided

½ cup oil

½ cup (1 stick) butter

4 eggs

Juice and zest (the grated yellow part of the lemon rind) of 1 lemon

2½ cups flour

2½ teaspoons baking powder

½ teaspoon salt

2½ pounds apples (or other fresh fruit), thinly sliced (about 4 cups)

2 teaspoons cinnamon

½ cup chopped nuts or raisins (optional)

TO MAKE 1 CAKE

Preheat the oven to 325 degrees.

Butter and flour a rectangular cake pan. Set aside.

Mix 1 cup of the sugar with the oil and butter in a large mixing bowl. Add the eggs, lemon juice, and lemon zest. Blend well. Sift the flour, baking powder, and salt together in another bowl, and stir into wet ingredients.

In a separate bowl, stir the sliced fruit with the remaining ½ cup sugar and cinnamon. Add raisins and nuts if desired.

Pour two-thirds of the batter into the cake pan. Spread around to cover the bottom completely. Cover with fruit. Dot top with remaining dough (it will spread in baking).

Bake for 1 hour, or until a cake tester comes out clean from the center.

"IF GOD HAD INTENDED US TO FOLLOW RECIPES, *He wouldn't have given us* GRANDMOTHERS." —LINDA HENLEY

GREEK LOVE
By Arianna Huffington

Memories of my mother are inextricably tied to food. As you entered our home, there was always a big basket filled with pistachio nuts, dried figs, and other delicious things to nibble on. No one could ring our doorbell without being asked, indeed *urged*, to come in, sit down, and try whatever she was cooking. And no one ever left the house without a goody bag filled with food.

When my sister Agapi and I would come home after school, there was always a wonderful meal, prepared by our mother, waiting for us. It might be lamb chops and salad; the traditional avgolemono soup; feta cheese, bread, roasted potatoes, and tsoureki, a Greek sweet bread with extra honey. Don't ask me how we could do anything but sleep after this meal—let alone still do our homework. But somehow we did.

Our late lunch was the biggest meal of the day. The most important thing that happened during those afternoon banquets was having our mother sit down and join us to talk about our day. The three of us would talk about what had happened at school, about our teachers, schoolmates, challenges, aspirations, and our dreams. We would talk about boys, girlfriends, family, books—anything and everything that was on our minds. It was our ritual—one filled with love and life lessons. It would leave us deeply satisfied, or as my mother used to put it, "with body and soul fed."

KIRSTIN'S NANNA'S FRIKADELLER
(These Are Not Swedish Meatballs)

My amazing Danish grandmother's name was appropriately Nanna. She was not a fancy cook. As most people, she had just a few dishes she would make, but because she made each dish almost once a week, she made them so well.

One of my favorite things to do was to sit in her kitchen on a winter Sunday, the snow flying on the fields outside, the fire roaring inside. She would heat up a leftover frikadelle, put it on a piece of generously buttered pumpernickel bread, and plop some homemade black currant jam on top. The butter would melt, the jam was sweet, tangy, tasting like summer, and the frikadelle ... as my grandmother would say, heaven in a mouthful.

I have changed her recipe a bit, using chicken instead of pork (I am sure she would approve). But they are still just as good, whether on a dinner plate with a side of cucumber salad, or on a piece of bread and butter, with jam on top.

KIDS CAN

Tear the parsley to little bits.
Crack the eggs.
Stir the bread crumb mixture.

YOU NEED

1 cup cold water

⅔ cup unseasoned bread crumbs

2 eggs, lightly beaten

2 teaspoons salt

1 teaspoon pepper

1 tablespoon white wine or apple cider vinegar

¼ cup chopped fresh parsley

1 small finely chopped onion

3 pounds ground organic chicken

Vegetable oil, for frying

TO MAKE 32 MEATBALLS, SOME FOR TODAY AND SOME FOR TOMORROW

In a big bowl, mix everything but the chicken and the vegetable oil. Stir until it is all mixed well together. Let it rest in the fridge for about 10 minutes, giving the bread crumbs time to absorb the liquids.

Add the ground chicken to the bowl and stir well.

Heat the oven to 350 degrees. Oil a baking sheet and put aside.

Heat a large nonstick pan over medium heat and add a drizzle of vegetable oil.

Now you need a bowl of cold water and a large dinner spoon. Dip the spoon and your hands in the water, scoop up a spoonful of the chicken mixture, and smack it lightly into your hand. Scoop it up again, forming it with the spoon. You might have to do this a few times until it forms an egg-shaped meatball. (If it is round, it will look like a Swedish meatball. You don't want that.)

Slide the frikadelle into the pan, and continue forming them, sliding them into the pan as you go.

As the frikadeller turn golden brown, flip them. When they are brown on both sides, but still raw in the middle, put them on the baking sheet and finish cooking them in the oven for about 20 minutes.

DANISH CUCUMBER SALAD THE JAPANESE WAY

YOU NEED

1 hothouse cucumber, peeled and thinly sliced crosswise

½ cup *seasoned* Japanese rice vinegar

TO MAKE ABOUT 1½ CUPS

Toss the ingredients together. Add chopped dill if you please.

Leftover Tip *Put half of the meatballs in the freezer, and save for a lucky day. Or heat them up the next day and serve on a slice of pumpernickel with a dollop of black currant jam, or on a toasted English muffin topped with the cucumber salad.*

We Said,

"NO GRANDMOTHERS"

By Davia Nelson and Nikki Silva

Hidden kitchens. We go in search of them: Tales of secret, unexpected, below-the-radar cooking across America; stories of little-known kitchen cultures and traditions—how communities come together through food. We chronicle them in the *Hidden Kitchens* series that airs on NPR's *Morning Edition*.

When we opened up the Hidden Kitchens Hotline, we had but one stipulation: "Please, no grandmothers. Do not call in and tell us about your grandmother and her cooking." We know. It sounds cold and heartless. Kitchens and grandmothers, the two are inextricably linked. That's what we were afraid of. We knew if we gave grandmother stories an inch, the hotline would melt down. It would be a flood, an endless sea of grandmothers and their cookies, pies, and advice. Fortunately for us, most everyone ignored our plea, like this one:

"My grandmother was Mary Bridges. Mary used to make pies for families of people who died. On the day of her death, we began to receive pie plates. At first, we didn't really take notice because all these pie plates were empty, but as the day went on, we realized that they were her pie plates that she had given out to her community when someone had died. Before the day was over, we had received nearly fifty empty pie plates, all with her name on the back."

Dozens of confessional messages flowed in, grandmothers reaching out from the grave to their children and grandchildren through the long arm of the kitchen. Even our own grandmothers made their presence known. Just listen to Nikki Silva:

"My grandmothers, Narcissus and Rosebud, passed on their secrets in two very different kinds of kitchens. Narcissus came over from Portugal when she was twelve, was married off at thirteen, and had five kids by the time she was twenty. Narcissus was the matriarch of our family, holding everyone hostage with her soupage and carne vino d'alhos, her legendary Portuguese soup and meat. She canned, preserved, and tended a little kitchen garden. She held court at the stove—bestowing and withholding approval and love to her sons, daughters, and grandchildren who arrived unannounced throughout the day for coffee, cookies, and to

make sure their position as "her favorite" was secure.

"Rosebud on the other hand never cooked a meal in her life, at least as far as I knew. Rosebud was a hillbilly, played ukulele, and called me Doll Baby. When I was growing up, she owned a little closet of a diner called Ruby's Broiled Burgers. Ruby was long gone, but Rosebud kept the name and was called Ruby by all. She tended the counter and three booths, making shakes and flirting with the cops. Everyone loved Ruby."

We did receive one distressing message on the Hidden Kitchens Hotline from Barbara Rowland, Tacoma, Washington, who has been teaching food and nutrition at Stadium High School in Tacoma for thirty-five years. This grandmother has always required her students to cook something at home, but in the last few years this has become harder. "Many of these kids have no measuring cups or spoons or other kitchen tools in their home. One girl in the class told me that she had never had a home-cooked meal. All the food her family eats comes from the deli. Somebody picks it up on the way home."

So Barbara has been buying the cooking tools and sending them home with her students. "The generation that just passed through my classes will sit around when they are old and remember fondly Totino's frozen pizzas and Pepito's microwave burritos. They will not remember how Mama's house smelled with a pork roast cooking. We are losing a generation of food memories—of what Grandma cooked, childhood memories of the house smelling good."

We were surprised in our search for vanishing kitchen traditions that the family table was among them. Over the last decades the family dinner has transformed and in some families all but disappeared. Sometimes, not always, it's grandmothers and grandfathers, their recipes and traditions that hold part of the key to gathering the tribe around the table. The kitchen, it conjures up conversation, comfort. It's the room in the house that counts the most, and that smells the best, where families gather, where all good parties begin and end. The room where the best stories are told.

LAURIE'S MOM, LOLA
Hostess with the Mostest

My mother loved to entertain. Everything about it appealed to her. She loved the anticipation of it, planning the menu, getting the house ready, preparing the food, and selecting the right outfit for the occasion. I have warm memories of lying on her bed with my sister Lisa, our feet swinging in the air, watching her as she dressed for a weekend party, putting on perfume and pearls, being careful not to mess up her big beauty-parlor hairdo. And then Lisa and I would ooh and ahh at the final results. Saturday nights seemed so glamorous and exciting.

For days before the party my mother cooked up a storm, filling the house with food aromas long before the big event. But nothing was more fun than the anticipation of the arrival of the first guest. My father, freshly shaved and spiffy, would mix and pour the six o'clock preparty cocktails. My special job always included pouring the bridge mix into Mom's "company"

glass bowls, and helping her set the table with the "good china" and sterling silver. "Make sure the edge of the knife points toward the plate," she would always remind me.

My mother's entertaining skills extended to her immediate family during the week, like clockwork, Monday through Friday. Dinner was always a full three-course meal: salad, protein, two vegetables, a starch, and a dessert. In true midcentury style, most of the ingredients came from either the freezer or a can. Her Friday-night ritual of rye bread and chopped liver hors d'oeuvres signaled that the weekend was upon us.

Here is one of her most dependable staples, because of the speed with which it can be made. The leftovers are also great for lunch and delicious cold right out of the fridge. It has the worst possible name, Salmon Loaf, but don't let that turn you off. It stands the test of time. My other sister Bonnie made it yesterday, first time in years, and it brought us all right back to that well-used kitchen on Long Island. Bonnie's version was copied right from Lola's original recipe card. As for the bridge mix? We tried that again, too. Not nearly as tasty as I remember it!

LOLA'S SALMON LOAF

3 slices bread, soaked in . . .

1 cup milk

2 14-ounce cans of salmon, mashed (you can use tuna instead)

½ medium onion, grated

½ green pepper, diced (optional)

3 eggs, beaten

Salt and pepper to taste

Grated Parmesan cheese

Paprika

1 tablespoon butter

Preheat the oven to 350 degrees.

Soak the bread in the milk, then fold together with the next five ingredients and pour into an oiled loaf pan. Generously sprinkle grated cheese on top. Finish with a dusting of paprika. Dot with butter. Bake for 1 hour, or until the center is firm.

TWO HOMES, ONE TABLE

Family Dinner After Divorce

~14~

"Life is **UNEVEN AND UNPREDICTABLE. RITUALS HELP STABILIZE** and anchor us."

—MARSHALL P. DUKE, PhD, Candler Professor of Psychology, Emory University

MY FAMILY DINNER AFTER DIVORCE

I would be remiss in writing a book about family dinner if I didn't include families who are dealing with divorce, myself included. Today half of all marriages end in divorce. That's an awful lot of family dinners in jeopardy. It's unfortunate that just as kids need rituals most, when they are the most fragile and insecure, a great stabilizer like family dinner is often the first thing to go. Lots of factors contribute to this: the pain of the empty seat (no one wants to sit there, and if they did they would regret it when the reprimand came: "But that's Dad's seat!"); the emotional wreckage of the remaining parent; the sadness of the kids, often masked by sullenness; the convenient mindless tempting escape of the television . . . the list is endless.

When marriages break up, kids need the comfort of routine more than ever. When life is suddenly unpredictable and scary, rituals come to the rescue doing what they do best, providing a sense of predictability and normalcy, stability and security, comfort and love. I speak from personal experience. All the rituals I had spent years establishing helped me and my kids enormously, and Larry, too. Continuing them sent the message loud and clear that although our family was changing, life would go on, routines would continue, dinner would be served.

The first month of transition out of my marriage is a complete blur now, but I do remember insisting on dinners as usual every night at six thirty with my daughters. No one felt much like eating, but that didn't really matter.

Soon after, Larry and I decided to try something a little unorthodox. It's called "nesting." A split couple move back and forth in and out of the shared house so that the kids don't have to. Larry got an apartment, but had dinner with the girls and stayed at the house every Monday and Wednesday night. I would leave right before dinner and stay at my sister's house nearby.

Nesting isn't something everyone can do; both parties really have to cooperate and have the resources to do it. Luckily for us, it worked: Rituals remained intact, bedrooms stayed the same, even Dad coming home two nights a week helped everyone ease into the change. Still, I remember a lot of brooding meals and awkward, forced conversation between bites. I also remember making a lot of pleading phone calls to family members and friends begging them to come to dinner to help relieve the tension and provide some distraction. Skipping organized dinners and letting everyone do their own thing would have taken some of the pressure off the kids and me, but only temporarily. I was desperate to get back to feeling "normal" as soon as possible, and the fewer things that changed, the better off we would all be.

If family dinner had stopped, the lesson to my kids (and to myself) would be that we weren't whole anymore, that something was broken forever. I honestly didn't believe that to be true. The message I did believe, and the one our continuing dinners provided was—This family is changing, we are in a transition, but we are still a family! Not only that, but we are a family that is going to get through this and come out strong and connected.

Family dinner helped all of us weather the rough days by forcing us to deal with one another, by reminding all of us every day that we were still a family. Thank goodness for that toolbox of table games. When things got uncomfortable and no one was talking, I would toss out a spelling challenge, or play the Pet Peeve game. My new full-time job was to make sure that despite this change, my family didn't fall apart. Our dinner rituals, thank goodness, helped me accomplish that.

Then I took this concept one step farther. I had the notion (hope) that eventually I could even get my ex back to the table, with me sitting at it, for a once-a-month, dare I say once-every-other-week, family dinner. Crazy, you say? Maybe it was, but I was eager to try. I wanted a different divorce model for my kids. They had lots of friends who were from broken homes (okay, that is a crazy expression we have to stop using. Could we make people feel even worse than they already do?), and whose parents were in constant battle. I didn't want to put my girls through that. They were innocent bystanders and deserved better.

Furthermore, I wanted them to understand that just because the marriage ended, it didn't mean you no longer care about the other person or wanted them cut out of your life completely. I believe it's possible to have a loving divorce. It takes an enormous amount of courage to change your life. No one wants a marriage to end; no one wants to have that heart-crushing conversation with his or her kids, but it happens.

Most parents going through a divorce want to do what is best for their kids, and that is always, always going to be an amicable split and co-parenting arrangement. I wanted an open line to my girls' dad so that we could be in sync as we headed into those turbulent teen seas. I wanted access and a united front for all the important decisions and issues looming ahead. I wanted both homes to have consistent values and rules if possible. I wanted to disarm my kids'

potential bag of tricks. You know, the game where they play one parent against the other: "But Dad said . . ." or "At Dad's I can . . ." I wanted communication and transparency.

I also didn't want to cheat myself out of seeing one of my kids' most important relationships change and evolve as they got older. I didn't want to be excluded from all the laughs and inside jokes they shared with their father, and I didn't want to have that awful sense of feeling left out of half of my kids' life. I didn't want my kids thinking that their two parents weren't in constant contact and in total agreement. I didn't want to lose too much parental power.

Ultimately, I wanted Larry and me to remain captains of our family ship, a perfect analogy coined by parenting guru Susan Stiffelman (*Parenting Without Power Struggles*). She says, "Kids need us to be the captain of the ship in their lives. This isn't about parents being in control; it's about being in charge. When we refuse to deal with reality as it is we leave the child without the sense of comfort that comes from knowing he has someone capable of getting him safely through whatever crisis he might be experiencing. When we fully inhabit the role of captain of the ship of our family, we set the stage for providing the quiet and comforting authority that our children so profoundly need."

Big agenda, I know, but I have taken on big challenges before! Family dinner would be the vehicle to get me there. Slowly, I started to ask Larry if he would have dinner with the kids and me on one of my nights. I received quite a few emphatic nos and then, lo and behold, I got a yes.

That first dinner was exactly what you can imagine: awkward and miserable, but mercifully quick. The girls downed their food in one gulp and hightailed it out of the kitchen with excuses of showers and homework. Larry left pretty quickly, too. Time was on my side, though. One meal turned into several, and soon enough we got back to our old family dinner ritual of "If It's Sunday We Must Be Eating Chinese Food." I would order the favorites and he would do the pickup on his way over to the house.

Eventually, the meals got a little longer, a little more relaxed; one night Larry even stayed for a movie afterward. Within the year, we branched out and started including local restaurants—still mostly Chinese, but at least we were out of the house! To this day I enjoy the surprised look on people's faces when they recognize Larry and realize he is having dinner with the kids and me! I'm sure one day I will read a gossip item saying how Larry was out to dinner with a woman who looks just like his ex-wife! Ha. It is his ex!

I wanted a happier, more inclusive divorce than what is generally the norm. I fought for it, but I couldn't do it alone. It took both parents, and two great kids, and a hexagon-shaped table, all the interactive recipes in this book, and all the word games that forced us to laugh even when we were hurting. During the most challenging time in my life, family dinner provided the space to reconnect with one another, to shore one another up, to remind us that we were okay. The shared meal was the path in. Amen.

Marina's DIVORCE BROWNIES

YOU NEED

8 1-ounce squares unsweetened chocolate

1 cup (2 sticks) butter

5 eggs

3 cups sugar

1 tablespoon vanilla

1½ cups flour

1 teaspoon salt

2½ cups chopped pecans or walnuts, toasted

1 teaspoon orange zest

TO MAKE 24 BROWNIES

Preheat the oven to 375 degrees. Grease a 9-by-13-inch pan.

Over low heat, melt the chocolate and butter in a saucepan. Set aside.

Beat the eggs, sugar, and vanilla at high speed for 10 minutes in a mixer. Fold in the chocolate mixture, flour, and salt until just mixed. Stir in the nuts and lastly, the orange zest. Pour into the prepared pan.

Bake for 35 minutes or until a toothpick comes out clean. (Don't overbake.) Let cool at room temperature.

This can be served slightly warm with ice cream. It's delicious with berries, too.

...⌘...

THE KITCHEN NOOK
By Marina Drasnin

On a not-so-beautiful spring day, our family table was derailed. It moved from the dining room to the small kitchen nook near my stove. It happened unintentionally, as train wrecks often do. The man I was married to for ten years walked out the door and formal dining was no longer necessary. Although I wanted to hide under the covers and escape reality, my five-year-old son had other plans. He needed nourishment.

I grew up in a house where good smells constantly emanated from the kitchen. When I got home from school, there was comfort in those aromas and now, looking back, I realize those foods defined my childhood. Despite the divorce, I wanted to give my son the same sensory delights.

Freshly baked brownies and hot cocoa became our ritual, served in our tiny kitchen nook. The space reminded me of being on a train in Europe. The kind where you sit across from total strangers and by the time you reach your destination you are sharing wine, cheese, and e-mail addresses. During those first few tough years, nobody sat there without enjoying a wonderful meal or knowing a little more about whom they were eating with.

It turned out that this tiny nook, where we sat shoulder-to-shoulder, was more intimate and better suited for conversation than any dining room could ever be.

At a time when my world was falling apart and I worried about how I was going to pay the bills, my beautiful son, Harry, did not feel or know any of this. In a small nook, in a corner by the stove, with delightful smells wafting around him, he felt safe. Little did I know that the way to get my life back on track was to keep the meals coming, right on schedule.

"*A family meal* REVIVES OUR SENSE OF TOGETHERNESS. *Life is not over. It's just different.*"

—JILL BROOKE, founder of Blended Families of America

GRACE
IS GRATITUDE
~ 15 ~

WAYS TO SAY THANK YOU AND APPRECIATE LIFE'S GIFTS

"Gratitude does not come naturally," says Wendy Mogel, PhD, author of one of my all-time favorite parenting books, *The Blessing of a Skinned Knee*. "It's like a muscle that must be built up and strengthened throughout childhood." If that's true, and I believe it is, then we have our work cut out for us, parenting in a world where so much is available and so much is taken for granted.

How do you teach kids to be grateful when their life experience affords so much immediate gratification and when we do so much for them that they really should be doing for themselves? It's an everyday quandary—how to foster gratitude and ensure that our kids are going to be able to make it on their own in the big and more challenging, constantly shifting and less forgiving real world.

Raising grateful kids has got to be one of the most daunting and difficult challenges we face as parents. "There is a consensus among parents I know," says the author of *Can I Have a Cell Phone for Hanukkah?* and mom of four Sharon Duke Estroff. "That it's our job to wait on our kids hand and foot, doing everything for them and never letting them be upset. But we really aren't doing them or us any favors by raising 'silver platter' kids (as in everything served up on a silver platter not to be confused with 'silver spoon' which could be bad, too). It really comes back and bites us in the long run."

One thing is for certain: There is no downside to getting those "gratitude muscles" in shape, and the dinner table is an effective place to start. We're all together, and there's something right in front of us to be grateful for: food! Yes indeed. Of course, this isn't a new idea, but I think it's one that is getting lost in our culture of convenience and speed. Expressing thanks for food is as basic a ritual as exists in the world.

"THE CHILD IS A WITNESS.
The child looks for cues as to how one ought to behave and finds them galore as we parents go about our lives."

—ROBERT COLES, MD, Harvard University, Pulitzer Prize–winning author of *The Moral Intelligence of Children*

Every religion from Buddhism to Islam, Judaism to Christianity, has its version of thanks for the blessings of food—and it's not optional. Gratitude, in fact, is *commanded* by most of the world's religions. Every culture, every civilization recognized nature's preeminent role in keeping us alive by providing all the elements—earth, sun, water—needed to feed us.

"FOOD HAS TO BE SACRED. *There is something very unique about sharing the nourishment of food with your loved ones.* **I FEAR WE ARE FORGETTING THAT."** —DR. MEHMET OZ, cardiothoracic surgeon, host of *The Dr. Oz Show*

Respect for food starts the moment a baby is born and is calmed by his or her mother's milk; early Native American Indians went so far in their gratitude that they had prayers asking for forgiveness from the animal or plant for taking its life. Imagine if we had that thought in our head every time we ate. Factory farming would never have become an acceptable way to feed America. It just doesn't get more primal than acknowledging our dependence on Mother Nature.

One of the beautiful things about gratitude is that the more you practice feeling it, the better you get at recognizing it. Estroff is particularly sage on this issue, having been raised by Marshall Duke, the revered psychologist at Emory University who spent his career studying family rituals and practicing what he learned at home. Imagine the dinners at that house! With such great role models, Sharon has continued the traditions she grew up with in her current household in Atlanta, and she sees the results of exercising the "gratitude muscle" every week with her four kids. "It's at the point now where something simple but pleasant will happen to my kids on a Wednesday, and they'll say, 'Oh that's what I'm going to say I am grateful for on Friday at Shabbat,'" she says. "They know the gratitude discussion is coming and they have to participate so they are looking for things to be grateful for all week long."

The Reverend Ed Bacon, the inspiring rector of All Saints Church in Pasadena, California, a four-thousand-member multiethnic urban Episcopal parish, doesn't hesitate a second when asked if gratitude can and should be taught. "If you don't learn gratitude as a child, you can grow up to be an ingrate—and that is one of the worst possible human conditions. The essence of life is a gift. What do you do when you receive a gift? It is a diminishment of the human soul not to know that life is a gift."

So the question isn't *should* we teach and encourage gratitude, the question is *how* we teach it. One time-tested place to start is at the dinner table. A thousand years of tradition provides us the model: the simple act of saying grace,

making a toast, or just simple words of thanks expressed before the meal begins.

You can do this in a religious way or a secular way—what's important is the pause before eating to acknowledge that the food before us did not appear on its own. Someone, many people, contributed to its arrival on our plate. You don't have to believe in God to say grace or to sprinkle a little gratitude at the table. You just have to believe in the importance of being grateful for what you have, or for whatever blessings, small or large, came your way that day.

We all need practice expressing thanks for our family, our friends, our health, and our ability to walk, or breathe or laugh or cry. Our kids are watching; that is how they learn. At a recent dinner, I asked our group what were some things we take for granted that we should be grateful for. My friend's fourteen-year-old daughter said, "Weekends!" Yes, that's it. That is exactly the point. We *should* be grateful for weekends. What a great answer! A regular appointment with gratitude, around the table with people you love, is one of life's simple but most nutritious gifts.

My family's first exposure to a religious mealtime grace was at a dinner with Bobby and Mary Kennedy and their large brood of kids. We've shared many meals over the years, but it was our first family dinner together, when I watched and listened to them say grace, that I remember most. I hadn't been exposed to this ritual in this form before, and neither had my kids. The unfamiliarity and reverence of the moment was a trigger for my kids to try to muffle their giggles, but it was wonderful, too, and made a powerful impression on all of us (for one, we had never seen the Kennedy kids so quiet and reflective!).

"Every dinner growing up opened and closed with a prayer," Bobby later told me. "Nobody was allowed to touch their food until we had prayed. The reason we said prayers, and the reason I teach my kids to say them, is not just to learn the traditions of faith but also the importance of gratitude. My father wanted us to know that we should be grateful for what we had, that there were people who didn't have enough to eat, and that the privileges that we had were not assigned necessarily because of merit but because we were fortunate, we were trustees. What we were given was supposed to be used to benefit other people. Praying at dinner was, and is, a way of reminding ourselves of that."

Explore the possibilities of gratitude with your children by expressing it yourself and giving them a chance to do the same. Make it a part of your dinner ritual however often you can fit it in. Saying grace can be expressed in lots of different ways—with a formal prayer, a more casual blessing, a question for the table, quotes, stories, a few simple words of thanks. However you say it, gratitude is a basic ingredient to a healthy life.

Gratitude BLESSINGS FOR THE TABLE

Here is a collection of lovely prayers, sayings, blessings, and meaningful words and phrases to help get you started on expressing gratitude. Prewritten graces really come in handy when you want to give everyone at the table the opportunity to say one, but keep the experience stress-free for the young, bashful, or tongue-tied. Adrian Butash, author of *Bless This Food,* a superb collection of graces from around the world, remembers well those moments at dinner when the question would inevitably arise: "Who is going to say grace?" "All us kids would freeze in panic that we would be chosen," Adrian recalls. *Bless This Food* and the other recommended books in this section solves that problem; all you have to do is read.

Asking a friend or guest to recite a food blessing is an honor and a wonderful way to welcome that person into your family's circle. Of course, thoughts just from the heart, no matter how simple, are perfect, too. Any words of gratitude will enhance the experience for all who are present— and even make the food taste better!

"*A food blessing* TRANSFORMS EVERYONE *into a circle of friends.*"

—ADRIAN BUTASH, author of *Bless This Food*

Other ideas: Have each child pick out a poem or saying that reflects gratitude for a Friday-night dinner or a Sunday supper. Print out the gratitude quotes compiled in this chapter and put one under each person's plate (your youngest can help cut the quotes apart, draw colored boxes around them, or fold them and make place cards out of them). At an appropriate time, announce that everyone has a special quote under their plate and go around the table reading them. Earmark at least one day of the week for the ritual of saying thank you, and it will become a treasured tradition.

From Bless This Food: Ancient & Contemporary Graces from Around the World
by Adrian Butash

GRACE OF THE BODHISATTVA
This food comes from the earth and the sky,
It is the gift of the entire universe
And the fruit of much hard work;
I vow to live a life which is worthy to receive it.

CHILDREN'S PRAYER
God is great! God is good!
Let us thank Him for our food.

OVERHEARD CHILD'S PRAYER

God thank you for the sun, the trees, the mountains, and me.

BUDDHIST BLESSING FOR FOOD

Earth, Water, Fire, Air and Space
combine to make this food.
Numberless beings gave their lives
and labors that we may eat.
May we be nourished
that we may nourish life.

JEWISH BLESSING FOR THE CHALLAH

Blessed art Thou, Lord our God, King of the universe, who
brings forth bread from the earth.

CHRISTIAN PRAYER

Dear Lord, thank you for this food.
Bless the hands that prepared it.
Bless it to our use and us to your service.
And make us ever mindful of the needs of others.
Through Christ our Lord we pray.
For what we are about to receive, may the Lord make us
truly thankful.

CLASSIC SLEEP-AWAY CAMP BLESSING

Rub a dub dub
Thanks for the grub
Yea! God!

A Blessing for a Parent to Say to a Child
by Rabbi Naomi Levy

May all the gifts hidden inside you find
their way into the world.

May all the kindness of your thoughts
be expressed in your deeds

May all your learning lead to wisdom, may all your efforts
lead to success, may all the love in your heart be returned
to you, may God bless your body with health and your
soul with joy, may God watch over you night and day and
protect you from harm, may all your prayers be answered.

Some Traditional Blessings for
the Family Table

TRADITIONAL AMERICAN BLESSING Circa 1800s

Father, we thank Thee for this food.
For health and strength and all things good.
May others all these blessings share.
And hearts be grateful everywhere.

CATHOLIC GRACE

Bless us, O Lord, and these Thy gifts, which we are about to
receive from Thy bounty, through Christ our Lord.

Without Thy sunshine and Thy rain;
We would not have the golden grain;
Without Thy love we'd not be fed;
We thank Thee for our daily bread.

THANKSGIVING

For each new morning with its light,
For rest and shelter of the night,
For love and friends,
For everything Thy goodness sends.

—Ralph Waldo Emerson (1803–1882)

CHILD'S BLESSING

Thank you for the world so sweet,
Thank you for the food we eat.
Thank you for the birds that sing,
Thank you God for everything.

CHINESE PROVERB

When eating bamboo shoots
remember the man who planted them...

Dear Father, hear and bless
Thy beasts and singing birds;
And guard with tenderness
Small things that have no words.

"DINNER RITUALS *have nothing to do with class, or working women's busy lives, or any particular family structure. I've had dinners of boiled potatoes with families in Siberia. Suppers of deli cold cuts with single welfare mothers in Chicago, bowls of watery gruel in the Sahara—**ALL MADE MEMORABLE BY THE GRACE WITH WHICH THEY WERE OFFERED** and by the sight of youngsters learning through experience the art of human companionship."*

—FRANCINE DU PLESSIX GRAY, *The New Yorker*

Quotes of Gratitude for the Table

"The only people with whom you should try to get even are those who have helped you." *John E. Southard*

"As we express our gratitude, we must never forget that the highest appreciation is not to utter words, but to live by them." *John Fitzgerald Kennedy*

"Gratitude is a quality similar to electricity: it must be produced and discharged and used up in order to exist at all." *William Faulkner*

"Silent gratitude isn't much use to anyone."
Gladys Bronwyn Stern

"Feeling gratitude and not expressing it is like wrapping a present and not giving it." *William Arthur Ward*

"I would maintain that thanks are the highest form of thought; and that gratitude is happiness doubled by wonder." *Gilbert Keith Chesterton*

"We often take for granted the very things that most deserve our gratitude." *Cynthia Ozick*

"Gratitude is the best attitude." *Author unknown*

"Praise the bridge that carried you over." *George Colman*

"If a fellow isn't thankful for what he's got, he isn't likely to be thankful for what he's going to get." *Frank A. Clark*

"Not what we say about our blessings, but how we use them, is the true measure of our thanksgiving." *W. T. Purkiser*

"I feel a very unusual sensation—if it is not indigestion, I think it must be gratitude." *Benjamin Disraeli*

"The hardest arithmetic to master is that which enables us to count our blessings." *Eric Hoffer*

"Most human beings have an almost infinite capacity for taking things for granted." *Aldous Huxley*

"May we eat with mindfulness and gratitude so as to be worthy to receive it." *Thich Nhat Hanh, Vietnamese Buddhist monk*

SHOPPING FOR GRATITUDE

One eye-opening gratitude exercise is learning about how much food costs (literally and figuratively). If you're getting your children involved in cooking and kitchen chores, shopping should be part of the drill. Take them with you and make them look at and compare prices. Is cheaper always better? How much food do you need to feed the family for a week and how much does it cost? Better yet, give them $25 and tell them to shop for a nutritious, balanced dinner themselves and see what they come up with. They will appreciate meals so much more when they know firsthand the work, time, and money that go into them.

...⚬◦⚬...

Thank God for home,
and crisp, fair weather,
and loving hearts,
That meet together—
And red, ripe fruit
And golden grain—
And dear Thanksgiving
Come again!

—*Nancy Byrd Turner (1880–1971)*

WHERE DOES Dinner Come From?

Like magic, presto! Dinner is on the table. But it's not magic, as anyone who is responsible for the finished product knows. The following list will help illuminate for everyone how many hands touched the food on the way to the plate. It might even help improve the number of thank yous at the end of your meals. The list would also make an interesting dinner grace (say "thank you" after each statement, for example). How many on the list below can your family come up with?

- A farmer plows, tills, plants, weeds, and waters the food.
- A rancher tends to and harvests livestock.
- The weather does its job: The sun shines and the rain falls.
- Farmworkers harvest the food.
- The farmer sells his or her food to the market.
- Food is transported from the farm to the supermarket.
- Mom/Dad/helper goes to the store or market.
- Food is put in grocery cart, unloaded on the counter, and paid for.
- Grocery bags are loaded and carried to the car.
- Shopper drives home.
- Grocery bags are unloaded from the car and carried into the house.
- Grocery bags are unpacked and everything put away.
- Recipes taken out, pots taken out, ingredients taken out.
- Food is prepared: mixed, baked, sautéed.
- Table is set with plates.
- Forks, knives, and spoons are put on table.
- Napkins, glasses, and condiments put on the table.
- Pitcher of water on the table.
- Food is brought to the table.
- Family is called to dinner, everyone eats!

The Most Precious Gift of All: A TRUE STORY for the Table

Once upon a time there was a young man named Tuan, who immigrated to the United States from his war-torn country, Vietnam. Although Tuan had been a goldsmith in his tiny fishing village, he knew no one in this new land. He was very poor and had few options, so he became a day laborer on the streets of Los Angeles.

His mother, concerned for his welfare, reached out to her community and spoke to someone who knew someone who knew someone, who contacted a Vietnamese American jewelry designer by the name of Chan Luu.

Chan took a chance and hired Tuan off the street to make jewelry for her. Every day, he worked hard, molding gold and setting diamonds. And every day, tiny shards of the metal would drift to the floor—the scraps from his delicate work. At day's end over the sink, he would laboriously scrape off the gold dust from his hands and fingernails before heading home.

Many years went by. Tuan helped Chan build her business, and soon the company had more than two hundred employees. Chan helped Tuan buy a home of his own. One day, Tuan presented her with a gift: a heavy, solid-gold, handcrafted bangle. "Where did this come from?" Chan exclaimed. "It is a fortune in gold and exquisitely crafted!"

With a sweet, shy smile, Tuan replied, "I made you this bracelet from the little gold scraps I collected over the last fifteen years. It is my way of saying thank you."

Chan was speechless. To this day, it remains her most precious gift.

DISCUSSION FOR THE DINNER TABLE: How are the themes of gratitude, loyalty, and honesty depicted in this story? How can we strive to exemplify these values in our own lives?

"We have the capacity to **CHANGE THE PACE AND TONE OF OUR LIVES IN AN INSTANT.** We can gobble down our food **WITHOUT EVEN PAYING ATTENTION** to what we are eating or we can take a moment and stop." —RABBI NAOMI LEVY, author of *Talking to God*

"THE SABBATH COMES LIKE A CARESS, *wiping away fear, sorrow, and somber memories."*

—RABBI ABRAHAM HESCHEL, Jewish theologian and philosopher

SHABBAT FRIDAY: A Weekly Appointment with Gratitude

Sometime around my daughter's fifth birthday, I started to look into the idea of starting a Friday-night Shabbat dinner ritual. I must have gone to one at a friend's house at the time (probably Heidi's) and liked it, but I really can't remember specifically. I do know that once I was exposed to a ready-made night of rituals, food, and family, I was full-steam-ahead determined to incorporate it into our week.

Observant Jews have a version of Shabbat that is very different from what I started to do in my house, but I knew I could modify the tradition to suit the needs of modern life and my family while keeping its essence intact. The *spirit* of Shabbat is what felt most important to me.

In fact, I think Shabbat is a perfect concept for any family, regardless of religion. It's just too great an idea not to do your own version: a special night once a week where everyone knows they will sit leisurely around the table, take stock of the week's highs and lows, and savor family, food, and friends. Pick and choose the rituals you like about Shabbat, make up a few new ones, and do your own version one night a week that fits your schedule, calling it Friday Family Dinner, or Special Sunday Lunch, or whatever you come up with.

To determine how I would create my Shabbat, I took a two-hour class my neighborhood temple was offering and brought my receipt home to wave at my husband to prove I was serious and it was time to get started.

I have to confess I didn't do it for religious reasons; I did it out of a joy for rituals. I love celebration, and I'll make the most of my own religion's holidays and anyone else's, for that matter. That's a genetic and cultural predilection that comes from being raised in a Jewish reform household that celebrated more holidays than those available in the Jewish catalog.

I'm not sure why my parents hid baskets of chocolate eggs, Marshmallow Peeps, and stuffed floppy-eared rabbits every Easter morning for us to find, or why they embraced Christmas morning with presents piled high and stockings on the staircase. (No Christmas tree, though—that's where they drew the line. Every year I asked for a tree and every year I got the same answer: "No tree, we're Jewish!") I can't explain it, but I am glad they did it, because the memories are so delicious. As expected, I continued my childhood family traditions with my children, evidence that rituals do help define who we are as a family and get passed down from generation to generation.

Strangely, though, Friday Shabbat dinner was never in my mother's repertoire. I had to discover it for myself—but once I did, I immediately loved it. First, it took the pressure off making plans for Friday nights. Shabbat required everyone to be home by sundown and to stop working. Second, it provided the perfect excuse to invite friends over (so I get to socialize but I don't have to go out!).

Third, it sets a tone of fun by mandating that the night is for celebration. It's a Shabbat law that you are forbidden from talking about anything sad during Shabbat dinner: only happiness and gratitude. What a perfect framework to start those gratitude juices flowing. In preparation, we spiff up the house, the table, and ourselves, roast a chicken and potatoes, and welcome the weekend with a loving, focused celebration around the table.

How clever that the Jewish ancestors more than two thousand years ago understood the importance of setting aside a sacred time for dinner; a time to take a break from the pressures of the week and purposely bring family together. It's incredibly powerful to ponder that way back then, they recognized the importance of a shared meal.

SHABBAT

To cease, end, or rest. It begins at sundown each Friday and ends Saturday one hour after sundown, or when three stars are visible in the sky. Shabbat dinner is the meal celebrated at sundown Friday. Shabbat is a time for reflection, prayer, renewing of the spirit, friends, and family.

The Shabbat table is filled with the symbols of Jewish history, but they are just as relevant today. The candlesticks, the challah, the wine all represent contemporary goals: a regularly scheduled moment to pause, to express gratitude for the food we eat, to bless our children and one another. Whatever our religion, the core truths are universal: gratitude for all that we have, compassion for those who have less, family togetherness, peace in the home, love and hope for the future.

Four Rituals for Shabbat Friday

- **Blessings** over the candles, wine, and challah.
- **Gratitudes.** Around the table, everyone says something they are grateful for.
- **Highs and lows.** Everyone shares their high and/or low from the week.
- **Tzedaka.** A special box is used to collect everyone's loose change for those in need. When the box is full, the family decides on a worthy cause to contribute it to.

TWO QUESTIONS
For Rabbi Morley Feinstein

University Temple, Brentwood, Los Angeles

1. The Talmud talks about the sacredness of the home and holiness of the "meal table." Why is the table considered the holiest place in the house?

Think of the homes we had in ancient times. People barely had room to sleep, beds were shared, but there was always one table. And that table was where one studied, that was the table where one argued, where one ate. That was the table where one mended clothes or prepared food. The table was the place where conversation and communication took place. Even today it is the one common space in modern homes and it is still the place where everyone gravitates.

2. If someone isn't Jewish, can the concept of Shabbat be adapted to his or her family dinner?

The Jewish model of observing the Sabbath beginning with prayer and family time together over a meal is a model that can work for anyone. Speaking words from the heart, tying it into your own tradition, having family time is all part not only of making your family healthy but of passing on the most important values that are essential to a family. All that is crystallized in a Shabbat meal.

*"One of **THE GREAT JOYS OF MY WEEK WAS A SHABBAT DINNER** a good friend of mine would host every Friday. The night became so popular, guests would have to bring their own folding chairs. It was an **AMAZING GATHERING OF PEOPLE** of all faiths, and it marked the rhythms of my week."*

—THE REVEREND MARI CASTELLANOS, United Church of Christ

"HE IS A WISE MAN *who does not grieve for the things which he has not,* **BUT REJOICES FOR THOSE WHICH HE HAS."** —EPICTETUS, Greek philosopher

"YOU KNOW IT'S A RITUAL *when you do it a little wrong and one of the* *kids says,* **'THAT'S NOT HOW WE DO IT.'"** —BRADD SHORE, PhD, professor and director, Center for Myth and Ritual in American Life, Emory University

Sunday Dinner
WITH SOLEDAD

SOLEDAD O'BRIEN *is a correspondent for CNN and one of five siblings, all of whom graduated from Harvard. A year ago, Soledad and her husband, Bradley, had a problem. Both were traveling nonstop, she with her high-pressure reporting, and he as an investment banker. Family time was suffering. Dinner for their four kids was a crazy countertop affair with Mom and Dad hovering nearby. A time-out was needed; not for the kids, but for the parents. The solution: a new commitment to family dinner.*

"We decided to institute a ritual Sunday Dinner. I am talking four-course meal, sitting at the table for an hour and a half. That is a huge deal for five-year-old twins! It was my husband's idea. He realized we were missing out on important family traditions because we were all too busy. It's very easy in a family with two working parents to lose track of everything. You just never have these moments together, unless you make a decision to do it.

"My husband cooks, and the kids have gotten completely involved in helping him with the meal. The results have been incredible. First of all, we have gotten them to eat better. My daughter, who never met anything healthy that she likes, is now in love with salad. My nine-year-old said to me the other day, "You know I've really gotten close to Daddy helping him make dinner." Our five-year-olds clear the table; I fill and empty the dishwasher. They sit, we all talk. They've learned manners, too; they now know where their napkins go.

"It is so important to carve out family time as a way of remaining close to your roots and sharing them with your kids. Family dinner is one way to do that. My parents understood that. As parents we see it now, too. When I was growing up, my family had dinner together every night. I think part of that was there wasn't gymnastics practice that went until 7 PM like my daughter has. There was no swim team across the city. That didn't exist. People did everything at school and then there was a five thirty bus that brought you home in time for dinner.

"My dinners growing up had a huge impact on me because it forced us to spend so much time with each other. We discussed everything at dinner. I remember when I was in high school and my brothers and sisters would come home from college and we would sit at dinner and argue about law cases (they were all pre-law). We'd argue over movies. There was an unwritten rule in my big family that you had to defend your position. You had to argue your point of view. That was great life training."

Shabbat or Sunday **ROAST CHICKEN**

When you sit down for a traditional roast chicken dinner, be it Shabbat, Sunday, or a Tuesday in March, know that at tables all over the world, people are doing exactly the same thing: lighting candles, gathering their families, quietly counting their blessings, and sharing a roast chicken.

A whole roast chicken is simple, elegant, and not difficult to make. Serve the chicken with Crispy Smashed Potatoes (page 59), perhaps some Roasted Vegetables (page 109), and a crisp endive salad. Sit down and know that you are in good company.

YOU NEED

For the Chicken

1 chicken, 4–4½ pounds, preferably organic and kosher

1 tablespoon salt

8 shallots, peeled and halved (or 3 onions, peeled and quartered)

2 whole heads garlic, clean, unpeeled, and cut in half

Olive oil

Salt and pepper

2 cups chicken stock

3 tablespoons Dijon mustard

For the Herb Butter

4–5 3-inch sprigs thyme

1 3-inch sprig of rosemary

3 scallions, minced

5 sage leaves, minced

Zest of 1 lemon

1 teaspoon honey

3 tablespoons room-temperature butter

TO MAKE 6 SERVINGS

Remove the giblets from the chicken's cavity, if there are any. If there are two fatty flaps inside the chicken, pull them out as well. Rinse the chicken and pat it dry with paper towels . . . this is important, you want it really dry for crisp skin. Sprinkle it with 1 tablespoon of salt.

Pull the leaves off 2 of the thyme sprigs and the whole rosemary sprig, chop them, and, in a small bowl, combine them with the remaining herb butter ingredients.

Toss the shallots and garlic with a drizzle of olive oil.

Fill a shallow medium-size roasting pan with the shallots, garlic, and leftover thyme. If you got one of those V-shaped roasting racks for your wedding, now is the time to use it. (If you didn't, don't worry about it; the chicken will still be comfortable.) Oil the rack well. Put the pan in the oven and heat the oven to 425 degrees.

Meanwhile, rub the chicken all over with 2 tablespoons of the herb butter, pushing some under the skin of the breast as well.

Remove the hot pan from the oven. Lay the chicken on one side (on the V-rack, if you are using it, or nestled among the shallots if you are not), wing-up. Roast for 20 minutes, then flip the chicken other-wing-side up, and roast for 20 minutes. If the pan starts to smoke, add a few tablespoons stock or wine to the shallots and stir.

Finally, flip the chicken breast-side up. Slather the breast with the remaining herb butter. Continue roasting for 15 to 20 more minutes, until the juices from the cavity run clear, or an instant-read thermometer inserted into the thigh registers between 165 and 170 degrees. Transfer the chicken to a cutting board, give it a grind of pepper, and let it rest 20 minutes.

Now you have time to remove the shallots, thyme twigs, and garlic from the pan with a slotted spoon (discard the thyme). Scrape loose any tasty brown bits that might be stuck to the bottom of the pan. Pour the juices into a saucepan (or a fat separator if you have one). With a spoon, gently try to remove most of the fat floating on the surface. Add the chicken stock, shallots, and mustard to the juices in the saucepan. Simmer for about 10 minutes. Season with salt and pepper.

Carve the chicken and serve it garnished with the roasted garlic-shallot mixture, a few pieces of coquettishly placed sage, and the pan juice gravy.

> **Cook's Tip**
>
> *If you know that dinnertime will be a little hectic, roast and carve the chicken earlier in the day. Right before dinner, slide the chicken pieces into the middle of the oven and broil them for just a few minutes until they are hot and crispy again.*

HOMEMADE CHALLAH

Here is a recipe for soft, rich, beautiful challah bread. It won't take you much more than half an hour of hands-on time, but take the rising time into consideration when you plan your day.

This recipe makes two regular loaves or one big one. If you want to keep one in the freezer, carefully wrap it after you have braided it, before the last rising, then freeze. To defrost, take it out, unwrap it, cover it lightly with oiled parchment paper and a dishtowel, and let it defrost and rise for about 5 hours.

TIME: About 1 hour, plus 2½ hours' rising time

YOU NEED

1½ tablespoons active dry yeast (about 1½ packages)
Pinch of crumbled saffron (optional)
½ cup honey, divided
1¾ cups warm water
½ cup vegetable oil or nut oil
1 tablespoon salt
6 large eggs, divided
7 cups all-purpose flour (approximately)
½ cup raisins, plumped in hot water and drained (optional)
Poppy or sesame seeds, for sprinkling (optional)

TO MAKE 2 LOAVES

In a large bowl, whisk the yeast, saffron, and 1 tablespoon of the honey with 1¾ cups water that is quite warm, but not too hot to put your pinkie in it. When the yeast has dissolved and is creamy, whisk the oil, the remaining honey, and the salt into the bowl, then 4 of the eggs 1 at a time.

Stirring vigorously with a wooden spoon, add 1 cup of flour at a time until the dough cleans the sides and is kneadable. Turn the dough out onto a floured surface, put a little oil on your hands, and knead the dough until it is smooth and elastic . . . this can take awhile, at least 8 minutes (you won't need to go to the gym today).

When you are done kneading, fold in the raisins if you're using them, and plop the dough into a large oiled bowl. Flip the dough so its top ends up oiled as well. Cover with parchment paper and a clean towel.

Put the dough in a warm place (such as an oven that has been heated to 100 degrees and *then turned off*) and let it rise for 1 hour or until almost doubled in size. Punch it down and let it rise again in a warm place for half an hour.

Line one or two baking sheets with parchment paper.

Punch down the dough and divide it into 2 loaves. Cut each loaf into 3 and roll the pieces into ropes about 12 inches long. Braid them, pinching under the ends when you are done. Alternatively, you can braid a big challah and a small one, and rest the small loaf on top of the large loaf, so you end up with a beautiful double-decker loaf.

Beat the remaining eggs and brush half of the mixture on the loaves, saving the leftover egg wash. Let the loaves rise for another hour until puffy and almost doubled.

Preheat your oven to 375 degrees.

Brush the loaves with the remaining egg wash and sprinkle with the seeds. Bake in the middle of the oven for about 40 minutes or until the loaves sound hollow when they are thumped on the bottom. Cool the loaves on a rack.

Danish Tip

Cardamom is not usually found in challah, but its beautiful fragrance is very present in Danish baking. I like to sneak ½ teaspoon of cardamom and some orange zest into my challah.

"SHABBAT DINNER *is a big production that I would never consider doing on a daily basis. But it caps our week, slows us down, and* **DRAWS US TOGETHER** *in a powerful way."* —WENDY MOGEL, PhD, author of *The Blessing of a Skinned Knee*

"WHEN WE VALUE IT MORE, WE WASTE LESS." —ANONYMOUS

CHALLAH TIME

Challah is a loaf of white bread containing eggs and leavened with yeast; it's often formed into braided loaves and glazed with eggs before baking. When you're ready to eat, don't use a knife; just use your hands to pull pieces off. But before you dig in, there are a couple of fun challah games to play, including the Silent Game, which is perfect when the table is full of guests—particularly little ones. After the prayer, the first person tears a small piece of challah and passes the rest to the next—but no one is allowed to speak until the bread has made it completely around the table. (Good luck! Nothing is more guaranteed to raise giggles than saying, "Silence please.") The other game is Tug of War. Two kids pull from either side of the challah at the same time, and the person with the biggest piece is extra blessed that night (just like the wishbone)!

TWO MORE TIPS: You can find challah at many grocery stores, but if you can't it's fun to make your own (see our recipe on page 204) and a great family cooking project. Depending on the season and the store, you might even be lucky enough to find chocolate chip or raisin challah. Whichever one you find, it all makes the best French toast the next morning!

RECIPES

HOW DO YOU KNEAD?

Whatever style you had with Play-Doh is probably fine, as long as the dough is being stretched and folded, but if you need some pointers:

• On a lightly floured surface, flatten the dough slightly into a disk shape. Use the heels of your hands to push the dough out and away from you. Pick up the edge farthest away from you and fold it toward you, bringing the dough back to its original spot on the counter.

• Turn the dough a quarter turn. Repeat, repeat, repeat.

HOW DO I KNOW I AM DONE KNEADING?
You are tired. And your dough is even, soft, smooth, and feels and looks like a baby's bottom.

HOW DO I KNOW THE DOUGH HAS FINISHED RISING?
When it has risen to almost double in size, gently poke the dough with your finger. If the impression you made stays, you can continue with the recipe. If the indent quickly disappears, it needs a little more time; cover and let it rise longer.

Lazy Tip

Yes, you can use your dough mixer for this, for 4 or 5 minutes, but you will still have to knead it by hand for another 5 minutes, so why not just join all your ancestors who have been kneading bread for thousands of years? Remember them, or something you have to be grateful for, with each turn of the bread.

Leftover Tip

Challah makes great French toast! Beat 3 eggs with 1½ cups milk, ½ cup maple syrup, vanilla, cinnamon, and salt. Dip 8 thick slices of challah into the egg mixture and sauté on a hot buttered pan.

PLAY WITH YOUR
DESSERT

Great Games for After Dinner

16

WE LOVE DESSERT!

When we say *dessert*, we mean one last chance to savor one another's company. Ten or fifteen minutes more to relax and enjoy before life's pressures return in the form of homework and e-mails.

A few slices of fruit, two small squares of dark chocolate, a cup of soothing tea is all it takes. It's dessert *time* that we love. Stay a little bit longer before this kitchen is closed for the night.

Of course, for those evenings when dinner can be the evening's entire activity, here are great desserts and after-dinner games to keep everyone engaged and having fun as the candles burn down low . . .

LITTLE CHOCOLATE POCKET PIES

If you have yet to try the chocolate hazelnut spread Nutella . . . today is your lucky day. Make these cute little pastries and try not to grab a spoon, swoon into a chair, and finish off the rest of the Nutella jar.

Although Nutella and bananas are filled with extra smiles, experiment with peanut butter, chocolate chips, apples, and pears.

YOU NEED

2 sheets defrosted puff pastry

1 cup Nutella or 1 cup chocolate chips

¾ cup chopped nuts (optional)

1 cup chopped bananas

1 egg, lightly beaten

½ cup granulated sugar

TO MAKE 16 PASTRIES

Preheat your oven to 400 degrees.

Cut the puff pastry into 5-by-5-inch squares. Press each square into a cupcake tin that has been lined with a square of parchment paper. Drop in a heaping teaspoon of Nutella or chocolate chips, and top with the fruit and nuts.

When the pie was opened
The birds began to sing—
Wasn't that a dainty dish
To set before the king?

—*Anonymous*

WRITE IT DOWN!

It is truly a gift to inherit family recipes. They make a very tangible connection with your past and are part of your family story. So if there is a favorite family recipe that you love and haven't written down yet, do it now with your mom, dad, aunt, uncle, or grandparent before it is forgotten. Cook it together, share it. And someday, when they are gone, you can still spend a little time in the kitchen together.

Take the corners of each pastry and fold down over the filling; pinch together to seal. Brush with the egg and sprinkle with sugar.

Bake for 12 to 15 minutes or until golden brown.

Remove the pies from the tins and cool.

Quick Tip

How to Make a Mango Porcupine!
First, remove the wide, disk-shaped pit by cutting two slices slightly off center, from the top of the mango down alongside the pit. (If it is hard to cut, you are hitting the seed. Just move your knife out a bit.) Take one of your two mango "cheeks." Score vertical and horizontal cuts across your mango, being careful not to cut through the skin. The cubes should stay attached to the skin. Turn the skin inside out, so the cubes are poking out like a porcupine's pins.

CHOCOLATE FONDUE

It only takes a few minutes to melt the chocolate, and a few more to assemble the dipables. But how long will it take your family to dip, swirl, swizzle, drizzle, and dollop every last sweet, luscious bite?

YOU NEED

1 cup half-and-half

12 ounces good-quality milk or dark chocolate

Pinch of salt

Something delicious to dip (see options below)

TO MAKE 4–6 SERVINGS

In a small pot, warm the half-and-half over moderate heat until it begins to simmer. Add the chocolate and whisk until smooth and fully incorporated.

Immediately transfer the mixture to a fondue pot heated over a low flame, or serve straight from the pot.

Arrange the fruits and sweets around the chocolate pot. Give everyone at the table a fondue fork, bamboo skewer, or fork so they can pierce one of the options below and swirl it into the warm melted chocolate.

The Fruity:
Any fruit you love, cut into bite-size pieces. Grilled bananas and pineapples are great, too.

The Sweetie:
Cubed angel food cake, pound cake, marshmallows, biscotti, cinnamon churros, Oreos, and meringues

The Salty:
Pretzels and potato chips

The Naughty:
Cubed frozen cheesecake, little cream puffs, tiny brownies, doughnut holes

The Nutty:
Set out bowls of chopped nuts to roll the chocolate-dipped treats in.

"DON'T CLEAR TOO QUICKLY, *let the empty plates sit a bit."* —MARIO BATALI, chef and author of *Molto Gusto: Easy Italian Cooking*

RECIPES

BRIDESMAID WITH A VEIL
A Danish Apple Dessert

Once upon a time, the bridesmaid (played by the cookies) tricked the groom into marrying her, instead of the bride, by hiding under a veil (the whipped cream). I am not sure what happened when the groom lifted the veil; perhaps he was relieved. Whatever the case, in Denmark we have been eating this dessert happily ever after.

YOU NEED

1½ cups crushed amaretto cookies (or gingersnaps)

3 cups tart applesauce (see recipe at right, or use store-bought)

2 cups heavy cream, whipped

¼ cup black currant jam (or a tart berry jam)

TO MAKE 4–6 SERVINGS

Place a layer of cookies in the bottom of a glass bowl. Add a layer of applesauce, then another layer of cookies. Keep on alternating the layers until nothing is left. Top with soft dollops of whipped cream and decorate with dots of currant jam.

APPLESAUCE

YOU NEED

8 medium-sized apples, peeled, cored, and chopped (Gala and Fuji are good)

½ cup water

⅓ cup honey

Pinch of cinnamon

TO MAKE 3 CUPS

Bring the apples, water, honey, and cinnamon to a boil in a medium-size heavy pot, stirring occasionally. Then reduce the heat and simmer, covered, for 15 minutes.

Remove the lid and simmer until most of the liquid is evaporated, about 5 to 10 minutes.

Mash the apples with a potato masher or a fork to a coarse sauce, and then cool.

When You Really Need
CHOCOLATE PUDDING FAST

YOU NEED

½ cup sugar

2 tablespoons cocoa powder

3 tablespoons cornstarch

3 cups regular milk

4 ounces good-quality milk or semisweet chocolate, finely chopped

1 teaspoon vanilla extract

¼ teaspoon salt

TO MAKE 6 SMALL OR 4 GENEROUS SERVINGS

Stir the sugar, cocoa powder, and cornstarch together in a medium-size saucepan. Gradually stir in the milk. Heat, whisking constantly, until the sugar dissolves and the mixture begins to boil and thicken, about 10 minutes.

Add the chocolate. Turn off the stove. Gently whisk until the chocolate is completely melted.

Stir in the vanilla and salt. Pour into small custard cups. Serve warm or at room temperature.

Tasty Tip

Use great chocolate for this (like Scharffen Berger), and you will have great pudding that will make you smile and hum, while slowly rocking back and forth.

Blanca's Locally Famous **HEALTHY FRUIT POPSICLES**

YOU NEED

1 pound organic mixed sweet ripe berries, like strawberries, blackberries, and blueberries (or 1 pound organic frozen, defrosted berries)

2 ripe bananas, cut into chunks

6 ounces vanilla yogurt (optional)

1 cup orange juice

¼ cup honey, or to taste (just remember that once frozen, anything will taste less sweet)

Popsicle molds (or small empty yogurt containers and craft sticks)

TO MAKE ABOUT 12–15 POPSICLES

Put all the ingredients in a blender and blend until smooth. Pour the fruit into molds; insert the sticks, and freeze until solid, about 4 hours. Meanwhile, go jump into the sprinklers.

Cook's Tip

After these Popsicles are all eaten up, let your kids experiment with new flavors. How about watermelon blended with honey, lime, and mint ? Or crushed pineapple and coconut milk? Fresh peaches, ripe raspberries, and orange yogurt?

DANISH CRÊPES!

*On my father's birthdays, we would put two big uphol-
stered armchairs, flowers, pillows, and lots of blankets
on the back of a long tractor wagon. My grandparents
would sit laughing on the chairs as we all drove down to
the woods. There under the tall whispering pines we would
pick tiny blueberries. The ones that made it into our buckets were brought back to the picnic blankets. My mother
had fresh crêpes, ice cream, and whipped cream waiting
to be smothered in the berries and eaten after the birthday
songs were sung.*

YOU NEED

2 cups all-purpose flour

2½ cups milk

4 eggs

2 tablespoons butter, melted

Zest of ½ lemon

Pinch of salt

½ teaspoon vanilla extract

Vegetable oil, for the pan

TO MAKE ABOUT 15 CRÊPES

Combine all the ingredients, except for the oil, in a
blender. Pulse a few times until smooth. Let the batter
rest for 30 minutes in the fridge. If the batter is thicker
than heavy cream, add a little more milk.

Heat up a large nonstick pan. Pour a little vegetable
oil onto a folded paper towel, and wipe the pan evenly.
Keep the paper towel at hand while preparing the crêpes,
in case you want to give it another wipe.

Pour in 2 to 3 tablespoons of the crêpe batter and
quickly move the pan around so that the batter spreads
evenly, covering the whole surface with a thin layer.

Let cook for about 1 minute, until the crêpe's surface
is no longer shiny. Then flip it with a spatula and cook the
other side for about 30 seconds.

Repeat these steps until you are out of batter, stack-
ing the cooked crêpes on a plate.

The first few will probably be a bit crumpled and
unpresentable. They belong to the cook as a snack,
sprinkled with sugar.

Serving Ideas

Top your crêpes with jam or Nutella, fresh sliced fruit and
whipped cream, or keep them simple with a sprinkle of
sugar and a squeeze of lemon juice.

Then either fold the crêpes into quarters, or roll them
up, or stack them on top of one another as a very fine
layer cake.

Crêpes for Dinner!

Add a little more salt to the batter, skip the vanilla, and,
if you like, toss in a few tablespoons of chopped tender
herbs, like basil, dill, or chives. Make according to the
above directions.

Fold the cooked savory crêpes around roast chicken,
pesto, peas, and Monterey Jack cheese. Or sautéed
spinach and mushrooms, mixed with a little Parmesan
and ricotta. Perhaps some feta with chopped broccoli and
tomatoes. Drizzle with a little tomato sauce and heat in
the oven until warm.

A FROZEN YOGURT PARLOR
at Your Table (No Ice Cream Maker Needed)

*Here is the easiest way in the world to make frozen yogurt.
You just throw all the ingredients into the food processor,
pulse a few times, and ta-da, it is ready, no waiting necessary. Offer some toppings to go alongside and you have a
bright, tangy, and good-for-you dessert.*

YOU NEED

For the Frozen Yogurt

**1 pound frozen good-quality fruit like strawberries,
raspberries, or mangoes (do not defrost!)**

½ cup honey

1 cup plain Greek yogurt

1 teaspoon fresh lemon juice

1 teaspoon vanilla

Pinch of salt

For the Toppings

Chopped fresh fruit like strawberries, mangoes, and bananas

Crunchy cereal

Chocolate chips

Chopped nuts

TO MAKE 4–6 SERVINGS

Combine the frozen fruit and honey in a food processor. Pulse quickly until coarsely chopped.

Add the yogurt, lemon juice, vanilla, and salt. Process until smooth and creamy, scraping down the sides of the bowl once or twice.

The frozen yogurt should be firm enough to be served directly from the food processor, but if it is a little soft, let it harden in the freezer for about 30 minutes.

Leftover Tip

Frozen yogurt is a great way to use up uneaten cut-up fruit, the berries in the fridge that are just hanging in there, and the fruit you bought too much of . . . Spread the fruit out on baking sheets so the pieces freeze individually, put them in the freezer, and when they are frozen put them in containers so they are ready for the next time you need them.

NANNA'S HAPPY CHOCOLATE CHIP COOKIES

I know I am biased, but these are my favorite chocolate chip cookies in the world. Thin, crispy and chewy, buttery and chocolatey all in one happy bite. Make a double or triple batch of cookie dough; it doesn't really take much longer, and the dough actually gets better after a few days in the freezer. With cookie dough in the freezer, you will never be more than twenty minutes away from warm home-baked cookies, and isn't that a bit of happiness?

YOU NEED

12 ounces good-quality chocolate (milk, semisweet, or dark—whatever you are in the mood for), chopped into chunks

2½ cups flour

½ teaspoon baking soda

1 teaspoon salt

1½ cups (3 sticks) room-temperature butter

1 cup granulated sugar

1 cup light brown sugar

2 eggs

TO MAKE ABOUT 60 COOKIES

Preheat the oven to 350 degrees.

In a small bowl, mix the chocolate, flour, baking soda, and salt.

In your favorite cookie-making bowl, mix the butter and sugars, then vigorously mix in the eggs until it is all well combined. Fold in the flour and chocolate.

If you have the patience, chill the dough in the fridge for at least half an hour. Otherwise drop grape-size balls onto a greased baking sheet. They will spread, so space them about 3 inches apart.

Bake for 8 to 10 minutes, until the edges are golden brown. Let the cookies cool for a moment before gently lifting them off with a wide spatula and placing them on a cookie rack to cool.

Cook's Tip

Pull off a large piece of waxed or parchment paper. Along the bottom of the short edge, put a "roll" of cookie dough (I use an ice cream scoop to do this). Tightly roll up the paper so you have a roll of cookie dough. Wrap it in foil and label it. It will last at least 3 months in the freezer. When you are ready to bake the cookies, just take the roll out of the freezer. You do not have to defrost it—simply slice the still-frozen dough with a serrated knife. Put the slices on a cookie sheet and bake at 350 degrees for 8 to 10 minutes.

Recipes

Growing Up

IN THE KITCHEN

SCOTT PEACOCK *is a Southern chef extraordinaire—
a food expert whose vision of Southern cuisine
emphasizes fresh, seasonal, regionally grown
ingredients. He is the co-author, with Edna Lewis, of
The Gift of Southern Cooking: Recipes and Revelations
from Two Great American Cooks.*

"I was always fascinated watching my mother, my
grandmother, and Gertrude Moore (who worked for my
family) cooking, so I was in the kitchen a lot. My grandmother gave me my first kitchen job cracking coconuts at
Thanksgiving and Christmas for the cakes and ambrosia
when I was four years old.

"By the third grade I was making oatmeal for everyone in the family for breakfast. In the fifth and sixth
grade, I was reading cookbooks, making my own cookies,
and things like that. By the time I was thirteen, I had my
first dinner party.

"I had this notion from TV that a dinner party had
to consist of seven courses, but I had no idea how you
might design a menu or what those seven courses would
be. Dessert was the easy part. My big one at that time was
Julia Child's chocolate mousse, which I thought was really
something. I heard about it on TV and it sounded so exotic.
It had rum in it, which was a big deal because I lived in
a dry county. Negotiating with my parents, who did not
drink, to get alcohol for the recipe was rather involved.

"Another strong memory I have was making cakes
around the holidays. We only had square cake pans, and
at the time (and as a gay kid who was struggling to keep
that under wraps and survive in the 1960s) those square
cakes were just one more thing that made me feel like I or
we were different from everybody else. Of course, I love
square cakes now!

"The point I'm leading up to is that the dinner table
is a wonderful place where you can help instill that sense
of the importance of identity, and the wonderful feeling
of being different and not having to fit in—but still belonging. Your cakes can be different from someone else's
and that's kind of fantastic."

DINNER GUEST RECIPE

Very Good CHOCOLATE CAKE

BY SCOTT PEACOCK

This is a super-easy recipe that requires no mixer or other fancy equipment to make. Once you have assembled the ingredients, it will take less than 10 minutes till you're popping it into the oven.

You will be rewarded with a luscious chocolatey, very moist cake with a generous amount of rich frosting, crying out for a glass of icy cold whole milk.

YOU NEED

For the Cake

2 cups granulated sugar

$1\frac{1}{2}$ cups cake flour

$\frac{1}{2}$ teaspoon salt

$\frac{3}{4}$ teaspoon baking soda

1 cup double-strength brewed coffee (or decaf coffee)

4 ounces unsweetened chocolate, finely chopped

2 eggs, at room temperature

$\frac{1}{2}$ cup vegetable oil

$\frac{1}{2}$ cup sour cream, at room temperature

$1\frac{1}{2}$ teaspoons vanilla extract

TO MAKE 1 8-BY-8-INCH CAKE

Preheat the oven to 325 degrees.

Sift together the sugar, flour, salt, and baking soda in a bowl. In another bowl, pour the hot coffee over the finely chopped chocolate, and allow the chocolate to melt completely.

In a separate bowl, whisk together until well blended the eggs and vegetable oil, followed by the sour cream, vanilla, and coffee-chocolate mixture. Stir this liquid mixture into the dry ingredients until completely blended. Pour the batter into a buttered and floured parchment-lined 8-by-8-inch cake pan. Drop the cake pan once onto the counter from a height of 3 inches, to remove any large air pockets. Bake in the preheated oven for 30 to 40 minutes, until the cake springs back slightly when gently tapped in the center. Remove immediately to a cooling rack, and allow to rest for 5 minutes before turning out of the pan.

YOU NEED

For the Frosting

$\frac{1}{2}$ cup heavy cream

8 tablespoons (1 stick) unsalted butter, cut into $\frac{1}{2}$-inch pieces

3 tablespoons granulated sugar

$\frac{1}{4}$ teaspoon salt

$\frac{1}{2}$ pound semisweet chocolate, finely chopped

2 tablespoons hot double-strength brewed coffee (or decaf coffee)

1 teaspoon vanilla extract

Heat the cream, butter, sugar, and salt in a heavy saucepan until the butter is melted. Add the chocolate and cook over very low heat, whisking constantly, just until the chocolate is melted and the mixture is smooth. Remove from the heat and mix in the coffee and vanilla. Transfer the frosting to a bowl to cool, stirring occasionally, until it is of spreading consistency—about 1 hour, depending on the temperature of the kitchen. (If your kitchen is very warm, move the frosting to a cooler area to cool and thicken, but do not refrigerate or chill over ice water.)

When the frosting is of spreading consistency and the cake completely cooled, generously frost the top and sides of the cake. For best results, allow the cake to sit for 2 or more hours before slicing. Store, covered, at room temperature.

Cook's Tip

For the richest, darkest frosting possible, resist the urge to whisk or beat to cool faster. Excessive stirring incorporates air, which will cool and set the frosting more quickly, but will also dilute its dark color and flavor. And because it takes a little while to cool to the proper consistency, have all the ingredients ready and make the frosting as soon as the cake is in the oven.

THE SWEET SIMPLICITY OF FRUIT!

I often think: If only you could invent a dessert just like an orange. *You would start by making the packaging, a beautiful fragrant orb. The dessert itself would be segments filled with juicy tear-shaped droplets, the perfect balance between wonderfully sweet and just tart enough. What if we could make a dessert just like that, or like a ripe peach, a vibrant kiwi, or a sun-ripened strawberry, and magically make it incredibly healthy as well! Aren't we lucky that nature figured it out for us? That juicy, fresh, tart, sweet, crunchy, amazing, healthy fruit just grows for us to pick!*

My best advice, other than to enjoy its simple pleasures, is to pick well. Whether from the tree or the market, fruit wants to be picked when it is ripe and in season, so wait until the time of year when it is calling out Pick me! *with its scent drifting from across the aisle. It will reward you by being simply perfect.*

Berries

- Slice 1 pound of fresh strawberries; toss with 1 tablespoon honey and the juice of 1 orange. Serve in wineglasses.
- Put out a big bowl of ripe strawberries and surround it with little bowls of brown sugar, yogurt, or crème fraîche, to dip them in.
- Strawberry bruschetta . . . Chop 1 pound of strawberries, and toss with a bit of honey and cinnamon. Toast slices of bread or pound cake, slather with honey-sweetened cream cheese, and top with a generous amount of strawberries.
- In the summer, when the farmer's markets are filled with sweet ripe berries, stock up your freezer for smoothies or to eat frozen all year long.
- Toss blackberries, blueberries, or raspberries with a little honey, vanilla, and yogurt. Chill until very cold, and serve in a pretty glass.

Grapes

Freeze grapes and they will turn into little balls of sorbet all by themselves. Serve with a few squares of chocolate.

Oranges and Grapefruit

Cut the peel and white pith off different sizes and types of citrus, slice and arrange on a platter. Sprinkle with cinnamon or fresh mint.

Serve slices of oranges topped with a sauce of frozen raspberries blended with a little honey and orange juice.

Watermelon

A light sprinkling of lime juice and fresh mint makes watermelon sparkle. Or cut the watermelon into wedges and freeze.

Apples

Cut into wedges and serve with honey or caramel (sold in jars and easily warmed in the microwave) for dipping and drizzling.

Nanna's Frozen Apple Snow

Cut apples in half and freeze. Quickly, while they are still frozen, roughly grate the apples and toss with cold yogurt. Add vanilla and honey to sweeten, and serve right away. In the fall when apples are abundant, make them into applesauce (page 212) and serve a bowl with yogurt or a spoonful of cream.

Fruit Salad

Cut fresh seasonal fruit into slices, dices, or wedges. Serve in chilled martini glasses topped with toasted nuts or shaved chocolate.

Passion Fruit

One of our great food discoveries this year was passion fruit. It's the funniest-looking thing, with its egg-shaped purple shell that wrinkles. Slice it in half, scoop out the juice and seeds for a taste sensation not to be beat. Grown in Hawaii, Florida, and California, passion fruits are rich in vitamins C and A. One passion fruit has only sixteen calories and is an excellent source of fiber. Serve over ice cream, toss it in a fruit salad, or just eat right out of the shell with a small spoon.

Cook's Tip *The heavier the fruit, the better it will be. In the store, lift up different pieces of the same fruit. You will notice that some pieces, although the same size, are heavier. These will be juicier and much more delicious! (Use this trick when looking for fresher onions and garlic, too!)*

GAMES TO PLAY
After Dinner

One of the things I hate about board games is reading directions. (In fact, the entire David family has an aversion to it.) I just don't have the patience, and even if I did the directions are always too complicated and confusing; by the time you explain them, you've lost your crowd. So I am really in favor of games that require little equipment and are simple for everyone to learn. With that requirement in mind, here are some of my favorites for dessert.

He Said, She Said

Supplies needed: Full-size paper, pens

This David family favorite is a table version of Mad Libs (hey, those would be great for the table, too). It's hilarious and teens love it (at least mine does, and she's discerning).

How to Play

Each dinner guest gets a blank piece of paper and a pen. The leader reads the beginning of a sentence, and then everyone writes it and makes up the rest of the sentence on the top of their slip of paper. When everyone is done, guests narrowly fold the paper over so that the sentence is covered and pass their paper to the person on their right. The leader says the next sentence and the pattern repeats.

The sentences read aloud are . . .

They met . . .

She wore . . .

He wore . . .

She said . . .

He said . . .

She thought . . .

He thought . . .

It all ended . . .

When all the sentences are written and passed to the next person for the last time, the leader selects someone to read his or her sheet aloud . . . lots of laughs ensue!

Celebrity

Supplies needed: Scrap paper, pen, timer (borrow from a board game)

Do you want to keep everyone together after dinner? This is a perfect choice to extend your together time around the table.

How to Play

Hand out ten (or more) small pieces of paper for your group to fill out with popular culture names from movies, television, books, music, politics, animation, or sports. After you have written your names (like Julia Roberts, Jack Black, Kermit the Frog, Fred Flintstone, Willie Mays, Miley Cyrus, SpongeBob, and F. Scott Fitzgerald), fold the pieces of paper in half and put them all in a large bowl in the center of the table.

Split your group into teams of two. One team at a time goes and has one minute to pick the names out of the bowl and give clues to their teammate by describing who that person is. If they can't guess it, the name goes back in the bowl and time is up. Try to guess as many as you can in your round. At the end of the game (usually when all the names have been used), count all the slips of paper you have guessed correctly; the team with the most correct guesses wins.

For example: We turn the timer over, and I pick my first slip of paper. It says "Mickey Mouse." Quickly, I start my clues. Okay, I say: "He has big ears, children love him, Walt Disney created him"—by now my partner yells, "Mickey Mouse." I then grab another sheet from the bowl. I say: "He was a reassuring president during difficult times, he was in a wheelchair, his chats made everyone's fireside a bit warmer"—by this time my teammate is shouting "Franklin Roosevelt!" I make sure I tell my teammates how clever they are!

Identity

Supplies needed: Scraps of paper, pen

How to Play

This is a fun version of Celebrity. Give everyone one small piece of paper to write a famous name on. It could be someone past or present, alive or dead; a fictional character or anyone the group knows. The names have to be recognizable to everyone. Then everyone passes the name they wrote down to their right, and without looking, on the count of three, everyone puts their slip up on their forehead (a Scotch tape dispenser on the table is handy about now). Then one at a time each person gets to ask the group a question about his or her name. Is it a politician? Is it a male? Is he under forty? Go around the table until someone guesses the identity!

Slammin' Gramma

Supplies needed: Playing cards—two decks if there are more than six players

I guarantee no one in America knows this card game . . . yet. It's a Danish doozy that Kirstin adapted from a family favorite and it's great for all ages, genders, and political views. The more the merrier. Clear the plates, pour the tea, and hunker down for a lot of laughs. Bear with me, though, for I have broken a golden rule: I do have to give you some directions. But it will be worth it, I promise.

How to Play

- Each suit (spades, hearts, diamonds, clubs) has a special sound and an action you perform when two in a row are put down on the table. The numbers on the cards don't matter.

- If there are 2 spades on top of each other: Slap your hand down on the table and make a *phududderphudder* sound like a whoopee cushion.

- 2 diamonds: Point to the closest window and make a sound as if you ate a bad mushroom (*ooooaaahhhhth*).

- 2 hearts: Slap your heart and sound surprised (*hhhhuuuuuh!*).

- 2 clubs: Scratch your head and make a monkey sound (*ah ah ah*).

- Joker: If one (not two) joker is put out, stand up and sing the first bar of any song the group has agreed on beforehand. We usually alternate between singing "Oh boogie wooggy" with both hands opened wide and "Old MacDonald Had a Farm." Change the joker song halfway through the game just to befuddle everyone.

- As a group, practice the sounds and actions a few times.

- Deal out the entire deck facedown (two decks if you have a lot of people), and keep the cards facedown. The object of the game is to get rid of all your cards.

Okay, now go around the table so that one at a time the players, in order of seating, quickly put one card down from their pile. Be sure to open your card *away* from you as you place it in the center of the table (just so you don't get a peek first before everyone else). If there are two of the same suit put on top of each other, one immediately after the other, you quickly make the correct sound and action for the suit. Whoever does this last takes the pile and puts it on the bottom of their existing cards. However, anyone who does the wrong sound or action also gets the pile. If there's more than one late or wrong person, split the pile.

If you at any time accidentally make a sound or a jerky motion because you think you saw two cards of the same suit, but you were wrong, then you get the pile. The faster you put out the cards, the more fun it is. Once you get rid of your cards, you have to stay in the game for one more round before you are declared the winner. But with this card game, everyone wins because it is so much fun!

The Poetry Game

Supplies needed: Pens, paper, a poetry book

This is a great game to play with one of the poetry books recommended in Resources at the end of this book.

How to Play

The leader selects a poem from a book and announces the title. Next, the leader writes the actual first four lines of the poem on a slip of paper, folds it in half, and puts it into a bowl.

Meanwhile, everyone else writes down their names plus the first four lines of the poem, which they make up themselves (remind everyone to write very neatly!). On a second sheet of paper, everyone writes the numbers 1 through 10 (or one number for each player, plus one for the famous poet) to create a scorecard. The host randomly picks one slip out of the bowl and reads it convincingly to the group.

Everyone has to guess which person the poetic masterpiece belongs to and writes the answers on their scorecard. The leader continues pulling out slips and reading them. The group also has to try to identify which four lines are the real stanzas. When all the poems have been read aloud, the host identifies who wrote which poem. The winner is the person who correctly identifies the most writers. This game is a hoot—everyone gets to use their imagination, and realize that we all have a little poet hiding deep down within ourselves. Legend has it that President Kennedy played a rollicking version of this game in the White House with his special dinner guest, Robert Frost!

Younger Version

Everyone teams up, younger with older, and works on their lines together. The leader reads one poem at a time, and the group guesses right then who they think the poet is.

The Novel Game

This is the same as the poetry game, but with a novel. Read the title and author, then everyone writes down a made-up first or last line to the book. Have everyone guess the true line.

The Dictionary Game

This is the same as the Novel Game but using a dictionary. Choose words no one knows. Everyone makes up a definition for the word. Read them along with the real definition and see who guesses right.

"One of the **LUCKIEST** things that can happen to you in life is, I think, to have a **HAPPY CHILDHOOD.**" —DAME AGATHA CHRISTIE, author of crime novels

AFTERWORD
Kernels of Thanks

BY JONATHAN SAFRAN FOER,
author of *Eating Animals*

Throughout my childhood, we celebrated Thanksgiving at my uncle and aunt's house. My uncle, my mother's younger brother, was the first person on that side of the family to be born on this side of the Atlantic. My aunt can trace her lineage back to the *Mayflower*.

That unlikely pairing of histories was no small part of what made those Thanksgivings so full, and memorable, and, in the very best sense of the word, American.

We would arrive around two o'clock. The cousins would play football on the sloping sliver of a front yard until my little brother got hurt, at which point we would head up to the attic to play football on the various video game systems. Two floors beneath us, Maverick (RIP) salivated at the stove's window, my father talked politics and cholesterol, and my grandmother, surrounded by grandchildren, conducted her interior monologue in Yiddish, the language of her dead relatives.

In 1949, the first Thanksgiving my family celebrated in America, a card table and three folding chairs would have accommodated everyone. More recently, we have required two dozen mismatched chairs, which circumscribe four tables of slightly different heights, widths, and trustworthiness, pushed together and covered in similar (if not matching) cloths. No one is fooled into thinking this setup is perfect, but it is perfect. My aunt always places a small pile of popcorn kernels on each plate, which, in the course of the meal, we are supposed to transfer to the table as symbols of things we are thankful for. This ritual happens silently and in one's own good time, and that assures sincerity. Out of the corner of my eye I might catch a parent, sibling, uncle, or cousin transferring a kernel. It's impossible not to wonder what this person is thinking about. The wondering enriches the ritual: The gratitude is not performed, but shared, and in its mysteriousness, alive.

Dishes come out continuously; some go clockwise, some counter, some zigzag down the length of the table: sweet potato casserole, homemade rolls, green beans with almonds, cranberry concoctions, yams, buttery mashed potatoes, my grandmother's wildly incongruous kugel, trays of gherkins and olives and marinated mushrooms, and a cartoonishly large turkey that had been put in the oven when last year's was taken out. We talk and talk, to and over one another, about the Orioles and Redskins, changes in the neighborhood, our accomplishments and the anguish of others (our own anguish is off-limits), and all the while, my grandmother goes from one end of the table to the other and back, making sure no one is starving.

Thanksgiving is the dinner that encompasses all others. The meal we aspire for other meals to resemble. The Thanksgiving table is not a sanctuary from the world, but a representation of our best hope for it.

Of course most of us can't (and wouldn't want to) cook all day every day, and of course such food would be fatal if consumed with regularity. But it's nice to imagine all meals being so deliberate. Of the thousand-or-so meals we eat every year, Thanksgiving dinner is the one that we try most earnestly to get right. It holds the hope of being a *good* meal, whose ingredients, efforts, setting, and consuming are expressions of the best in us. More than any other meal, it is about good eating and good thinking. And it's about transmitting values.

I live in New York now and only rarely—at least according to my grandmother—get back to DC. No one who was young is young anymore. Some of those who transferred kernels to the table are gone. And there are new family members. (*I* am now *we*.) As if the musical chairs I played at birthday parties were preparation for all of this ending and beginning.

This will be the first year we celebrate in my home, the first time I will prepare the food, and the first Thanksgiving meal at which my son will be old enough to eat the food the rest of us eat. So what will he eat? And what kinds of conversations will we have? Which rituals will I perpetuate and which will I dispense with? What will I invent? At stake when setting the Thanksgiving table is more than the placement of silverware. To set the table, in this case, is to announce your vision of how things ought to be.

When thinking about future Thanksgivings, I find myself returning to past ones. I return to those pushed-together tables. At the end of every Thanksgiving dinner, much of what began on top of them ended up beneath them. Maverick never had to beg, and the various rugs became imprints of our celebrations. The kernels inevitably scattered, and it was not uncommon, upon visiting my uncle and aunt's house in the summer, to find—under the living room sofa, at the base of a bookshelf—an artifact of someone's gratitude. It was impossible to know just how old that thankfulness was. *That* is my vision of how things ought to be. Thankfulness is not a precious thing. It is not a speech, or well-composed letter. It is not segregated from the rest of the year, or, ideally, possessed by anyone.

We give more thought to Thanksgiving than any other meal, but every meal is an opportunity and a burden. Every meal—whether had in a car or a tent, at an airport food court or a candlelit dining room table—matters. Every meal is a chance to get it right or get it wrong, to approach or withdraw from our ideals. Does anything in our lives matter more than how we set our tables?

Of course it's only a coincidence that my son's favorite food is popcorn. We make it together most nights of the week. I pour the oil, he scoops in the kernels one little handful at a time, I turn on the heat, and we stand there—he balanced on a chair—waiting for the first pop. That waiting is more delicious than the popcorn could ever be. And then, after centuries, there is a pop. And then another. And then a barrage of popping: a celebration. It always overflows.

A FEW LAST THOUGHTS Before I Blow Out the Candles . . .

BY LAURIE DAVID

Writing and compiling this book has been a fantastic, emotional journey for me. When I first discovered the importance of family dinner, I was at a stage in my life where I was desperate for some fulfilling family moments. When I started looking at dinnertime as a gift in the day, I was rewarded with my most joyful parenting moments. My best family times are not on weekends, vacations, or even holidays. They are around the kitchen table, just sitting together meal after meal after meal.

It's still too soon to fully evaluate the job I did as a parent (maybe you never can) and it hasn't always been easy. In fact for me, it has often been hard. Looking back, I do find some comfort knowing that I can account for some of the time that might otherwise have evaporated—fleeting time that disappeared as quickly as my kids went from the car seat to the driver's seat.

I know that on most days for at least an hour, sometimes more, we all stopped what we were doing and sat down together as a family. We talked, we laughed, we fought, we ate, we told stories, and we played games. We discussed values, dilemmas, and newspaper articles. We even occasionally read a poem. That time has been spent wisely; it's done and no one can undo it.

As Jonathan Safran Foer says so perfectly in his afterword, "every meal counts." That's exactly how I feel and that's how I hope my kids will feel when they are living their own lives. Dinner is home.

ACKNOWLEDGMENTS

Thank you to **LARRY, CAZZIE,** and **ROMY** who for a decade sweetly and patiently (mostly) tested recipes, played games, and gave plenty of helpful feedback. Thank you to my wonderful sisters, **BONNIE** and **LISA,** who have always been right by my side through thick and thin. To **JENNIFER, JULIE, LAUREN,** and **AMY** for posing for pictures and cheering me on.

It took a large, dedicated, and hardworking extended family to bring this book to life, starting with the amazing **DAWN WOOLLEN,** who was our secret ingredient to pulling it all together. Dawn did the job of ten, acting as researcher, scheduler, organizer, and wise counsel on many fronts. Dawn, we literally couldn't have done it without you!

Thank you to **DORIAN KARCHMAR,** who represented this book so passionately (is it wrong to love your agent so much?). Thank you, **KATHY FRESTON,** for introducing us to **JENNIFER RUDOLPH WALSH,** who then brilliantly connected us to Dorian. Rounding out our great William Morris Endeavor team, our thanks also go out to **ALICIA EVERTT.** To our Grand Central team, starting with head honcho **JAMIE RAAB** who, as a product of family dinner herself, immediately understood our idea. Thank you to our wondrous editor and all-around champion **KAREN MURGOLO,** who personally raised this baby with loving care every step of the way. Thank you to Karen for also putting together her A team to help, including **DIANE LUGER, PHILIPPA WHITE, TARETH MITCH, PEGGY HOLM, MELISSA BULLOCK, LEAH TRACOSAS,** and **LAURA JORSTAD.**

Thank you to my guardian angels **DR. HARVEY KARP** and **NINA MONTEE KARP.** Truly, there isn't enough room on this page to pay proper tribute to them both. Thank you also for introducing me to **JONATHAN SAFRAN FOER**—and Jonathan, thank you for your support and collaboration!

Thank you to **MARYELLEN BAKER,** our phenomenal photographer who threw her heart, soul, and talent into this project and magically turned our ideas into beautiful pictures. She also turned out to be a great proofreader! We were also blessed with three more great artists: our illustrator **SARAH COLEMAN** and our designer **LAURA PALESE,** whose first pass at a designed page brought shrieks of joy from all of us! And to **RANDI BAIRD** for our great vineyard shots.

To **JESSIE NELSON, CAMI GORDON,** and **EMILY WHITESELL** for their tweaks, suggestions, and years of friendship. I am especially lucky to have friends who are also writers!

Thank you to **RITA WILSON, ARIANNA HUFFINGTON, LYN LEAR, KELLY MEYER, KIMBERLY BROOKS, HEIDI HADDAD,** and **CHAN LUU** for doing what precious girlfriends do so well, offering all the encouragement, enthusiasm, and advice a gal needs to keep on going.

Thank you to the many friends, families, and associates who helped along the way, including my NRDC family: **ROBERT F. KENNEDY JR., GINA SOLOMON,** and **JONATHAN KAPLAN, FRANCESCA KOE, VALERIE JAFFEE,** and **WENDY GORDON.** To **BRENDAN DEMILLE** for his rapid response, great research, and sharp pen! Thank you to **CAMERON STRACHER, ELLEN GALINSKY, SHARON DUKE ESTROFF, DAVIA NELSON, MONINA VAN OPEL,** and **EDWARD MILLER.** Thank you to **BLANCA** for all your support and **CLAUDIA** for being everyone's sunshine.

Thank you, **KAREN KELLY,** you are the gift that keeps on giving! **JILL BROOKE,** you were an enormous help, thank you! Also gratitude to **PAUL CUMMINS, MARY ANN HOBERMAN, DANIEL WATERS, ELIZABETH PLANET, ROY SEKOFF, ALEX LEO, JEAN BRADY, ROMI LASSALLY, DOMINIQUE BROWNING, ELLEN SEIDMAN, JUDY CHOATE,** and **DANIEL ROEMER.**

Thank you to **MATTHEW BALLAST** and **HEATHER LYLIS,** not for what they did to help with the book, but for what they are going to do!

Thank you to all of the people who contributed their stories and advice, helped us test recipes, and opened their homes and hearts to us.

Thank you to **BART** and **BELLA** for adding so much joy to my life and for teaching me the true pleasures of growing your own food. Thank you to your entire extended family, the **HICKEYS,** the **HANSENS,** and **BARBARA** and **JIM** too, for making room for me in your beautiful, loving family.

ONE LAST THANK YOU JUST FROM KIRSTIN

LAURIE, you fearlessly move mountains with grace, plant tiny seeds that become sequoias . . . all the while cooking up a homegrown stir-fry (with copious amounts of onions). You are a constant inspiration, and the very best dinner collaborator . . . in the land. I am brimming with Shiny. Sparkling. Gratitude!!! To my Danish family, the love around our dinner table has been the backbone of my life.

And **JOHN,** you will always be the heart that beats in it.

RESOURCES
Help Is on the Way

The following resource list includes brand-name products we love, books we've dog-eared, Web sites we've looked to time and again, best-loved games we've won and lost, and other tasty tips for your table.

IN THE PANTRY

Dried beans, Arborio rice, and spices: Surfas, surfasonline.com.

Ethnic groceries (everything from curry pastes to rice paper wrappers): templeofthai.com; kalustyans.com; ethnicfoodsco.com.

Grains, beans, seeds, and corn: Bob's Red Mill, bobsredmill.com.

How to Compost: howtocompost.org.

Kitchen Gardeners: kitchengardeners.org. A global community cultivating change.

Meat raised traditionally, humanely, and sustainably: Niman Ranch, nimanranch.com.

Meatless Monday: meatlessmonday.com. This organization strives to reduce meat consumption in the United States by 15 percent—and they make it easy with fabulous recipes, quick meal suggestions, and advice to get your family on board.

Organic Consumers Association: organicconsumers.org. Information, advocacy, recipes, and more about living organically.

Organic vegetable and herb seeds: seedsofchange.com.

Revolution Foods: revfoods.com. A company committed to providing healthy food to all students.

Simple Steps: simplesteps.org. For better health and sustainable living.

Slow Food USA: slowfoodusa.org. Supporting good, clean, and fair food.

Spices: The Spice House, thespicehouse.com.

Sustainable seafood information at Monterey Bay Aquarium: mbayaq.org (click on "Seafood Watch").

Wholesome Baby Food: wholesomebabyfood.com.

Reusable Lunch and Dinner Items

Graze Organic: grazeorganic.com.

Lunchsense: lunchsense.com.

Kids Konserve: kidskonserve.com.

Rebel Green: rebelgreen.com.

Reusable bags: 1 Bag at a Time, onebagatatime.com.

Tiffin lunch boxes: Can be found at Indian and Thai markets or online at amazon.com.

Custom-made lazy Susans: JamesRHickey@Gmail.com.

. . . And if there is anything you can't find, or are curious about look it up online!

BOOKS
Food and Family

Diet for a New America by John Robbins (H. J. Kramer, 1998).

Dinner with Dad: How One Man Braved Traffic, Battled Picky Eaters, and Found His Way Back to the Family Table by Cameron Stracher (Random House Trade Paperbacks, 2008).

Eating Animals by Jonathan Safran Foer (Little, Brown, 2009).

Fast Food Nation by Eric Schlosser (Harper Perennial, 2005).

Food Matters: A Guide to Conscious Eating with More than 75 Recipes by Mark Bittman (Simon & Schuster, 2009).

How to Raise a Drug-Free Kid: The Straight Dope for Parents by Joseph Califano Jr. (Fireside, 2009).

The Intentional Family: Simple Rituals to Strengthen Family Ties by William J. Doherty (Harper Paperbacks, 1999).

The Lost Art of Listening: How Learning to Listen Can Improve Relationships by Michael P. Nichols, PhD (Guilford Press, 2009).

Mind in the Making: The Seven Essential Life Skills Every Child Needs by Ellen Galinsky (HarperStudio, 2010).

Mindless Eating: Why We Eat More than We Think by Brian Wansink, PhD (Bantam, 2006).

The Moral Intelligence of Children: How to Raise a Moral Child by Robert Coles, MD (Plume, 1998).

More Home Cooking: A Writer Returns to the Kitchen by Laurie Colwin (Harper Perennial, 2000).

Near a Thousand Tables: A History of Food by Felipe Fernandez-Armesto (Free Press, 2003).

The Omnivore's Dilemma: A Natural History of Four Meals by Michael Pollan (Penguin, 2007).

Putting Family First: Successful Strategies for Reclaiming Family Life in a Hurry-Up World by William J. Doherty and Barbara Carlson (Holt Paperbacks, 2002).

The Rituals of Dinner by Margaret Visser (Penguin, 1992).

Rituals in Families and Family Therapy, revised edition, by Evan Imber-Black, Janine Roberts, Richard Alva Whiting, and Richard Whiting (W. W. Norton, 2003).

Secrets of Feeding a Healthy Family by Ellyn Satter (Kelcy Press, 1999).

The Surprising Power of Family Meals: How Eating Together Makes Us Smarter, Stronger, Healthier, and Happier by Miriam Weinstein (Steerforth, 2006).

Words and Knowledge

Keep these books on a shelf near the kitchen table—they provide smarts and snickers!

500 Key Words for the SAT, and How to Remember Them Forever!, 10th edition, by Charles Gulotta (Mostly Bright Ideas, 2007).

The Big Book of Words You Should Know by Michelle Bevilacqua, Justin Cord Hayes, and David Olsen (Adams Media, 2009).

The Book of General Ignorance by John Lloyd and John Mitchinson (Harmony, 2007).

Dictionary of Word Origins: A History of the Words, Expressions and Clichés We Use by Jordan Almond (Citadel, 2000).

I Didn't Know That: From "Ant in the Pants" to "Wet Behind the Ears"—The Unusual Origins of the Things We Say by Karlen Evins (Scribner, 2007).

The Facts on File Dictionary of Clichés: Meaning and Origins of Thousands of Terms and Expressions by Christine Ammer (Checkmark Books, 2006).

The Little, Brown Book of Anecdotes by Clifton Fadiman (Little, Brown, 1991).

The Mega Book of Useless Information by Noel Botham (John Blake, 2009).

Picture These SAT Words!, 2nd edition, by Philip Geer and Susan Geer (Barron's Educational Series, 2008).

The New Book of Lists: The Original Compendium of Curious Information by David Wallechinsky and Amy Wallace (Canongate U.S. 2005).

The Road to Success Is Paved with Failure: How Hundreds of Famous People Triumphed Over Inauspicious Beginnings, Crushing Rejection, Humiliating Defeats and Other Speed Bumps Along Life's Highway by Joey Green (Little, Brown, 2001).

The Superior Person's Book of Words by Peter Bowler (David R. Godine, 1985).

Poetry

The 20th Century Children's Poetry Treasury edited by Jack Prelutsky (Knopf Books for Young Readers, 1999).

Bartlett's Poems for Occasions edited by Geoffrey O'Brien (Little, Brown, 2004).

Ballistics: Poems by Billy Collins (Random House Trade Paperbacks, 2010).

A Child's Anthology of Poetry edited by Elizabeth Hauge Sword (Ecco, 2006).

Essential Pleasures: A New Anthology of Poems to Read Aloud edited by Robert Pinsky (W. W. Norton, 2009).

A Family of Poems: My Favorite Poetry for Children by Caroline Kennedy (Hyperion, 2005).

The Llama Who Had No Pajama: 100 Favorite Poems by Mary Ann Hoberman (Sandpiper, 2006).

Poem in Your Pocket: 200 Poems to Read and Carry by the Academy of American Poets (Abrams Image, 2009).

Poetry for Young People series by various authors, including Robert Frost, Langston Hughes, Maya Angelou, Lewis Carroll, Edgar Allan Poe, Emily Dickinson, and many more (Sterling, 2005).

The Poets' Corner: The One-and-Only Poetry Book for the Whole Family compiled by John Lithgow (Grand Central Publishing, 2007).

Where the Sidewalk Ends, 30th Anniversary Edition by Shel Silverstein (HarperCollins, 2004).

Gratitude

Bless This Food: Ancient and Contemporary Graces from Around the World by Adrian Butash (New World Library, 2007).

Crisp Toasts: Wonderful Words That Add Wit and Class to Every Time You Raise Your Glass (Thomas Dunne Book) by William R. Evans and Andrew Frothingham (St. Martin's Press, 2007).

Saying Grace: Blessings for the Family Table edited by Sarah McElwain (Chronicle Books, 2003).

WEB SITES
Sustainability

Natural Resources Defense Council: nrdc.org.

The Edible Schoolyard: edibleschoolyard.org.

Feeding America: feedingamerica.org. For information on where your local foodbanks are.

Priscilla Woolworth's Your Eco Friendly General Store: priscillawoolworth.com.

Parenting

AARP: aarp.org.

Ancestry: ancestry.com.

Blended Families of America: blendedfamiliesofamerica.com.

Families with Purpose: familieswithpurpose.com.

National Center on Addiction and Substance Abuse at Columbia University: casacolumbia.org.

Passionate Parenting: passionateparenting.net.

Poetry and Culture

The Emory Center for Myth and Ritual in American Life: marial.emory.edu.

Funny-Poems: funny-poems.co.uk/kids. Can't get to the bookstore? Download sidesplitting verse here.

The Kitchen Sisters: kitchensisters.org. Off-beat, original, award-winning storytelling.

Poetry Foundation: poetryfoundation.org.

Poetry Out Loud: poetryoutloud.org.

The Splendid Table: splendidtable.publicradio.org.

Wee Sing: weesing.com.

GAMES

Table talk question guides and boxes available for purchase include:

Apples to Apples: mattel.com. A hilarious game of comparisons that helps teach new words and concepts.

Bananagrams: bananagrams-intl.com. This classic anagram word game for the whole family comes in numerous languages, including English, Spanish, French, and Norwegian!

The Game of Scattergories: scattergories.net.

Szergy: A table crossword game great for after dinner.

Table Topics: tabletopics.com. Boxed games and quizzes to keep the conversation rolling during dinner.

FOR MORE CONVERSATION STARTERS

we recommend our favorite by The Box Girls, started by our very own Taco Tuesday Heidi Haddad and her girlfriend CeCe Feiler. The Box Girls have sets for all groups and occasions—from families and teens to holidays, parties, and road trips. Go to theboxgirls.com to order your box and a portion of the sale goes to charity!

NOTES

CHAPTER 1: Why Family Dinners Matter: Raise Healthier, Smarter, and More Confident Kids

In this chapter and throughout the book, we relied on "The Importance of Family Dinners," a series of reports prepared by the National Center on Addiction and Substance Abuse at Columbia University. Project Eating Among Teens (Project EAT), led by Dr. Dianne Neumark-Sztainer, provided statistics regarding family dinner and eating disorders in young women. The number of children who are overweight or obese in the United States is drawn from "Obesity Threatens a Generation: 'Catastrophe' of Shorter Spans, Higher Heath Costs," published in the *Washington Post* on May 17, 2008. Information about family dinner's impact on childhood obesity is in "Household Routines and Obesity in U.S. Preschool-Aged Children" by Sarah E. Anderson and Robert C. Whitaker, MD. Ellen Galinsky's book *Mind in the Making: The Seven Essential Life Skills Every Child Needs* included Catherine Snow's "The Home School Study of Language and Literacy Development," which shed light on family dinner's impact on language skills. "Supper's On! Adolescent Adjustment and Frequency of Family Mealtimes" by Bowden and Zeisz supplied data about how family dinners affect a child's adjustment, depression, and motivation.

Statistics on the average number of hours kids are using electronic media came from the Kaiser Family Foundation's "Generation M2: Media in the Lives of 8- to 18-Year-Olds." Research on when people first go online in the morning came from "Breakfast Can Wait: The Day's First Stop Is Online" published in *The New York Times* on August 9, 2009. "More than Half the Homes in US Have Three or More TVs" from *Nielsen Wire* on July 20, 2009, provided the average number of TVs in the home. Testimony about how parents use TV is from "Study Shows How Kids' Media Use Helps Parents Cope," published by the Kaiser Family Foundation. The number of meals eaten in the car was reported in *The Omnivore's Dilemma* by Michael Pollan.

"Videophilia: Implications for Childhood" by Patricia A. Zaradic and Olwer R. W. Pergams includes statistics on TV and the Internet's impact on family time. Brian Wansink's book *Mindless Eating: Why We Eat More than We Think* provided information concerning inattention and overeating. "TV Eating Up Family Mealtime" published by *Nutrition & Your Child,* Children's Nutrition Research Center, offered data about overweight children and television. Data concerning food ads were pulled from "Food for Thought: Television Food Advertising to Children in the United States" by the Kaiser Family Foundation; "The Impact of Industry Self-Regulation on the Nutritional Quality of Foods Advertised on Television to Children" published by Children Now sheds light on the content of those ads. The Robert Wood Johnson Foundation provided statistics on the number of children who are either overweight or obese in America. Statistics about teen desires for time with parents is from the Opinion Research Corporation.

CHAPTER 4: Fast Recipes That Can Save Weekday Dinners

Information about water used to grow lettuce and produce one portion of steak was drawn from *The Curious Gardener's Almanac* by Niall Edworthy. Microwave usage in the last three years is from *Time* magazine's November 2009 issue.

CHAPTER 8: Meatless Mondays: Why Eating More Vegetarian Dinners Will Save Your Health, Money, and the Earth

The Natural Resources Defense Council and *Food, Inc.,* edited by Karl Weber have been invaluable resources throughout this chapter and book. The impact of animal agriculture was outlined in "Livestock and Climate Change" by Robert Goodland and Jeff Anhang, published in *World Watch Magazine*'s November–December 2009 issue and the 2006 UN report "Livestock's Long Shadow: Environmental Issues and Options." The impact of a vegetarian diet on health is discussed in "Position of the American Dietetic Association: Vegetarian Diets" published in the *Journal of the American Dietetic Association*'s July 2009 issue. The rise in chicken consumption is outlined in *Eating Animals* by Jonathan Safran Foer, citing W. Boyd and M. Watts, "Agro-Industrial Just-in-Time: The Chicken Industry and Postwar American Capitalism," in *Globalising Food: Agrarian Questions and Global Restructuring,* edited by D. Goodman and M. Watts. Overall daily meat consumption is available in the American Meat Institute 2009's U.S. Meat and Poultry Production & Consumption Fact Sheet. Facts about decreasing meat consumption's impact on health is displayed on

MeatlessMonday.com. The percentage of overweight citizens in the United States is available in "Prevalence and Trends in Obesity Among U.S. Adults, 1999–2000," by Flegal, Carroll, and Johnson, published in *JAMA* in 2002.

Statistics about meat purchased in the United States that comes from factory farms is a Farm Forward calculation based on U.S. Department of Agriculture, *2002 Census of Agriculture,* June 2004, and Environmental Protection Agency, *Producers' Compliance Guide for CAFOs,* August 2003. "Most U.S. Antibiotics Fed to Healthy Livestock" by Kristin Leutwyler in *Scientific American*'s January 10, 2001, issue and the Union of Concerned Scientists' study "Hogging It!: Estimates of Antimicrobial Abuse in Livestock" from 2001 provided data on the amount of antibiotics fed to livestock. Information on the number of foodborne illnesses is contained in "Foodborne Illness" prepared by the Centers for Disease Control and Prevention. Medical costs related to meat consumption are charted by Dr. Colin Campbell of Cornell University in "United States Leads World Meat Stampede" published by Worldwatch Institute on July 2, 1998, and "The Medical Costs Attributable to Meat Consumption," by N. D. Barnard, A. Nicholson, and J. L. Howard in *Preventive Medicine.* Statistics regarding the percentage of farmland involved in livestock production is from Mark Bittman's book *Food Matters.* Water usage to grow soy tofu in California comes from "Water Inputs in California Food Production," 1991, by Kreith and published by Water Education Foundation in Sacramento, California. Total projected water usage and savings is in "The Math Behind Meatless Mondays" at MeatlessMonday.com.

CHAPTER 9: Kids in the Kitchen: Recipes Kids Can Make That Their Friends and Family Will Love

The percentage of money spent on food away from home was pulled from *Social Policy Report*'s "Reclaiming the Family Table: Mealtimes and Child Health and Wellbeing," authored by Barbara H. Fiese and Marlene Schwartz in 2008. The amount of juice boxes that end up in landfills every year was provided by the Container Recycling Institute.

CHAPTER 10: Your Green Table: Why Your Choices Matter

The percentage of food each household in America discards was drawn from "Using Contemporary Archaeology

and Applied Anthropology to Understand Food Loss in the American Food System" by Timothy W. Jones, PhD. The Natural Resources Defense Council provided the information regarding how far food travels and the journey grapes take from Chile to California. Statistics about calories from soda, in general, and in children and teenagers, specifically, was pulled from Mark Bittman's column, "Soda: A Sin We Sip Instead of Smoke?" from February 12, 2010's *New York Times*. The effect of BPA in the human body is outlined in "The Problems with Plastics" by Bruce Fellman in *Yale Magazine*'s fall 2009 issue. *The Wall Street Journal* provided data regarding plastic bags. The EPA's Ground Water and Drinking Frequently Asked Questions Web site shares information on the safety of bottled water. Soft drink consumption in America was summarized in "Changes in Beverage Intake Between 1977 and 2001" published in the *American Journal of Preventive Medicine* 27 by Nielsen and Popkin. The number of pesticides found on washed blueberries was pulled from the USDA's Pesticide Data Program Annual Summary, calendar year 2007, published in December 2008.

CHAPTER 12: Read Around the Table: From News to Poetry—Inspiration Is Your Dinner Guest

"Influence of Family Dinner on Food Intake of 4th to 6th Grade Students" by Cullen Baranowski, presented at the American Dietetic Association's Food and Nutrition Conference in October 2000, includes research on achievement levels of children. "What's Behind Success in School?" by Rachel Wildavsky, in *Reader's Digest*'s October 1994 issue, has statistics on higher achievement test scores. The "What Were They Thinking" suggestion was drawn from *Mind in the Making: The Seven Essential Life Skills Every Child Needs* by Ellen Galinsky.

CHAPTER 13: Grandparents and the Extended Family: Words of Wisdom

The average age of first-time grandparents is according to the AARP.

CHAPTER 15: Grace Is Gratitude: Ways to Say Thank You and Appreciate Life's Gifts

The quote from Francine du Plessix Gray was published in the October 16, 1995, issue of the *New Yorker*.

CONTRIBUTORS

DR. MAYA ANGELOU is a teacher, celebrated poet, novelist, and civil rights activist. She is the author of numerous books, including the memoir *I Know Why the Caged Bird Sings, Hallelujah! The Welcome Table,* and *Celebrations: Rituals of Peace and Prayer.* Web site: mayaangelou.com.

THE REVEREND ED BACON is the rector at All Saints Church in Pasadena, California. Web site: allsaints-pas.org.

DAN BARBER is the executive chef and co-owner of Blue Hill, Blue Hill at Stone Barns, and Blue Hill Farm. He is a locally grown and organic food advocate and has written pieces for *The New York Times, Gourmet, Saveur,* and *Food & Wine* magazine. Web site: bluehillfarm.com.

MARIO BATALI is the chef and owner of fifteen restaurants, including his flagship, Babbo, in New York City. He is also a host of several TV shows and author of eight cookbooks, including *Molto Italiano, The Babbo Cookbook,* and *Molto Gusto: Easy Italian Cooking.* Web site: mariobatali.com.

ED BEGLEY JR. is an actor, an environmentalist, and the author of several books, including *Ed Begley, Jr.'s Guide to Sustainable Living.* He and his wife, Rachelle Carson, star in the Planet Green show *Living with Ed.* Web site: edbegley.com.

LEANN BIRCH is the Distinguished Professor of Human Development at Penn State. Her landmark research focuses on both predictors and consequences of eating behavior from infancy to adolescence, including family influences on food choices. Web site: psu.edu.

MARK BITTMAN is a journalist, *New York Times* columnist, and author of several books, including *How to Cook Everything, Food Matters,* and *Kitchen Express.* Web site: markbittman.com.

JILL BROOKE is blogger, columnist, and a certified Stepfamily Foundation coach. She is the founder of Blended Families of America and author of *Don't Let Death Ruin Your Life.* Web site: blendedfamiliesofamerica.com.

DOMINIQUE BROWNING Former editor in chief of *House & Garden,* she is the author of three books: *Around the House and in the Garden: A Memoir of Heartbreak, Healing, and Home Improvement; Paths of Desire: The Passions of a Suburban Gardener;* and *Slow Love.* Web site: dominiquebrowning.com.

ADRIAN BUTASH is a producer, Holocaust scholar, and the author of *Bless This Food: Ancient & Contemporary Graces from Around the World* and *Bless This Food: Amazing Graces in Thanks for Food*. Web site: adrianarts.com.

JOSEPH CALIFANO is a lawyer and former secretary of health, education, and welfare under the Carter administration. He is currently the chairman of the National Center on Addiction and Substance Abuse (CASA) at Columbia University and author of several books, including *How to Raise a Drug-Free Kid: The Straight Dope for Parents*. Web site: casacolumbia.org.

THE REVEREND MARI CASTELLANOS is a public policy advocate with the United Church of Christ, founded in 1957 as the union of several different Christian traditions. Web site: ucc.org.

ROBERT COLES, MD, is a social psychiatrist, professor of literature, and Pulitzer Prize–winning author of hundreds of articles and more than fifty books, including *Children of Crisis, The Spiritual Life of Children,* and *The Moral Intelligence of Children*.

BILLY COLLINS is a professor and poet. From 2001 through 2003 he served two terms as the U.S. poet laureate and is the author of several books of poetry, including *Nine Horses, Sailing Alone Around the Room: New and Selected Poems,* and *Picnic, Lightning*. Web site: www.billy-collins.com.

CAT CORA is the first female American Iron Chef, founder and president of Chefs for Humanity, and author of the cookbooks *Cat Cora's Kitchen: Favorite Meals for Family and Friends* and *Cooking from the Hip: Fast, Easy, Phenomenal Meals*. Web site: catcoracooks.com.

PAUL CUMMINS, PhD, is an educator, the co-founder of Crossroads and New Roads schools in Los Angeles, and currently the executive director of the New Visions Foundation. He has authored several books, including *Proceed with Passion: Engaging Students in Meaningful Education*. Web site: newvisionsfnd.org.

MARINA DRASNIN is an interior designer, artist, and photographer. She has a card line with Chronicle Books, in addition to the "Marina Collection" with the Winn Devon Art Group. Web site: marinaartiste.com.

MARSHALL DUKE, PhD, is the Candler Professor of Psychology at Emory University and co-authored the books *Teaching Your Child the Language of Social Success* and *Helping the Child Who Doesn't Fit In*. Web site: psychology.emory.edu.

NORA EPHRON is a screenwriter, producer, author of several books, and director of *Julie and Julia*, among other films.

SHARON DUKE ESTROFF is a parenting columnist, educator, and author of *Can I Have a Cell Phone for Hanukkah?* Web site: sharonestroff.com.

RABBI MORLEY FEINSTEIN is senior rabbi of University Synagogue in Los Angeles, California. Web site: unisyn.org.

ROBYN FIVUSH, PhD, is the Samuel Candler Dobbs Professor of Psychology at Emory University. Her work focuses on early memory, trauma, and coping. Web site: psychology.emory.edu.

JONATHAN SAFRAN FOER is a Brooklyn-based novelist (*Everything Is Illuminated, Extremely Loud and Incredibly Close*) and the author of the nonfiction work *Eating Animals*. Web site: eatinganimals.com.

ELLEN GALINSKY is the co-founder and president of the Families and Work Institute and author of several books, including *The Six Stages of Parenthood* and *Mind in the Making: The Seven Essential Life Skills Every Child Needs*. Web site: familiesandwork.org.

MARY HARTZELL, MA, is a child development expert, parent educator, and director of First Presbyterian Preschool in Santa Monica, California. She is also the co-author of the book *Parent/Child Relationships: Communicating with Your Child: Building Self-Esteem and Avoiding Power Struggles*. Web site: maryhartzell.com.

MARY ANN HOBERMAN is the U.S. children's poet laureate and critically acclaimed author of more than forty books for children, including *A House Is a House for Me, The Llama Who Had No Pajama,* and *The Seven Silly Eaters*. Web site: maryannhoberman.com.

ARIANNA HUFFINGTON is the co-founder and editor in chief of The Huffington Post, a nationally syndicated columnist, and author of twelve books, including *Becoming Fearless . . . in Love, Work, and Life;* and *Pigs at the Trough.* Web site: huffingtonpost.com.

HARVEY KARP, MD, is a nationally renowned pediatrician, child development specialist, and assistant professor of pediatrics at the UCLA School of Medicine. He is also the author of *The Happiest Baby on the Block* and *The Happiest Toddler on the Block.* Web site: happiestbaby.com.

LYNNE ROSSETTO KASPER is a distinguished authority on food, and host of the popular public radio show *The Splendid Table,* produced and distributed by American Public Media. She is the author of *The Splendid Table: Recipes from Emilia-Romagna, the Heartland of Northern Italian Food,* and *The Italian Country Table: Home Cooking from Italy's Farmhouse Kitchens,* and co-author with producer Sally Swift of *The Splendid Table's How to Eat Supper: Recipes, Stories, and Opinions from Public Radio's Award-Winning Food Show.* Web site: splendidtable.publicradio.org.

ROBERT F. KENNEDY JR. is a professor, chief prosecuting attorney for the Hudson Riverkeepers, president of Waterkeeper Alliance, and senior attorney at the Natural Resources Defense Council. He is the best-selling author of articles and books, including *Crimes Against Nature, Saint Francis of Assisi: A Life of Joy,* and *The Riverkeepers.* Web site: robertfkennedyjr.com.

THE KITCHEN SISTERS—Davia Nelson and Nikki Silva—are award-winning NPR documentary producers who have been working together for more than twenty-five years. They are the creators of the popular *Hidden Kitchens* series on *Morning Edition,* the NPR series *Lost & Found Sound,* and the authors of *Hidden Kitchens: Stories, Recipes and More from NPR's The Kitchen Sisters.* Web site: kitchensisters.org.

PHOEBE LAPINE co-pens the blog Big Girls, Small Kitchen—a food and recipe guide for twenty-something cooks. The blog has recently spawned a book, *Cara and Phoebe's Quarter-Life Kitchen,* to be published in May 2011. Web site: biggirlssmallkitchen.com.

RABBI NAOMI LEVY is founder and spiritual leader of Nashuva, a Jewish outreach organization based in Los Angeles. She is the author of *To Begin Again* and *Talking to God.* Web site: nashuva.com.

CHAN LUU, originally from Vietnam, is a groundbreaking fashion, jewelry, and accessories designer. Her original designs are sold all over the world. Web site: chanluu.com.

PRESTON MARING, MD, is an ob-gyn physician. His passion for cooking with the best and freshest ingredients led him to establish the Friday Fresh Farmers' Market at the Kaiser Permanente Oakland Medical Center in May 2003. Web site: permanente.net.

WENDY MOGEL, PhD, is a nationally recognized clinical psychologist, speaker, and author of numerous articles and books, including the classic *The Blessing of a Skinned Knee.* Web site: wendymogel.com.

LORI MOZILO is a film editor, TV producer, interior decorator, and blogger for the Mindful Mom. Web site: mindfulmom.com.

PAT AND GINA NEELY are co-owners of the very successful Neely's Bar-B-Que restaurants, stars of their own Food Network cooking shows *Road Tasted with the Neelys* and *Down Home with the Neelys* and authors of the best-selling cookbook *Down Home with the Neelys.* Web site: neelysbbq.com.

SOLEDAD O'BRIEN is an award-winning journalist, producer, and anchor on CNN. Web site: cnn.com.

JAMIE OLIVER is a British chef committed to using seasonal and local food, host of nine TV shows around the world, and best-selling cookbook author of eleven cookbooks, including *Jamie's Kitchen, Jamie's America,* and *Jamie's Food Revolution: Rediscover How to Cook Simple, Delicious, Affordable Meals.* Web site: jamieoliver.com.

SCOTT PEACOCK is a Southern food expert whose vision of the region's cuisine emphasizes fresh, seasonal, locally grown ingredients. He is the co-author, along with Edna Lewis, of *The Gift of Southern Cooking.*

CAROL PETERS is a music industry veteran, manager of Heart and other artists.

CORKY POLLAN is a writer, former *New York Magazine* columnist, and former style editor at *Gourmet* magazine. She is also Michael Pollan's mother.

MICHAEL POLLAN is a professor, journalist, and award-winning author of the best-selling books *In Defense of Food, The Omnivore's Dilemma,* and *Food Rules.* Web site: michaelpollan.com.

MARICEL PRESILLA is a culinary historian and chef specializing in Latin American and Spanish cuisine. She is the author of *Cooking from Sun Country* and *The New Taste of Chocolate.* Web site: maricelpresilla.com.

TRI ROBINSON is the pastor of the Vineyard Boise Church in Boise, Idaho, and author of *Saving God's Green Earth* and *Small Footprint, Big Handprint.* Web site: timberbuttehomestead.com.

 TAL RONNEN is a vegan chef and the best-selling author of *The Conscious Cook.* Web site: talronnen.com.

RABBI DAVID SAPERSTEIN is the director and counsel of the Religious Action Center of Reform Judaism, as well as a speaker and author of numerous articles and books, including *Jewish Dimensions of Social Justice: Tough Moral Choices of Our Time.* Web site: rac.org.

ELLYN SATTER, MS, RCD, CISW, BCD, is an authority on eating and feeding and the author of *Child of Mine: Feeding with Love and Good Sense* and *Secrets of Feeding a Healthy Family.* Web site: ellynsatter.com.

 JUDGE JUDY SHEINDLIN is a former family court and supervising judge in Manhattan and star of the syndicated television show *Judge Judy.* She is the author of several books, including *Beauty Fades, Dumb Is Forever* and *Keep It Simple, Stupid: You're Smarter than You Look.* Web site: judgejudy.com.

BRADD SHORE, PhD, is the Goodrich C. White Professor at Emory University, director of The Emory Center for Myth and Ritual in American Life (MARIAL), and author of *Culture in Mind: Cognition, Culture, and the Problem of Meaning.* Web site: marial.emory.edu.

SUSAN STIFFELMAN is a marriage, child, and family therapist, parenting coach, and author of *Parenting Without Power Struggles.* Web site: passionateparenting.net.

BRYANT TERRY is an award-winning eco-chef, food activist, and author of *Vegan Soul Kitchen* and *Grub: Ideas for an Urban Organic Kitchen.* Web site: bryant-terry.com.

JOSH VIERTEL is an educator, organic farmer, activist, and the president of Slow Food USA, an organization devoted to promoting clean, healthy, whole food. Web site: slowfoodusa.com.

DANIEL WATERS is an award-winning poet, artist, and printmaker. In 2006, he proudly served as the first poet laureate of West Tisbury, Massachusetts. His poetry and prints can be found online. Web site: http://indianhillpress.com.

ALICE WATERS is a chef, restaurateur at the world-renowned Chez Panisse, and author of books including *The Art of Simple Food.* She is also the founder of The Edible Schoolyard. Web site: chezpanisse.com.

MIRIAM WEINSTEIN is a journalist and author of *The Surprising Power of Family Meals.* Web site: poweroffamilymeals.com.

NANCY WILSON is a singer-songwriter, guitarist, and with her sister Ann, member of the band Heart. She has also composed music for movies, including *Jerry Maguire, Almost Famous,* and *Vanilla Sky.* Web site: heart-music.com.

"DINNER IS NOT WHAT YOU DO IN THE EVENING *before something else.* DINNER IS THE EVENING." —ART BUCHWALD

INDEX

ABCs of Afternoon Snacks and Tea, 130
ABCs of Feeling Better, 138
Ad Hoc at Home (Keller), 45
All'Arrabbiata, 66
Almond, Jordan, 165
Almonds, Moroccan Chicken Tagine with Apricots, and Olives, 87
Anderson, Sarah E., 13
Angelhair Pasta Alla Checca, 54
Angelhair with Broccoli and Cheese, 40
Angelou, Maya, 172, 173
    recommended poems or poets, 174
Animal, Vegetable, Miracle (Kingsolver), 34
Apple(s)
    Applesauce, 212
    Asian, Vinaigrette, 71
    Bridesmaid with a Veil, 212
    Cider Chicken with Caramelized Onions and, 89, 91
    fresh, for dessert, 221
    A Grand Family-Size Turkey, and Cheese Panini, 126
    Grandma Helen's, Cake, 183
    Nanna's Frozen, Snow, 221
    Whole Wheat Crackers, Cheese, and Sliced, 130
Apricots, Moroccan Chicken Tagine with, Almonds, and Olives, 87
Arroz Con Pollo, 97
Artichoke(s)
    how to eat, steam, pick, 123
    toppings to serve with, 123
Art of Simple Food, The (Waters), 42
Asian Apple Vinaigrette, 71
Asian Beef Stir-Fry, 48–49
Asian Shrimp Cakes, 88
Asparagus
    roasting, seasoning, 109
    Sesame, 89
Aunt Isabelle's Icebox Cookies, 182
Avocado(s)
    Guacamole, 134
    as side dish, 61, 97
    as topping, 9, 69, 70, 76, 94

Bacon, Rev. Ed, 32, 194
Balsamic Vinaigrette, 123
Bananas, Caramelized, 44
Bang, Bang Chicken Parmesan, 55
Barber, Dan, 58, 130
Batali, Mario, 58, 118, 210
Bean(s)
    Chili Con, 94
    Crazy Water, 52
    Crispy, Bean Cakes, 106

Deep Dark Black, Soup with Fixin's, 82
Gary's T-Night Tacos, 9
Lynne Rossetto Kasper on, 52
Quick Black, 44
Savory Sausage and White, Stew, 51–52
Vegetable and, Wrap, 40
White, and Tiny Pasta Soup, 84
White, with Shrimp, 40
Beef
    Asian Stir-Fry, 48–49
    organic, grass-fed, 150
Begley, Ed, 151
Berry Cones, 130
Beverages
    Hot Lemonade, 138
    Milk and Honey, 138
    mulled cider, 23
    soda, calories from, daily, 145
    soda, not buying, 150
    Vanilla Milk, 138
    water, 21, 23
    wine for adults, 23
Big Peas and Little Peas, 46
Birch, Leann, 23
Bittman, Mark, 101, 105
Blanca's Locally Famous Healthy Fruit Popsicles, 213
Blessing of a Skinned Knee, The (Mogel), 158, 193, 204
Bless This Food (Butash), 195–96
Botham, Noel, 165
BPA (bisphenol A), 145
Brault, Robert, 31
Bread. *See also* Croutons
    Challah, 204
    French Toast, 207
    kneading/raising dough, 206, 207
    stale, for breadcrumbs or croutons, 148
Breakfast
    for dinner nights, 61
    as family meal, 7, 16, 62
    grilled cheese sandwich for, 68
    Pho soup for, 73
    quinoa for, 117
    wheat berries for, 60
Bridesmaid with a Veil (Danish Apple Dessert), 212
Bridges, Mary, 186
Broccoli
    Angelhair with, and Cheese, 40
    crispy, and sausage night, 61
    Noodlepanpie with, and Cheese, 122
    Pizza Potato, 40
    steamed, browned, with cheese, 62
Brooke, Jill, 191
Brownies, Marina's Divorce, 191
Browning, Dominique, 152
Bruschetta
    Alla Checca tomato sauce for, 54
    Strawberry, 221
Brussels sprouts, 111
Butash, Adrian, 195
Butterfly Pasta with Kale, 115–16

Butternut squash
    Fall Favorite Risotto, 53

Cabbage
    and Noodles, 51
    Salad, 75
    Slaw, 106, 108
Caesar Pita Pizza Pies, 124
Caesar Salad, 124
Cake
    frosting tip, 219
    Grandma Helen's Apple, 183
    Very Good Chocolate, 219
Califano, Joseph, 12
Can I Have a Cell Phone for Hanukkah? (Estroff), 193
Capers, 59
Caramelized Bananas, 44
Caramelized Sweet Potatoes with Quinoa and Greens, 116–17
Carrot(s)
    Pita Chips, Celery, and, 130
    roasting, seasoning, 111
Cassoulet, 51–52
Castellanos, Rev. Mari, 200
Cat Cora's Kitchen (Cora), 49
Celery
    Crunchy, Sticks with Tops Left, 130
    Pita Chips, and Carrots, 130
    Pretzels and, Sticks with Mustard and Chive Cream Cheese, 130
Challah
    Danish tip, 204
    French Toast, 207
    games, 205
    Homemade, 204
    two more tips, 205
Chan Luu, 198
    Tofu Summer Rolls with Peanut Sauce, 137
Cheese
    Angelhair with Broccoli and, 40
    Easy Cheesy Dinner Frittata, 127
    A Grand Family-Size Turkey, Apple, and, Panini, 126
    Greek Meatballs in a Fragrant Tomato Sauce with Feta, Orzo, and a Greek Salad, 99
    Kebabs, 130
    Mac 'n,' Please, 56
    Noodlepanpie with Broccoli and, 122
    Oven Grains, Greens, and, Please, 108–9
    Parmesan rind for soup, 79, 81, 84
    Quesadilla, 40
    for salad bar, 70
    Sliced Organic Turkey with Sliced, 130
    Whole Wheat Crackers, and Sliced Apples, 130
    Your Favorite Grilled, 68–69
Chesterton, Gilbert Keith, 197
"Chickadee's Lament" (Waters), 175
Chicken
    Arroz Con Pollo, 97

Bang, Bang, Parmesan, 55
Biryani, 97
Crunchy, Schnitzel, 45
Curry in a Hurry, 95
Greek Meatballs, 98
Kirstin's Nanna's Frikadeller, 185
leftover tips, 59, 91
Moroccan, Tagine with Apricots, Almonds, and Olives, 87
Neelys baked, dinner, 33
Organic, Legs Braised with Tomatoes, Onions, and Garlic, 42
organic kosher, buying, 88
Pho Broth, 73
Piccata, 59
quick rotisserie, soup, 62
Shabbat or Sunday Roast, 203
Slooooooow Cooker Curry, 95
Thai, Wraps, 66–67
Chickpeas
    Hummus/Tahini Sauce, 133
Child, Julia, 93
Chili Con Beans, 94
Chinese chopsticks, 73
Chinese Takeout Sunday, 7
    table setting and ambiance for, 27
Chipotle Orange Shrimp, 42–44
Chocolate
    brand, recommended, 213
    Fondue, 210
    Little, Pocket Pies, 209
    Marina's Divorce Brownies, 191
    Nanna's Happy, Chip Cookies, 217
    Pudding Fast, 213
    Very Good, Cake, 219
Chores for children, 23, 25
Christie, Agatha, 225
Cilantro, Summer Corn, Tomato, and, Salad, 152
Citrus Shrimp, 75
Claiborne, Craig, 66
Clark, Frank A., 197
Cleaning supplies, 150, 151
    Drain Opener, 151
    Glass and Surface Cleaner, 151
    Household Cleanser, 151
Cole, William, 56
Coles, Robert, 193
Collins, Billy, 174
Colman, George, 197
Colwin, Laurie, 88
Composting, 142
Conscious Cook, The (Ronnen), 118
Cookies
    Aunt Isabelle's Icebox, 182
    freezing the dough, 217
    Nanna's Happy Chocolate Chip, 217
Cook's Tips
    on cake frosting, 219
    capers, 59
    croutons, making your own, 124
    double portion for freezing, 55
    freezing cookie dough, 217
    fresh or frozen shrimp, 75
    frittatas, making individual, 127

ABOUT THE AUTHORS

LAURIE DAVID is an environmentalist, author, and producer of the Academy Award–winning film *An Inconvenient Truth* and the HBO documentary *Too Hot Not to Handle*. She executive produced *Earth to America!*, a prime-time comedy special about global warming, which earned her a Gracie Allen Award for Individual Achievement. A trustee of the Natural Resources Defense Council, Laurie founded the Stop Global Warming Virtual March, and launched the Stop Global Warming College Tour with Sheryl Crow.

Laurie has written *Stop Global Warming: The Solution Is You,* and with Cambria Gordon, co-authored *The Down-to-Earth Guide* to *Global Warming,* which received the prestigious Green Earth Book Award. She has also served as guest editor at *Elle* magazine.

Laurie has received numerous awards, including the prestigious Stanley Kramer Award from the Producers Guild of America, a Humanitas Prize Special Award, the Audubon Society's Rachel Carson Award, and the Feminist Majority's Eleanor Roosevelt Award. She was named the 2006 *Glamour* Woman of the Year and was awarded the prestigious NRDC 2006 Forces of Nature award.

Laurie is a regular blogger for the Huffington Post and continues her work with the NRDC, but her favorite activity is having dinner with her family as often as possible.

KIRSTIN UHRENHOLDT grew up on a fruit farm in Denmark, picking 'n' pruning and making pie. She then, by a stroke of good luck, ended up on a cargo ship to Greenland, doing, among other things, a lot of dishes. A lot . . . More than you can imagine. She escaped and became a beer wench in Appenzelle, Switzerland, where they speak a language no one understands. Eventually, she landed in L.A. where, lo and behold, she was kidnapped by some actors, some heavy rockers, and some kosher people. Presently, she is living happily ever after.

WE INVITE YOU TO JOIN THE CONVERSATION AT TheFamilyDinnerBook.com.